92-97
107-111

2000 SUPPLEMENT

CONSTITUTIONAL LAW

THIRTEENTH EDITION

by

GERALD GUNTHER
William Nelson Cromwell Professor of Law Emeritus,
Stanford University

KATHLEEN M. SULLIVAN
Dean, Richard E. Lang Professor of Law, and
Stanley Morrison Professor of Law,
Stanford University

NEW YORK, NEW YORK
FOUNDATION PRESS
2000

ISBN 1–58778–014–3

TEXT IS PRINTED ON 10% POST CONSUMER RECYCLED PAPER

TABLE OF CONTENTS

Numbers on the left indicate where the new materials fit into the casebooks. Cases and legislative material set out at length are in **bold face**.

Chapter 14. The Religion Clauses: Free Exercise and Establishment

*

TABLE OF CASES

Principal cases are in bold type. Non-principal cases are in roman type. References are to Pages.

TABLE OF AUTHORITIES

References are to Pages.

*

2000 SUPPLEMENT

CONSTITUTIONAL LAW

*

CHAPTER 1

THE NATURE AND SOURCES OF THE SUPREME COURT'S AUTHORITY

SECTION 2. CONSTITUTIONAL AND PRUDENTIAL LIMITS ON CONSTITUTIONAL ADJUDICATION

Page 43. Add after Lujan v. Defenders of Wildlife:

Contrast with Lujan the decision in BENNETT v. SPEAR, 520 U.S. 154 (1997), which found adequate grounds for standing in another lawsuit brought under the Endangered Species Act (ESA). Pursuant to provisions of the ESA, the Bureau of Reclamation, which operated a water reclamation project, notified the Fish and Wildlife Service that the project might endanger two endangered species of fish. The Service issued a "Biological Opinion" concluding that the project "was likely to jeopardize the continued existence of" the two species and recommending the maintenance of minimum water levels in several reservoirs as a "reasonable and prudent alternative" to avoid such jeopardy. The Bureau notified the Service that it intended to operate the project in compliance with the Biological Opinion. Two irrigation districts that received water from the project and two ranches within those districts filed suit against officials of the Service and the Secretary of Interior. They challenged the Service's jeopardy determination and claimed that the ESA required economic impact to be taken into account under the circumstances. The district court, affirmed by the court of appeals, dismissed the action on the ground that the plaintiffs' economic, as opposed to environmental, interests in the case were not within the "zone of interests" contemplated by the citizen-suit provision of the ESA.

The Supreme Court unanimously reversed. Justice SCALIA, writing for the Court, reiterated that the "zone of interests" test is prudential, and that "prudential standing doctrine [applies] unless it is expressly negated." He then found any zone-of-interests obstacle here to be negated by the ESA's citizen-suit provision, which says that "any person may commence a civil suit on his own behalf (A) to enjoin any person, including the United States and any other governmental instrumentality or agency [who] is alleged to be in violation of any provision of this chapter or regulation issued under the authority thereof; or . . . (C) against the Secretary where there is alleged a failure of the Secretary to perform any act or duty which is not discretionary. . . ." He noted that this was an "authorization of remarkable breadth when compared with the language Congress ordinarily uses." He concluded that "the 'any person' formulation applies [not] only to actions against private violators of environmental restrictions, and not only to actions against the Secretary asserting under-enforcement, but also to actions against the Secretary asserting overenforcement."

Justice Scalia also found no constitutional obstacle to standing here. First, he found that the complaint alleged the requisite injury in fact. The plaintiffs claimed that "the restrictions on lake levels imposed in the Biological Opinion adversely affect [them] by substantially reducing the quantity of available irrigation water." Justice Scalia noted that "it is easy to presume specific facts under which petitioners will be injured—for example, the Bureau's distribution of the reduction pro rata among its customers." Second, he found the injury "fairly traceable" to the Service's Biological Opinion, notwithstanding that the Bureau of Reclamation retained ultimate responsibility for determining whether and how the Service's proposal should go forward. He explained: "While it does not suffice if the injury complained of is 'the result [of] the independent action of some third party not before the court,' that does not exclude injury produced by determinative or coercive effect upon the action of someone else." On his reading of the relevant regulations, the Service's Biological Opinion was technically advisory but "in reality [has] a powerful coercive effect. [An] agency is technically free to disregard the Biological Opinion and proceed with its proposed action, but it does so at its own peril (and that of its employees), for 'any person' who knowingly 'takes' an endangered or threatened species is subject to substantial civil and criminal penalties, including imprisonment." He thus concluded that "petitioners have met their burden—which is relatively modest at this stage of the litigation—of alleging that their injury is 'fairly traceable' to the Service's Biological Opinion and that it will 'likely' be redressed—i.e., the Bureau will not impose such water level restrictions—if the Biological Opinion is set aside."

Despite Lujan, Congress's power to confer standing on some broad classes of individuals to challenge government inaction was reaffirmed in FEC v. AKINS, 524 U.S. 11 (1998), in which the Court, by a vote of 6–3, held that a group of voters had standing to challenge the failure of the Federal Election Commission to treat the American Israel Public Affairs Committee (AIPAC) as a "political committee" subject to certain reporting and disclosure requirements under federal election law. The Federal Election Campaign Act provides that "any person who believes a violation of this Act ... has occurred, may file a complaint with the Commission," and that "any party aggrieved by an order of the Commission dismissing a complaint filed by such party ... may file a petition" in district court seeking review of that dismissal. Justice BREYER, writing for the Court, found that voters seeking to obtain information about a political committee were within the zone of interests that FECA sought to protect, precluding any prudential obstacle to their standing. He also found that their claim to standing satisfied the constitutional requirements of Article III: "The 'injury in fact' that respondents have suffered consists of their inability to obtain information—lists of AIPAC donors (who are, according to AIPAC, its members), and campaign-related contributions and expenditures—that, on respondents' view of the law, the statute requires that AIPAC make public. There is no reason to doubt their claim that the information would help them (and others to whom they would communicate it) to evaluate candidates for public office, especially candidates who received assistance from AIPAC, and to evaluate the role that AIPAC's financial assistance might play in a specific election. Respondents' injury consequently seems concrete and particular."

Justice Breyer similarly found the injury fairly traceable to the FEC and redressable by judicial action.

The majority opinion also rejected the claim that the lawsuit involved only a nonjusticiable "generalized grievance": "Whether styled as a constitutional or prudential limit on standing, the Court has sometimes determined that where large numbers of Americans suffer alike, the political process, rather than the judicial process, may provide the more appropriate remedy for a widely shared grievance. [Reservists; Richardson, see 13th ed., p.37]. [But such an obstacle] invariably appears in cases where the harm at issue is not only widely shared, but is also of an abstract and indefinite nature. [Often] the fact that an interest is abstract and the fact that it is widely shared go hand in hand. But their association is not invariable, and where a harm is concrete, though widely shared, the Court has found 'injury in fact.' [We] conclude that [the] informational injury at issue here, directly related to voting, the most basic of political rights, is sufficiently concrete and specific such that the fact that it is widely shared does not deprive Congress of constitutional power to authorize its vindication in the federal courts."

Justice SCALIA dissented, joined by Justices O'Connor and Thomas. The dissent argued that the claimants here, like the challengers seeking to compel publication of CIA expenditures in Richardson, had merely a generalized grievance, " 'undifferentiated and common to all members of the public.' " As he had in his Lujan opinion, Justice Scalia also suggested that conferring standing on citizens to compel government enforcement action "unconstitutionally transfers from the Executive to the courts the responsibility to 'take Care that the Laws be faithfully executed.' "

Raines v. Byrd

521 U.S. 811, 117 S.Ct. 2312, 138 L.Ed.2d 849 (1997).

[This case involved a challenge to the constitutionality of the Line Item Veto Act of 1996 by four Senators and two Congressmen who had voted against its passage in the 104th Congress. The Act provided that the President may "cancel" certain items appropriated for expenditure in any bill or joint resolution "that has been signed into law pursuant to Article I, section 7, of the Constitution." Such a cancellation would take effect upon receipt in both Houses of Congress of a "special message" from the President specifying the cancelled item, and the Congress could undo the cancellation only by passage of a "disapproval bill" signed by the President or reenacted by two thirds of each House over his veto. The Act specifically provided that "any Member of Congress" may bring an action alleging the unconstitutionality of any provision of the Act. Senator Byrd and the other appellees brought suit under this provision. The district court rejected a motion to dismiss for want of standing and found the act unconstitutional as a violation of the Presentment Clause, Art. I, § 7, and as an improper delegation of legislative power to the President. The Supreme Court heard an expedited direct appeal. Before the Court, both Houses of Congress filed amicus briefs urging reversal on the merits.]

Chief Justice REHNQUIST delivered the opinion of the Court.

[We] hold that appellees have no standing to bring this suit, and therefore direct that the judgment of the District Court be vacated and the complaint dismissed. Under Article III, § 2 of the Constitution, the federal courts have jurisdiction over this dispute between appellants and appellees only if it is a "case" or "controversy." This is a "bedrock requirement." One element of the case-or-controversy requirement is that appellees, based on their complaint, must establish that they have standing to sue. [We] have always insisted on strict compliance with this jurisdictional standing requirement. And our standing inquiry has been especially rigorous when reaching the merits of the dispute would force us to decide whether an action taken by one of the other two branches of the Federal Government was unconstitutional. [In] the light of this overriding and time-honored concern about keeping the Judiciary's power within its proper constitutional sphere,[1] we must put aside the natural urge to proceed directly to the merits of this important dispute and to "settle" it for the sake of convenience and efficiency. Instead, we must carefully inquire as to whether appellees have met their burden of establishing that their claimed injury is personal, particularized, concrete, and otherwise judicially cognizable.

We have never had occasion to rule on the question of legislative standing presented here. In Powell v. McCormack [1969; 13th Ed., p. 53], we held that a Member of Congress' constitutional challenge to his exclusion from the House of Representatives (and his consequent loss of salary) presented an Article III case or controversy. But Powell does not help appellees. First, appellees have not been singled out for specially unfavorable treatment as opposed to other Members of their respective bodies. [Second,] appellees do not claim that they have been deprived of something to which they personally are entitled—such as their seats as Members of Congress after their constituents had elected them. Rather, appellees' claim of standing is based on a loss of political power, not loss of any private right.

[The] one case in which we have upheld standing for legislators (albeit state legislators) claiming an institutional injury is Coleman v. Miller, 307 U.S. 433 (1939). [In] Coleman, 20 of Kansas' 40 State Senators voted not to ratify the proposed "Child Labor Amendment" to the Federal Constitution. [The] State's Lieutenant Governor, the presiding officer of the State Senate, cast a deciding vote in favor of the amendment, and it was deemed ratified. [The] 20 State Senators who had voted against the amendment [and other sitting legislators] filed an action in the Kansas Supreme Court seeking a writ of mandamus that would compel the appropriate state officials to recognize that the legislature had not in fact ratified the amendment. That court held that the members of the legislature had standing to bring their mandamus action, but ruled against them on the merits.

This Court affirmed. By a vote of 5–4, we held that the members of the legislature had standing. [We] emphasized that if these legislators (who were suing as a bloc) were correct on the merits, then their votes not to ratify the

1. It is settled that Congress cannot erase Article III's standing requirements by statutorily granting the right to sue to a plaintiff who would not otherwise have standing. We acknowledge, though, that Congress' decision to grant a particular plaintiff the right to challenge an act's constitutionality (as here) eliminates any prudential standing limitations and significantly lessens the risk of unwanted conflict with the Legislative Branch when that plaintiff brings suit. [Footnote by Chief Justice Rehnquist.]

amendment were deprived of all validity. [It] is obvious [that] our holding in Coleman stands (at most) for the proposition that legislators whose votes would have been sufficient to defeat (or enact) a specific legislative act have standing to sue if that legislative action goes into effect (or does not go into effect), on the ground that their votes have been completely nullified. It should be equally obvious that appellees' claim does not fall within our holding in Coleman, as thus understood. They have not alleged that they voted for a specific bill, that there were sufficient votes to pass the bill, and that the bill was nonetheless deemed defeated. In the vote on the Line Item Veto Act, their votes were given full effect. They simply lost that vote.[2]

[*Rule* — handwritten margin note]

[Nevertheless,] appellees rely heavily on our statement in Coleman that the Kansas senators had "a plain, direct, and adequate interest in maintaining the effectiveness of their votes." Appellees claim that this statement applies to them because their votes on future appropriations bills [will] be less "effective" than before, and that the "meaning" and "integrity" of their vote has changed: [Before] the Act, Members of Congress could be sure that when they voted for, and Congress passed, an appropriations bill that included funds for Project X, [either] the bill would become law and all of the projects listed in the bill would go into effect, or [the] bill would not become law and none of the projects listed in the bill would go into effect. [After] the Act, however, [there] is a third option: [that] the bill will become law and then the President will "cancel" Project X. Even taking appellees at their word about the change in the "meaning" and "effectiveness" of their vote for appropriations bills which are subject to the Act, we think their argument pulls Coleman too far from its moorings. [There] is a vast difference between the level of vote nullification at issue in Coleman and the abstract dilution of institutional legislative power that is alleged here. To uphold standing here would require a drastic extension of Coleman. We are unwilling to take that step.

[*vote nullification vs. abstract dilution.* — handwritten margin note]

[In] sum, appellees have alleged no injury to themselves as individuals (contra Powell) [and] the institutional injury they allege is wholly abstract and widely dispersed (contra Coleman). [We] attach some importance to the fact that appellees have not been authorized to represent their respective Houses of Congress in this action, and indeed both Houses actively oppose their suit. We also note that our conclusion neither deprives Members of Congress of an adequate remedy (since they may repeal the Act or exempt appropriations bills from its reach), nor forecloses the Act from constitutional challenge (by someone who suffers judicially cognizable injury as a result of the Act). Whether the case would be different if any of these circumstances were different we need not now decide.

[*SUMMARY* — handwritten margin note]

[Vacated with instructions to dismiss.]

Justice SOUTER, concurring in the judgment, with whom Justice GINSBURG joins, concurring.

[Under] our precedents, it is fairly debatable whether this injury is sufficiently "personal" and "concrete" to satisfy the requirements of Article III.

2. Just as appellees cannot show that their vote was denied or nullified as in Coleman, [so] are they unable to show that their vote was denied or nullified in a discriminato- ry manner (in the sense that their vote was denied its full validity in relation to the votes of their colleagues). [Footnote by Chief Justice Rehnquist.]

[In] Coleman v. Miller, [the Court] found the legislators had standing even though they claimed no injury but a deprivation of official voting power. Thus, it is at least arguable that the official nature of the harm here does not preclude standing. Nor is appellees' injury so general that, under our case law, they clearly cannot satisfy the requirement of concreteness. [Appellees] are not simply claiming harm to their interest in having government abide by the Constitution, which would be shared to the same extent by the public at large and thus provide no basis for suit, [but instead allege] that the Act deprives them of an element of their legislative power.

[Because] it is fairly debatable whether appellees' injury is sufficiently personal and concrete to give them standing, it behooves us to resolve the question under more general separation-of-powers principles underlying our standing requirements. [A] dispute involving only officials, and the official interests of those, who serve in the branches of the National Government lies far from the model of the traditional common-law cause of action at the conceptual core of the case-or-controversy requirement. Although the contest here is not formally between the political branches (since Congress passed the bill augmenting Presidential power and the President signed it), it is in substance an interbranch controversy about calibrating the legislative and executive powers, as well as an intrabranch dispute between segments of Congress itself. Intervention in such a controversy would risk damaging the public confidence that is vital to the functioning of the Judicial Branch by embroiling the federal courts in a power contest nearly at the height of its political tension.

While it is true that a suit challenging the constitutionality of this Act brought by a party from outside the Federal Government would also involve the Court in resolving the dispute over the allocation of power between the political branches, [such a suit] raises no specter of judicial readiness to enlist on one side of a political tug-of-war. The virtue of waiting for a private suit is only confirmed by the certainty that another suit can come to us. If the President "cancels" a conventional spending or tax provision pursuant to the Act, the putative beneficiaries of that provision will likely suffer a cognizable injury and thereby have standing under Article III.

Justice STEVENS, dissenting.

The Line Item Veto Act purports to establish a procedure for the creation of laws that are truncated versions of bills that have been passed by the Congress and presented to the President for signature. If the procedure were valid, it would deny every Senator and every Representative any opportunity to vote for or against the truncated measure that survives the exercise of the President's cancellation authority. Because the opportunity to cast such votes is a right guaranteed by the text of the Constitution, [Art. I, § 7,] I think it clear that the persons who are deprived of that right by the Act have standing to challenge its constitutionality. [Appellees] articulated their claim as a combination of the diminished effect of their initial vote and the circumvention of their right to participate in the subsequent repeal. Whether one looks at the claim from this perspective, or as a simple denial of their right to vote on the precise text that will ultimately become law, the basic nature of the injury caused by the Act is the same.

In my judgment, the deprivation of this right—essential to the legislator's office—constitutes a sufficient injury to provide every Member of Congress with standing to challenge the constitutionality of the statute. If the dilution of an individual voter's power to elect representatives provides that voter with standing—as it surely does, see, e.g., Baker v. Carr [13th ed., p. 47]—the deprivation of the right possessed by each Senator and Representative to vote for or against the precise text of any bill before it becomes law must also be a sufficient injury to create Article III standing for them. [Moreover, the] immediate, constant threat of the partial veto power has a palpable effect on [Members'] current legislative choices. [Thus,] they need not await an exercise of the President's cancellation authority to institute the litigation that the statute itself authorizes.

Justice BREYER, dissenting.

[I] concede that there would be no case or controversy here were the dispute before us not truly adversary, or were it not concrete and focused. But the interests that the parties assert are genuine and opposing, and the parties are therefore truly adverse. [The] harm is focused and the accompanying legal issues are both focused and of the sort that this Court is used to deciding. The plaintiffs therefore do not ask the Court "to pass upon" an "abstract, intellectual problem," but to determine "a concrete, living contest between" genuine "adversaries." Coleman v. Miller, (Frankfurter, J., dissenting).

Nonetheless, there remains a serious constitutional difficulty due to the fact that this dispute about lawmaking procedures arises between government officials and is brought by legislators. The critical question is whether or not this dispute, for that reason, is so different in form from those "matters that were the traditional concern of the courts at Westminster" that it falls outside the scope of Article III's judicial power. Justice Frankfurter explained this argument in his dissent in Coleman, saying that courts traditionally "leave intra-parliamentary controversies to parliaments and outside the scrutiny of law courts." [Although] the majority today attempts to distinguish Coleman, I do not believe that Justice Frankfurter's argument or variations on its theme can carry the day here. [The] Constitution does not draw an absolute line between disputes involving a "personal" harm and those involving an "official" harm. [Coleman] itself involved injuries in the plaintiff legislators' official capacity. [Moreover,] Justice Frankfurter's views were dissenting views, and the dispute before us, when compared to Coleman, presents a much stronger claim, not a weaker claim, for constitutional justiciability. [In contrast to a complaint about a single vote on a constitutional amendment, the] lawmakers in this case complain of a lawmaking procedure that threatens the validity of many laws (for example, all appropriations laws) that Congress regularly and frequently enacts. The systematic nature of the harm immediately affects the legislators' ability to do their jobs. [In] sum, I do not believe that the Court can find this case nonjusticiable without overruling Coleman.

Limits of Raines. After Raines, would a sitting member of Congress have standing to bring any of the following actions? (1) A suit challenging the constitutionality under the Incompatibility Clause, Art. I, § 6, of the membership of other members of Congress in the armed services Reserves. Cf. Schlesinger v. Reservists Committee [13th ed., p. 37]. (2) A suit challenging a law forbidding first-term Members from voting on appropriations bills. (3) A suit challenging a law disqualifying any Member of Congress from voting on major federal projects in his or his own district.

Who might have standing to challenge the line item veto if not members of Congress? The Line Item Veto Act also specifically authorized "any individual adversely affected" to bring a constitutional challenge. Shortly after the decision in Raines, President Clinton exercised his authority under the Act by canceling a provision of the Balanced Budget Act of 1997 that would have protected the State of New York from having to reimburse the federal government for up to $2.6 billion in taxes it had levied against Medicaid providers, and a provision of the Taxpayer Relief Act of 1997 that had allowed food processors to defer recognition of capital gains for tax purposes if they sold their stock to eligible farmers' cooperatives. Claiming they had been adversely affected, the City of New York and several hospital associations and health care employee unions filed an action challenging the cancellation of the New York Medicaid provision, and the Snake River Potato Growers, an Idaho farmers' cooperative formed in part in order to acquire potato processing facilities, filed an action challenging cancellation of the food processor capital gains provision. In CLINTON v. NEW YORK, 524 U.S. 417 (1998), the Court found that both groups of challengers had standing because they would suffer concrete economic injury from the President's cancellation. Writing for the Court, Justice STEVENS noted that, as a result of the Medicaid cancellation, "both the City of New York and the appellee health care providers will be assessed by the State for substantial portions of any recoupment payments that the State may have to make to the Federal Government." And he noted that the cancellation of the food processors' capital gains deferral had deprived the Snake River Potato Growers of a "statutory 'bargaining chip' " they might otherwise have used in acquiring processing facilities, as they were actively negotiating to do at the time of the cancellation. "Having found that both the New York and Snake River appellees are actually injured," he concluded, "traceability and redressability are easily satisfied—each injury is traceable to the President's cancellation [and] would be redressed by a declaratory judgment that the cancellations are invalid." Justice SCALIA, joined by Justice O'Connor in dissent, would not have found that the Snake River cooperative had standing to object to the President's cancellation of the limited tax benefit since it involved the tax treatment of third parties (i.e., food processors) with only indirect and speculative effects on Snake River, but agreed that the New York appellees had standing to challenge the President's cancellation of a new item of direct spending. Reaching the merits, the Court invalidated the Line Item Veto Act by a vote of 6–3, reasoning that it failed to meet the requirements of the Presentment Clause, Art. I § 7. For the opinions on the merits, see p. 42 below.

The Court declined to clarify the issue of legislative standing in DEPARTMENT OF COMMERCE v. UNITED STATES HOUSE OF REPRESENTATIVES, 119 S. Ct. 765 (1998), which involved challenges to the proposed use of statistical sampling to conduct the 2000 Decennial Census. Article 1, § 2, cl. 3 authorizes Congress to direct an "actual Enumeration" of the American public every ten years in order to provide a basis for apportioning congressional representation among the States. Congress delegated this authority by statute to the Department of Commerce, which proposed to use statistical sampling in 2000 in order to avoid undercounting minorities and other groups. In a 1998 appropriations act, Congress provided that "[a]ny person aggrieved by the use of any statistical method in violation of the Constitution or [other] provision of law [in] connection with the 2000 census or any later decennial census, to determine the population for purposes of the apportionment or redistricting of Members in Congress, may in a civil action obtain declaratory, injunctive, and any other appropriate relief against the use of such method." The act defined "aggrieved person" to include "either House of Congress." Reviewing consolidated appeals from two successful challenges to the proposed sampling before three-judge district courts, the Court found the constitutional requirements for standing satisfied by an individual resident of a state that was likely to lose a House seat under the proposed plan, and by several individual residents of counties that were likely to lose state legislative seats under the proposed plan because their states used federal census numbers for intrastate districting. Justice O'CONNOR, writing for the Court, stated that, as to these plaintiffs, "the threat of vote dilution through the use of sampling" was both particularized and concrete. On the merits, the majority affirmed, finding statistical sampling for purposes of apportionment barred by amendments to the Census Act, and thus declining to reach the question whether such a method was barred by the term "Enumeration" in the Constitution's Census Clause. Having reached this conclusion in the individual plaintiffs' case, the Court dismissed the appeal from a successful challenge by the House of Representatives, offering no opinion on whether that body had standing, as the district court had held it did. Dissenting, Justice STEVENS, joined by Justice Breyer, would have found that the "House has a concrete and particularized 'institutional interest in preventing its unlawful composition' that satisfies the injury in fact requirement of Article III," but found against the challengers on the merits. Justices Souter and Ginsburg also dissented.

CHAPTER 3

THE COMMERCE POWER

SECTION 1. INTRODUCTION

Page 159. Add after United States v. Lopez:

United States v. Morrison

120 S.Ct. 1740 (2000).

Chief Justice REHNQUIST delivered the opinion of the Court.

[This case arose from a rape claim brought by a student at Virginia Polytechnic Institute, Christy Brzonkala, against two football players also enrolled at the university. She filed a complaint under the Virginia Tech disciplinary system, but one of the accused was not punished and the other's punishment was eventually suspended. She dropped out of school and sued both men and Virginia Tech in federal district court under the challenged statute.]

In these cases we consider the constitutionality of 42 U.S.C. § 13981, which provides a federal civil remedy for the victims of gender-motivated violence. [Section] 13981 was part of the Violence Against Women Act of 1994, [which] states that "[a]ll persons within the United States shall have the right to be free from crimes of violence motivated by gender." To enforce that right, [the law] declares: "A person (including a person who acts under color of any statute, ordinance, regulation, custom, or usage of any State) who commits a crime of violence motivated by gender and thus deprives another of the right [to be free of such crimes] shall be liable to the party injured, in an action for the recovery of compensatory and punitive damages, injunctive and declaratory relief, and such other relief as a court may deem appropriate."

II. [We] turn to the question whether § 13981 falls within Congress' power under Article I, § 8, of the Constitution. Brzonkala and the United States rely upon the third clause of the Article, which gives Congress power "[t]o regulate Commerce with foreign Nations, and among the several States, and with the Indian Tribes." [United States v.] Lopez [1995; 13th ed., p. 142] emphasized [that] even under our modern, expansive interpretation of the Commerce Clause, Congress' regulatory authority is not without effective bounds. [Petitioners] seek to sustain § 13981 as a regulation of activity that substantially affects interstate commerce. Given § 13981's focus on gender-motivated violence wherever it occurs (rather than violence directed at the instrumentalities of interstate commerce, interstate markets, or things or persons in interstate commerce), we agree that this is the proper inquiry.

Since Lopez most recently canvassed and clarified our case law governing this third category of Commerce Clause regulation, it provides the proper framework for conducting the required analysis of § 13981. In Lopez, we held that the Gun–Free School Zones Act of 1990, 18 U.S.C. § 922(q)(1)(A), which made it a federal crime to knowingly possess a firearm in a school zone, exceeded Congress' authority under the Commerce Clause. Several significant considerations contributed to our decision.

First, we observed that § 922(q) was "a criminal statute that by its terms has nothing to do with 'commerce' or any sort of economic enterprise, however broadly one might define those terms." [Lopez's] review of Commerce Clause case law demonstrates that in those cases where we have sustained federal regulation of intrastate activity based upon the activity's substantial effects on interstate commerce, the activity in question has been some sort of economic endeavor. The second consideration that we found important in analyzing § 922(q) was that the statute contained "no express jurisdictional element which might limit its reach to a discrete set of firearm possessions that additionally have an explicit connection with or effect on interstate commerce." [Third,] we noted that [§ 922(q) lacked] "formal findings as to the substantial burdens that an activity has on interstate commerce." [Finally,] our decision in Lopez rested in part on the fact that the link between gun possession and a substantial effect on interstate commerce was attenuated.

[With] these principles underlying our Commerce Clause jurisprudence as reference points, the proper resolution of the present cases is clear. Gender-motivated crimes of violence are not, in any sense of the phrase, economic activity. While we need not adopt a categorical rule against aggregating the effects of any noneconomic activity in order to decide these cases, thus far in our Nation's history our cases have upheld Commerce Clause regulation of intrastate activity only where that activity is economic in nature.

explicit: economic activity

aggregation still allowed, but...

Like the Gun–Free School Zones Act at issue in Lopez, § 13981 contains no jurisdictional element establishing that the federal cause of action is in pursuance of Congress' power to regulate interstate commerce. Although Lopez makes clear that such a jurisdictional element would lend support to the argument that § 13981 is sufficiently tied to interstate commerce, Congress elected to cast § 13981's remedy over a wider, and more purely intrastate, body of violent crime.

In contrast with the lack of congressional findings that we faced in Lopez, § 13981 is supported by numerous findings regarding the serious impact that gender-motivated violence has on victims and their families. But the existence of congressional findings is not sufficient, by itself, to sustain the constitutionality of Commerce Clause legislation. [Congress] found that gender-motivated violence affects interstate commerce "by deterring potential victims from traveling interstate, from engaging in employment in interstate business, and from transacting with business, and in places involved in interstate commerce; . . . by diminishing national productivity, increasing medical and other costs, and decreasing the supply of and the demand for interstate products." [The] reasoning that petitioners advance seeks to follow the but-for causal chain from the initial occurrence of violent crime (the suppression of which has always been the prime object of the States' police power) to every attenuated effect upon interstate commerce. If accepted, petitioners' reasoning would allow Congress to regulate any crime as long as the nationwide, aggregated impact of that crime has substantial effects on employment, production, transit, or consumption. Indeed, if Congress may regulate gender-motivated violence, it

floood-gates

would be able to regulate murder or any other type of violence since gender-motivated violence, as a subset of all violent crime, is certain to have lesser economic impacts than the larger class of which it is a part.

Petitioners' reasoning, moreover, will not limit Congress to regulating violence but may, as we suggested in Lopez, be applied equally as well to family law and other areas of traditional state regulation since the aggregate effect of marriage, divorce, and childrearing on the national economy is undoubtedly significant. We accordingly reject the argument that Congress may regulate noneconomic, violent criminal conduct based solely on that conduct's aggregate effect on interstate commerce. The Constitution requires a distinction between what is truly national and what is truly local. In recognizing this fact we preserve one of the few principles that has been consistent since the Clause was adopted. The regulation and punishment of intrastate violence that is not directed at the instrumentalities, channels, or goods involved in interstate commerce has always been the province of the States. Indeed, we can think of no better example of the police power, which the Founders denied the National Government and reposed in the States, than the suppression of violent crime and vindication of its victims.

[In part III of the opinion, the Chief Justice found the violence against women law unsupported by Congress's power to enforce the Fourteenth Amendment. That part, and Justice Breyer's response in dissent, are reported at p. 107 below.]

Justice THOMAS, concurring.

The majority opinion correctly applies our decision in [Lopez] and I join it in full. I write separately only to express my view that the very notion of a "substantial effects" test under the Commerce Clause is inconsistent with the original understanding of Congress' powers and with this Court's early Commerce Clause cases. [Until] this Court replaces its existing Commerce Clause jurisprudence with a standard more consistent with the original understanding, we will continue to see Congress appropriating state police powers under the guise of regulating commerce.

Justice SOUTER, with whom Justice STEVENS, Justice GINSBURG, and Justice BREYER join, dissenting.

Our cases, which remain at least nominally undisturbed, stand for the following propositions. Congress has the power to legislate with regard to activity that, in the aggregate, has a substantial effect on interstate commerce. The fact of such a substantial effect is not an issue for the courts in the first instance, but for the Congress, whose institutional capacity for gathering evidence and taking testimony far exceeds ours. By passing legislation, Congress indicates its conclusion, whether explicitly or not, that facts support its exercise of the commerce power. The business of the courts is to review the congressional assessment, not for soundness but simply for the rationality of concluding that a jurisdictional basis exists in fact. Any explicit findings that Congress chooses to make, though not dispositive of the question of rationality, may advance judicial review by identifying factual authority on which Congress relied.

[One] obvious difference from [Lopez] is the mountain of data assembled by Congress, here showing the effects of violence against women on interstate commerce. Passage of the Act in 1994 was preceded by four years of hearings, *(unlike Lopez)* which included testimony from physicians and law professors; from survivors of rape and domestic violence; and from representatives of state law enforcement and private business. The record includes reports on gender bias from task forces in 21 States, and we have the benefit of specific factual findings in the eight separate Reports issued by Congress and its committees over the long course leading to enactment. [Congress] thereby explicitly stated the predicate for the exercise of its Commerce Clause power. Is its conclusion irrational in view of the data amassed? True, the methodology of particular studies may be challenged, and some of the figures arrived at may be disputed. But the sufficiency of the evidence before Congress to provide a rational basis for the finding cannot seriously be questioned.

Indeed, the legislative record here is far more voluminous than the record compiled by Congress and found sufficient in Heart of Atlanta Motel, Inc. v. United States [1964; 13th ed., p. 203], and Katzenbach v. McClung [1964; 13th ed., p. 203], [where] the Court referred to evidence showing the consequences of racial discrimination by motels and restaurants on interstate commerce, [including] compelling anecdotal reports that individual instances of segregation cost thousands to millions of dollars [and] that the average black family spent substantially less than the average white family in the same income range on public accommodations, and that discrimination accounted for much of the difference.

(it supported other cases w/ massive evidence of economic effects)

While Congress did not, to my knowledge, calculate aggregate dollar values for the nationwide effects of racial discrimination in 1964, in 1994 it did rely on evidence of the harms caused by domestic violence and sexual assault, citing annual costs of $3 billion in 1990, and $5 to $10 billion in 1993. Equally important, though, gender-based violence in the 1990's was shown to operate in a manner similar to racial discrimination in the 1960's in reducing the mobility of employees and their production and consumption of goods shipped in interstate commerce. Like racial discrimination, "[g]ender-based violence bars its most likely targets—women—from full partic[ipation] in the national economy."

comparing gender violence w/ racism

If the analogy to the Civil Rights Act of 1964 is not plain enough, one can always look back a bit further. In Wickard [v. Filburn (1942); 13th ed., p. 189], we upheld the application of the Agricultural Adjustment Act to the planting and consumption of homegrown wheat. The effect on interstate commerce in that case followed from the possibility that wheat grown at home for personal consumption could either be drawn into the market by rising prices, or relieve its grower of any need to purchase wheat in the market. The Commerce Clause predicate was simply the effect of the production of wheat for home consumption on supply and demand in interstate commerce. Supply and demand for goods in interstate commerce will also be affected by the deaths of 2,000 to 4,000 women annually at the hands of domestic abusers, and by the reduction in the work force by the 100,000 or more rape victims who lose their jobs each year or are forced to quit. Violence against women may be found to affect interstate commerce and affect it substantially.

Civil Rights Act 1964

Wickard

The Act would have passed muster at any time between Wickard in 1942 and Lopez in 1995, a period in which the law enjoyed a stable understanding that congressional power under the Commerce Clause, complemented by the

Short class!

authority of the Necessary and Proper Clause, Art. I. § 8 cl. 18, extended to all activity that, when aggregated, has a substantial effect on interstate commerce. [The] fact that the Act does not pass muster before the Court today is therefore proof, to a degree that Lopez was not, that the Court's nominal adherence to the substantial effects test is merely that. Although a new jurisprudence has not emerged with any distinctness, it is clear that some congressional conclusions about obviously substantial, cumulative effects on commerce are being assigned lesser values than the once-stable doctrine would assign them. These devaluations are accomplished not by any express repudiation of the substantial effects test or its application through the aggregation of individual conduct, but by supplanting rational basis scrutiny with a new criterion of review.

[History] has shown that categorical exclusions have proven as unworkable in practice as they are unsupportable in theory. [For] significant periods of our history, the Court has defined the commerce power as plenary, unsusceptible to categorical exclusions, and this was the view expressed throughout the latter part of the 20th century in the substantial effects test. These two conceptions of the commerce power, plenary and categorically limited, are in fact old rivals. [In] the half century following the modern activation of the commerce power with passage of the Interstate Commerce Act in 1887, this Court from time to time created categorical enclaves beyond congressional reach by declaring such activities as "mining," "production," "manufacturing," and union membership to be outside the definition of "commerce" and by limiting application of the effects test to "direct" rather than "indirect" commercial consequences. Since adherence to these formalistically contrived confines of commerce power in large measure provoked the judicial crisis of 1937, one might reasonably have doubted that Members of this Court would ever again toy with a return to the days before NLRB v. Jones & Laughlin Steel Corp. [1937; 13th ed., p.185], which brought the earlier and nearly disastrous experiment to an end. And yet today's decision can only be seen as a step toward recapturing the prior mistakes. [Just] as the old formalism had value in the service of an economic conception [of laissez-faire], the new one is useful in serving a conception of federalism. It is the instrument by which assertions of national power are to be limited in favor of preserving a supposedly discernible, proper sphere of state autonomy to legislate or refrain from legislating as the individual States see fit.

[The] Court finds it relevant that the statute addresses conduct traditionally subject to state prohibition under domestic criminal law. [Again,] history seems to be recycling, for the theory of traditional state concern as grounding a limiting principle has been rejected previously. [See] Garcia v. San Antonio Metropolitan Transit Authority [1985; 13th ed. p. 209], which held that the concept of "traditional governmental function" [was] incoherent. [The] majority [rejects] the Founders' considered judgment that politics, not judicial review, should mediate between state and national interests as the strength and legislative jurisdiction of the National Government inevitably increased through the expected growth of the national economy. [Today's] majority [finds] no significance whatever in the state support for the Act based upon the States' acknowledged failure to deal adequately with gender-based violence in state courts, and the belief of their own law enforcement agencies that national action is essential. The National Association of Attorneys General supported the Act unanimously, and Attorneys General from 38 States urged Congress to enact the Civil Rights Remedy, [and] thirty-six [states] and the Commonwealth of Puerto Rico have filed an amicus brief in support of petitioners in these cases, and only one State has taken respondents' side. It is, then, not the least irony of these cases that the States will be forced to enjoy the new federalism whether they want it or not. [All] of this convinces me that today's ebb of the commerce power rests on error, and at the same time leads me to doubt that the majority's view will prove to be enduring law.

Justice BREYER, with whom Justice STEVENS joins, and with whom Justice SOUTER and Justice GINSBURG join as to Part I–A, dissenting.

I–A. Consider the problems [with the majority's approach]. The "economic/noneconomic" distinction is not easy to apply. Does the local street corner mugger engage in "economic" activity or "noneconomic" activity when he mugs for money? Would evidence that desire for economic domination underlies many brutal crimes against women save the present statute? [More] important, why should we give critical constitutional importance to the economic, or noneconomic, nature of an interstate-commerce-affecting cause? If chemical emanations through indirect environmental change cause identical, severe commercial harm outside a State, why should it matter whether local factories or home fireplaces release them? [Most] important, the Court's complex rules seem unlikely to help secure the very object that they seek, namely, the protection of "areas of traditional state regulation" from federal intrusion. [In] a world where most everyday products or their component parts cross interstate boundaries, Congress will frequently find it possible to redraft a statute using language that ties the regulation to the interstate movement of some relevant object, thereby regulating local criminal activity or, for that matter, family affairs. [How] much would be gained, for example, were Congress to reenact the present law in the form of "An Act Forbidding Violence Against Women Perpetrated at Public Accommodations or by Those Who Have Moved in, or through the Use of Items that Have Moved in, Interstate Commerce"?

[We] live in a Nation knit together by two centuries of scientific, technological, commercial, and environmental change. Those changes, taken together, mean that virtually every kind of activity, no matter how local, genuinely can affect commerce, or its conditions, outside the State—at least when considered in the aggregate. And that fact makes it close to impossible for courts to develop meaningful subject-matter categories that would exclude some kinds of local activities from ordinary Commerce Clause "aggregation" rules without, at the same time, depriving Congress of the power to regulate activities that have a genuine and important effect upon interstate commerce. Since judges cannot change the world, [Congress], not the courts, must remain primarily responsible for striking the appropriate state/federal balance.

SECTION 4. EXTERNAL LIMITS ON THE COMMERCE POWER: THE STATE AUTONOMY AND SOVEREIGNTY CONCERNS REFLECTED IN THE TENTH AND ELEVENTH AMENDMENTS

Page 225. Add after Note, "Some comments and questions on New York v. United States":

Does New York v. United States apply to federal commands directed at state or local *executive* officials, as opposed to legislatures? New York itself involved a federal command directed at state legislatures, not executive officials. But the Court in New York stated that "[t]he Federal Government may not compel the States to enact *or administer* a federal regulatory program." The Court reached the constitutionality of such compelled administration in the following case.

Printz v. United States

inconsistent w/ 10th Amend. What abt Commerce Clause?

521 U.S. 898, 117 S.Ct. 2365, 138 L.Ed.2d 914 (1997).

Justice SCALIA delivered the opinion of the Court.

The question presented in these cases is whether certain interim provisions of the Brady Handgun Violence Prevention Act commanding state and local law enforcement officers to conduct background checks on prospective handgun purchasers and to perform certain related tasks, violate the Constitution.

The Gun Control Act of 1968 establishes a detailed federal scheme [prohibiting] firearms dealers from transferring handguns to [various persons such as minors, convicted felons, fugitives, drug users, mentally ill persons, illegal aliens, and persons found to have engaged in domestic violence.] In 1993, Congress amended the GCA by enacting the Brady Act. The Act requires the Attorney General to establish a national instant background check system [and] immediately puts in place certain interim provisions until that system becomes operative. Under the interim provisions, a firearms dealer who proposes to transfer a handgun must [seek identifying information] from the transferee [and] provide [that information to the] "chief law enforcement officer" (CLEO) of the transferee's residence. [The CLEO] must "make a reasonable effort to ascertain within 5 business days whether receipt or possession would be in violation of the law, including research in whatever State and local recordkeeping systems are available and in a national system designated by the Attorney General." The Act does not require the CLEO to take any particular action if he determines that a pending transaction would be unlawful; he may notify the firearms dealer to that effect, but is not required to do so. If, however, the CLEO notifies a gun dealer that a prospective purchaser is ineligible to receive a handgun, he must, upon request, provide the would-be purchaser with a written statement of the reasons for that determination, [and if he] does not discover any basis for objecting to the sale, he must destroy any records in his possession relating to the transfer. [Any] person who "knowingly violates [the Act] shall be fined, [imprisoned] for no more than 1 year, or both." Petitioners Jay Printz and Richard Mack, the CLEOs for Ravalli County, Montana, and Graham County, Arizona, respectively, filed separate actions challenging the constitutionality of the Brady Act's interim provisions. [The] Court of Appeals [found] none of the Brady Act's interim provisions to be unconstitutional.

[The] Brady Act purports to direct state law enforcement officers to participate, albeit only temporarily, in the administration of a federally enacted regulatory scheme. [The] petitioners here object to being pressed into federal service, and contend that congressional action compelling state officers to execute federal laws is unconstitutional. Because there is no constitutional text speaking to this precise question, the answer to the CLEOs' challenge must be sought in historical understanding and practice, in the structure of the Constitution, and in the jurisprudence of this Court.

The Government contends [that] "the earliest Congresses enacted statutes that required the participation of state officials in the implementation of federal laws." [This] contention demands our careful consideration, since early congressional enactments "provide 'contemporaneous and weighty evidence' of the Constitution's meaning," Bowsher v. Synar. [Statutes] enacted by the first Congresses required state courts to record applications for citizenship, to transmit abstracts of citizenship applications and other naturalization records to the Secretary of State, [to] register aliens seeking naturalization and issue certificates of registry [and to perform functions] such as resolving controversies between a captain and the crew of his ship concerning the seaworthiness of the vessel, hearing the claims of slave owners who had apprehended fugitive slaves and issuing certificates authorizing the slave's forced removal to the State from which he had fled, taking proof of the claims of Canadian refugees who had assisted the United States during the Revolutionary War, and ordering the deportation of alien enemies in times of war.

These early laws establish, at most, that the Constitution was originally understood to permit imposition of an obligation on state judges to enforce federal prescriptions, insofar as those prescriptions related to matters appropriate for the judicial power. [We] do not think the early statutes imposing obligations on state courts imply a power of Congress to impress the state executive into its service. Indeed, it can be argued that the numerousness of these statutes, contrasted with the utter lack of statutes imposing obligations on the States' executive (notwithstanding the attractiveness of that course to Congress), suggests an assumed absence of such power. The only early federal law [that] imposed duties on state executive officers is the Extradition Act of 1793, which required the "executive authority" of a State to cause the arrest and delivery of a fugitive from justice upon the request of the executive authority of the State from which the fugitive had fled. That was in direct implementation, however, of the Extradition Clause of the Constitution itself, see Art. IV, § 2.

Not only do the enactments of the early Congresses [contain] no evidence of an assumption that the Federal Government may command the States' executive power in the absence of a particularized constitutional authorization, they contain some indication of precisely the opposite assumption. [When] the First Congress enacted a law aimed at obtaining state assistance [in] holding [federal] prisoners in state jails at federal expense [it] issued not a command to the States' executive, but a recommendation to their legislatures.

[The] Government also [points] to portions of The Federalist which [suggested] that Congress will probably "make use of the State officers and State regulations, for collecting" federal taxes, The Federalist No. 36 (A. Hamilton), and predicted that "the eventual collection [of internal revenue] under the immediate authority of the Union, will generally be made by the officers, and according to the rules, appointed by the several States," [The Federalist] No. 45 (J. Madison). The Government also invokes the Federalist's more general observations that the Constitution would "enable the [national] government to employ the ordinary magistracy of each [State] in the execution of its laws," [The Federalist] No. 27 (A. Hamilton), and that it was "extremely probable

sources of law

historical practice
- Congress
 reg. judicary
 not executive

recommeded instead
of imposed on
exec.
(jails)

taxes

that in other instances, particularly in the organization of the judicial power, the officers of the States will be clothed in the correspondent authority of the Union," [The Federalist] No. 45 (J. Madison). But none of these statements necessarily implies—what is the critical point here—that Congress could impose these responsibilities without the consent of the States. They appear to rest on the natural assumption that the States would consent to allowing their officials to assist the Federal Government, an assumption proved correct by the extensive mutual assistance the States and Federal Government voluntarily provided one another in the early days of the Republic.

[Justice Souter relies on The Federalist No. 27 (A. Hamilton), which reads:] "It merits particular attention ..., that the laws of the Confederacy as to the enumerated and legitimate objects of its jurisdiction will become the SUPREME LAW of the land; to the observance of which all officers, legislative, executive, and judicial in each State will be bound by the sanctity of an oath. Thus, the legislatures, courts, and magistrates, of the respective members will be incorporated into the operations of the national government as far as its just and constitutional authority extends; and will be rendered auxiliary to the enforcement of its laws." [Justice Souter reads this to mean] that the National Government will have "authority ..., when exercising an otherwise legitimate power (the commerce power, say), to require state 'auxiliaries' to take appropriate action." There are several obstacles to such an interpretation. First, [if] the passage means that state officers must take an active role in the implementation of federal law [as a consequence of their oaths], it means that they must do so without the necessity for a congressional directive that they implement it. But no one has ever thought [that] that is the law. The second problem [is] that it makes state legislatures subject to federal direction. We have held, however, that state legislatures are not subject to federal direction. New York v. United States. These problems are avoided, of course, if the [passage is] taken to refer to nothing more (or less) than the duty owed to the National Government, on the part of all state officials, to enact, enforce, and interpret state law in such fashion as not to obstruct the operation of federal law, and the attendant reality that all state actions constituting such obstruction, even legislative acts, are ipso facto invalid.

[Justice] Souter contends that his interpretation of Federalist No. 27 is "supported by No. 44," written by Madison. [In] fact, Federalist No. 44 quite clearly contradicts Justice Souter's reading. In that Number, Madison justifies the requirement that state officials take an oath to support the Federal Constitution on the ground that they "will have an essential agency in giving effect to the federal Constitution." If the dissent's reading of Federalist No. 27 were correct (and if Madison agreed with it), one would surely have expected that "essential agency" of state executive officers (if described further) to be described as their responsibility to execute the laws enacted under the Constitution. Instead, however, Federalist No. 44 continues with the following description: "The election of the President and Senate will depend, in all cases, on the legislatures of the several States. And the election of the House of Representatives will equally depend on the same authority in the first instance; and will, probably, forever be conducted by the officers and according to the laws of the States." It is most implausible that the person who labored for that example of state executive officers' assisting the Federal Government believed, but neglected to mention, that they had a responsibility to execute federal laws.

To complete the historical record, we must note that there is not only an absence of executive-commandeering statutes in the early Congresses, but there is an absence of them in our later history as well, at least until very recent years. [An 1882 law enlisting] state officials [to inspect, exclude and provide relief for arriving immigrants] did not [mandate] those duties, but merely empowered the Secretary of the Treasury "to enter into contracts with such State . . . officers as may be designated for that purpose by the governor of any State." [And a] World War I selective draft law that authorized the President "to utilize the service of any or all departments and any or all officers or agents of the United States and of the several States [in] the execution of this Act," [was not clearly] an authorization to compel the service of state officers. [In] implementing the Act President Wilson did not commandeer the services of state officers, but instead requested the assistance of the States' governors. [It] is impressive that even with respect to a wartime measure the President should have been so solicitous of state independence.

no Executive demands on Executive

The Government points to a number of federal statutes enacted within the past few decades that require the participation of state or local officials in implementing federal regulatory schemes. Some of these are connected to federal funding measures, and can perhaps be more accurately described as conditions upon the grant of federal funding than as mandates to the States; others, which require only the provision of information to the Federal Government, do not involve the precise issue before us here, which is the forced participation of the States' executive in the actual administration of a federal program. We of course do not address these or other currently operative enactments that are not before us. [Even] assuming they represent assertion of the very same congressional power challenged here, [their] persuasive force is far outweighed by almost two centuries of apparent congressional avoidance of the practice.

utilize ≠ compel demand ≠ request

conditions on funding provide info & participate

[We] turn next to consideration of the structure of the Constitution, to see if we can discern among its "essential postulates" a principle that controls the present cases. It is incontestable that the Constitution established a system of "dual sovereignty." Although the States surrendered many of their powers to the new Federal Government, they retained "a residuary and inviolable sovereignty," The Federalist No. 39 (J. Madison). This is reflected throughout the Constitution's text, including [the] prohibition on any involuntary reduction or combination of a State's territory, Art. IV, § 3; the Judicial Power Clause, Art. III, § 2, and the Privileges and Immunities Clause, Art. IV, § 2, which speak of the "Citizens" of the States; the amendment provision, Article V, which requires the votes of three-fourths of the States to amend the Constitution; [the] Guarantee Clause, Art. IV, § 4; [and] the Constitution's conferral upon Congress of not all governmental powers, but only discrete, enumerated ones, Art. I, § 8, which implication was rendered express by the Tenth Amendment's assertion that "the powers not delegated to the United States by the Constitution, nor prohibited by it to the States, are reserved to the States respectively, or to the people."

STRUCTURE

dual sovereignty

[The] Framers rejected the concept of a central government that would act upon and through the States [as had the Articles of Confederation], and instead designed a system in which the state and federal governments would exercise concurrent authority over the people—who were, in Hamilton's words, "the

orig. und. ↳ structure

only proper objects of government," The Federalist No. 15. The great innovation of this design was that "our citizens would have two political capacities, one state and one federal, each protected from incursion by the other." [U.S. Term Limits, Inc. v. Thornton, 1995; 13th Ed., p.115 (Kennedy, J., concurring).] This separation of the two spheres is one of the Constitution's structural protections of liberty. [To quote Madison:] "In the compound republic of America, the power surrendered by the people is first divided between two distinct governments, and then the portion allotted to each subdivided among distinct and separate departments. Hence a double security arises to the rights of the people. The different governments will control each other, at the same time that each will be controlled by itself." The Federalist No. 51. The power of the Federal Government would be augmented immeasurably if it were able to impress into its service—and at no cost to itself—the police officers of the 50 States.

We have thus far discussed the effect that federal control of state officers would have upon the first element of the "double security" alluded to by Madison: the division of power between State and Federal Governments. It would also have an effect upon the second element: the separation and equilibration of powers between the three branches of the Federal Government itself. The Constitution does not leave to speculation who is to administer the laws enacted by Congress; the President, it says, "shall take Care that the Laws be faithfully executed," Art. II, § 3, personally and through officers whom he appoints. The Brady Act effectively transfers this responsibility to thousands of CLEOs in the 50 States, who are left to implement the program without meaningful Presidential control. [Unity] in the Federal Executive [would] be shattered, and the power of the President would be subject to reduction, if Congress could act as effectively without the President as with him, by simply requiring state officers to execute its laws.

The dissent of course resorts to the last, best hope of those who defend ultra vires congressional action, the Necessary and Proper Clause. It reasons that the power to regulate the sale of handguns under the Commerce Clause, coupled with the power to "make all Laws which shall be necessary and proper for carrying into Execution the foregoing Powers," Art. I, § 8, conclusively establishes the Brady Act's constitutional validity, because the Tenth Amendment imposes no limitations on the exercise of delegated powers but merely prohibits the exercise of powers "not delegated to the United States." [But when] a "Law . . . for carrying into Execution" the Commerce Clause violates the principle of state sovereignty reflected in the various constitutional provisions we mentioned earlier, it is not a "Law . . . proper for carrying into Execution the Commerce Clause," and is thus, in the words of The Federalist, "merely [an] act of usurpation" which "deserves to be treated as such." The Federalist No. 33 (A. Hamilton).

[Finally,] we turn to the prior jurisprudence of this Court. Federal commandeering of state governments is such a novel phenomenon that this Court's first experience with it did not occur until the 1970's, when the Environmental Protection Agency promulgated regulations requiring States to prescribe auto emissions testing, monitoring and retrofit programs, and to designate preferential bus and carpool lanes. [Three] Courts of Appeals [invalidated] the regulations. [After] we granted certiorari to review the [validity] of the regulations,

only people are governed, not states

federalism

separation of powers

loss of presidential power

DISSENT:
state sovereignty more important than law for carrying into Execution Art I § 8 (necessary & proper)

JURISPRUDENCE

began w/ EPA laws

the Government declined even to defend them, and instead rescinded some and conceded the invalidity of those that remained. [Later] opinions of ours have made clear that the Federal Government may not compel the States to implement, by legislation or executive action, federal regulatory programs. In Hodel v. Virginia Surface Mining & Reclamation Assn., Inc., 452 U.S. 264 (1981), and FERC v. Mississippi, 456 U.S. 742 (1982), we sustained statutes against constitutional challenge only after assuring ourselves that they did not require the States to enforce federal law. [When] we were at last confronted squarely with a federal statute that unambiguously required the States to enact or administer a federal regulatory program, our decision should have come as no surprise. ["The] Federal Government," we held, "may not compel the States to enact or administer a federal regulatory program." [New York v. United States.]

The Government contends that New York is distinguishable on the following ground: unlike the "take title" provisions invalidated there, the background-check provision of the Brady Act does not require state legislative or executive officials to make policy, but instead issues a final directive to state CLEOs. It is permissible, the Government asserts, for Congress to command state or local officials to assist in the implementation of federal law so long as "Congress itself devises a clear legislative solution that regulates private conduct" and requires state or local officers to provide only "limited, non-policymaking help in enforcing that law." "The constitutional line is crossed only when Congress compels the States to make law in their sovereign capacities." The Government's distinction between "making" law and merely "enforcing" it, between "policymaking" and mere "implementation," is an interesting one. [But] executive action that has utterly no policymaking component is rare, particularly at an executive level as high as a jurisdiction's chief law-enforcement officer. [Is the] decision whether to devote maximum "reasonable efforts" or minimum "reasonable efforts" [to handgun purchaser background checks] not preeminently a matter of policy? It is quite impossible [to] draw the Government's proposed line at "no policymaking," and we would have to fall back upon a line of "not too much policymaking." [Such] an imprecise barrier against federal intrusion upon state authority is not likely to be an effective one.

Even assuming, moreover, that the Brady Act leaves no "policymaking" discretion with the States, we fail to see how that improves rather than worsens the intrusion upon state sovereignty. Preservation of the States as independent and autonomous political entities is arguably less undermined by requiring them to make policy in certain fields than by "reducing [them] to puppets of a ventriloquist Congress," Brown v. EPA, [521 F.2d 827, 839 (9th Cir.1975) (Sneed, J.)]. [It] is no more compatible with this independence and autonomy that their officers be "dragooned" [into] administering federal law, than it would be compatible with the independence and autonomy of the United States that its officers be impressed into service for the execution of state laws. The Government purports to find support for its proffered distinction of New York in our [decision] in Testa v. Katt, 330 U.S. 386 (1947). We [do not] find [this] case relevant. Testa stands for the proposition that state courts cannot refuse to apply federal law—a conclusion mandated by the terms of the Supremacy Clause ("the Judges in every State shall be bound [by federal law]"). As we have suggested earlier, that says nothing about whether state executive officers must administer federal law.

[The] Government also maintains that requiring state officers to perform discrete, ministerial tasks specified by Congress does not violate the principle of New York because it does not diminish the accountability of state or federal officials. This argument fails even on its own terms. By forcing state governments to absorb the financial burden of implementing a federal regulatory program, Members of Congress can take credit for "solving" problems without having to ask their constituents to pay for the solutions with higher federal taxes. And even when the States are not forced to absorb the costs of implementing a federal program, they are still put in the position of taking the blame for its burdensomeness and for its defects. See Merritt, Three Faces of Federalism: Finding a Formula for the Future, 47 Vand. L. Rev. 1563, 1580, n. 65 (1994). Under the present law, for example, it will be the CLEO and not some federal official who stands between the gun purchaser and immediate possession of his gun.

[Finally,] the Government [argues]: "The Brady Act serves very important purposes, is most efficiently administered by CLEOs during the interim period, and places a minimal and only temporary burden upon state officers." [Even assuming] all the mentioned factors were true, they might be relevant if we were evaluating whether the incidental application to the States of a federal law of general applicability excessively interfered with the functioning of state governments. But where, as here, it is the whole object of the law to direct the functioning of the state executive, and hence to compromise the structural framework of dual sovereignty, such a "balancing" analysis is inappropriate. It is the very principle of separate state sovereignty that such a law offends, and no comparative assessment of the various interests can overcome that fundamental defect.

[We] held in New York that Congress cannot compel the States to enact or enforce a federal regulatory program. Today we hold that Congress cannot circumvent that prohibition by conscripting the State's officers directly. The Federal Government may neither issue directives requiring the States to address particular problems, nor command the States' officers, or those of their political subdivisions, to administer or enforce a federal regulatory program. It matters not whether policymaking is involved, and no case-by-case weighing of the burdens or benefits is necessary; such commands are fundamentally incompatible with our constitutional system of dual sovereignty.

[Reversed.]

Justice O'CONNOR, concurring.

Our precedent and our Nation's historical practices support the Court's holding today. [Our] holding, of course, does not spell the end of the objectives of the Brady Act. States and chief law enforcement officers may voluntarily continue to participate in the federal program. [Congress] is also free to amend the interim program to provide for its continuance on a contractual basis with the States if it wishes. In addition, the Court appropriately refrains from deciding whether other purely ministerial reporting requirements imposed by Congress on state and local authorities pursuant to its Commerce Clause powers are similarly invalid, [e.g., requirements that] state and local law enforcement agencies [report] cases of missing children to the Department of Justice. The provisions invalidated here, however, which directly compel state officials to administer a federal regulatory program, utterly fail to adhere to the design and structure of our constitutional scheme.

Justice THOMAS, concurring. *(usually concurs/dissents alone?)*

In my "revisionist" view, the Federal Government's authority under the Commerce Clause, which merely allocates to Congress the power "to regulate Commerce ... among the several states," does not extend to the regulation of wholly intrastate, point-of-sale transactions. See United States v. Lopez [1995; 13th ed., p.142 (Thomas, J., concurring)]. Absent the underlying authority to regulate the intrastate transfer of firearms, Congress surely lacks the corollary power to impress state law enforcement officers into administering and enforcing such regulations. [Moreover, if] the Second Amendment is read to confer a personal right to "keep and bear arms," a colorable argument exists that the Federal Government's regulatory scheme, at least as it pertains to the purely intrastate sale or possession of firearms, runs afoul of that Amendment's protections. As the parties did not raise this argument, however, we need not consider it here. Perhaps, at some future date, this Court will have the opportunity to determine whether Justice Story was correct when he wrote that the right to bear arms "has justly been considered, as the palladium of the liberties of a republic." 3 J. Story, Commentaries § 1890, p. 746 (1833). In the meantime, I join the Court's opinion striking down the challenged provisions of the Brady Act as inconsistent with the Tenth Amendment.

Commerce Clause

violates 2nd Amend.?

STORY

Justice STEVENS, with whom Justices SOUTER, GINSBURG, and BREYER join, dissenting.

When Congress exercises the powers delegated to it by the Constitution, it may impose affirmative obligations on executive and judicial officers of state and local governments as well as ordinary citizens. This conclusion is firmly supported by the text of the Constitution, the early history of the Nation, decisions of this Court, and a correct understanding of the basic structure of the Federal Government.

*TEXT
HISTORY
PRECEDENT
STRUCTURE*

[Article] I, § 8, grants the Congress the power to regulate commerce among the States [including commerce in handguns.] The additional grant of authority in that section of the Constitution "to make all Laws which shall be necessary and proper for carrying into Execution the foregoing Powers" is surely adequate to support the temporary enlistment of local police officers in the process of identifying persons who should not be entrusted with the possession of handguns. [The] Tenth Amendment [confirms] the principle that the powers of the Federal Government are limited to those affirmatively granted by the Constitution, but it does not purport to limit the scope or the effectiveness of the exercise of powers that are delegated to Congress. Thus, the Amendment provides no support for a rule that immunizes local officials from obligations that might be imposed on ordinary citizens. Indeed, it would be more reasonable to infer that federal law may impose greater duties on state officials than on private citizens [given state officials' obligations under the Oath Clause, Art. VI, cl.3.]

*Commerce
Necessary & Proper
Tenth Amend.
purs limited but not
scope of purs granted*

TEXT

[The] historical materials strongly suggest that the Founders intended to enhance the capacity of the federal government by empowering it—as a part of

HISTORY

the new authority to make demands directly on individual citizens—to act through local officials. Hamilton made clear that the new Constitution, "by extending the authority of the federal head to the individual citizens of the several States, will enable the government to employ the ordinary magistracy of each, in the execution of its laws." The Federalist No. 27. Hamilton's meaning was unambiguous; the federal government was to have the power to demand that local officials implement national policy programs. [More] specifically, during the debates concerning the ratification of the Constitution, it was assumed that state agents would act as tax collectors for the federal government. Opponents of the Constitution had repeatedly expressed fears that the new federal government's ability to impose taxes directly on the citizenry would result in an overbearing presence of federal tax collectors in the States. Federalists rejoined that this problem would not arise because, as Hamilton explained, "the United States ... will make use of the State officers and State regulations for collecting" certain taxes. [The Federalist] No. 36. Similarly, Madison made clear that the new central government's power to raise taxes directly from the citizenry would "not be resorted to, except for supplemental purposes of revenue ... and that the eventual collection, under the immediate authority of the Union, will generally be made by the officers ... appointed by the several States." [The Federalist] No. 45. The Court's response to this powerful historical evidence is weak. The majority suggests that "none of these statements necessarily implies ... Congress could impose these responsibilities without the consent of the States." No fair reading of these materials can justify such an interpretation.

[Bereft] of support in the history of the founding, the Court rests its conclusion on the claim that there is little evidence the National Government actually exercised such a power in the early years of the Republic. [But] we have never suggested that the failure of the early Congresses to address the scope of federal power in a particular area or to exercise a particular authority was an argument against its existence. That position, if correct, would undermine most of our post-New Deal Commerce Clause jurisprudence. [More important,] the fact that Congress did elect to rely on state judges and the clerks of state courts to perform a variety of executive functions is surely evidence of a contemporary understanding that their status as state officials did not immunize them from federal service. [Statutes] of the early Congresses required in mandatory terms that state judges and their clerks perform various executive duties with respect to applications for citizenship. [Similarly,] the First Congress enacted legislation requiring state courts to serve, functionally, like contemporary regulatory agencies in certifying the seaworthiness of vessels. [The] use of state judges and their clerks to perform executive functions was, in historical context, hardly unusual. [See] Caminker, State Sovereignty and Subordinacy: May Congress Commandeer State Officers to Implement Federal Law?, 95 Colum. L. Rev. 1001, 1045, n. 176 (1995). [The] majority's insistence that this evidence of federal enlistment of state officials to serve executive functions is irrelevant simply because the assistance of "judges" was at issue rests on empty formalistic reasoning of the highest order.

[Indeed,] the majority's opinion consists almost entirely of arguments against the substantial evidence weighing in opposition to its view; the Court's ruling is strikingly lacking in affirmative support. Absent even a modicum of textual foundation for its judicially crafted constitutional rule, there should be a presumption that if the Framers had actually intended such a rule, at least one of them would have mentioned it.

[The] Court's "structural" arguments are not sufficient to rebut that presumption. [As] we explained in Garcia v. San Antonio Metropolitan Transit Authority, [1985; 13th ed., p. 209]: "The principal means chosen by the Framers to ensure the role of the States in the federal system lies in the structure of the Federal Government itself." [Given] the fact that the Members of Congress are elected by the people of the several States, with each State receiving an equivalent number of Senators in order to ensure that even the smallest States have a powerful voice in the legislature, it is quite unrealistic to assume that they will ignore the sovereignty concerns of their constituents. It is far more reasonable to presume that their decisions to impose modest burdens on state officials from time to time reflect a considered judgment that the people in each of the States will benefit therefrom. [Recent] developments demonstrate that [the political safeguards of federalism identified in Garcia have been] effective. [The] problem of federal actions that have the effect of imposing so-called "unfunded mandates" on the States has been identified and meaningfully addressed by Congress in [the Unfunded Mandates Reform Act of 1995.][1] [Whatever] the ultimate impact of the new legislation, its passage demonstrates that unelected judges are better off leaving the protection of federalism to the political process in all but the most extraordinary circumstances.

Perversely, the majority's rule seems more likely to damage than to preserve the safeguards against tyranny provided by the existence of vital state governments. By limiting the ability of the Federal Government to enlist state officials in the implementation of its programs, the Court creates incentives for the National Government to aggrandize itself. In the name of State's rights, the majority would have the Federal Government create vast national bureaucracies to implement its policies. This is exactly the sort of thing that the early Federalists promised would not occur, in part as a result of the National Government's ability to rely on the magistracy of the states.

[Finally, the holding in] New York v. United States [sheds] no doubt on the validity of the Brady Act. [That decision] clearly did not decide the question presented here, whether state executive officials—as opposed to state legislators—may in appropriate circumstances be enlisted to implement federal policy. The "take title" provision at issue in New York was beyond Congress' authority to enact because it was "in principle . . . no different than a congressionally compelled subsidy from state governments to radioactive waste producers," almost certainly a legislative act. The majority relies upon dictum in New York to the effect that "the Federal Government may not compel the States to enact or administer a federal regulatory program." But that language was wholly unnecessary to the decision of the case. It is, of course, beyond dispute that we are not bound by the dicta of our prior opinions.

1. The majority also [claims] that requiring state officials to carry out federal policy causes states to "take the blame" for failed programs. [But] to the extent that a particular action proves politically unpopular, we may be confident that elected officials charged with implementing it will be quite clear to their constituents where the source of the misfortune lies. [Footnote by Justice Stevens.]

[Margin annotations: STRUCTURE; benefit fm modest burdens; damage safeguards against tyranny; federal bureaucracy v. magistracy of states; compare dicta in NY v US; blame / pass the buck]

[The] majority either misconstrues or ignores [cases] that are more directly on point. [For example, in] Testa v. Katt, 330 U.S. 386 (1947), [the] Court unanimously held that state courts of appropriate jurisdiction must occupy themselves adjudicating claims brought by private litigants under the federal Emergency Price Control Act of 1942, regardless of how otherwise crowded their dockets might be with state law matters. [The majority suggests] that Testa rested entirely on the specific reference to state judges in the Supremacy Clause. [Even] if the Court were correct, [its] implied expressio unius argument that the Framers therefore did not intend to permit the enlistment of other state officials is implausible. [The] notion that the Framers would have had no reluctance to "press state judges into federal service" against their will but would have regarded the imposition of a similar—indeed, far lesser—burden on town constables as an intolerable affront to principles of state sovereignty, can only be considered perverse.

[The] provision of the Brady Act that crosses the Court's newly defined constitutional threshold is more comparable to a statute requiring local police officers to report the identity of missing children to the Crime Control Center of the Department of Justice than to an offensive federal command to a sovereign state. If Congress believes that such a statute will benefit the people of the Nation, and serve the interests of cooperative federalism better than an enlarged federal bureaucracy, we should respect both its policy judgment and its appraisal of its constitutional power.

Justice SOUTER, dissenting.

[In] deciding these cases, which I have found closer than I had anticipated, it is The Federalist that finally determines my position. [Hamilton] in No. 27 first notes that because the new Constitution would authorize the National Government to bind individuals directly through national law, it could "employ the ordinary magistracy of each [State] in the execution of its laws." Were he to stop here, he would not necessarily be speaking of anything beyond the possibility of cooperative arrangements by agreement. But he then addresses the combined effect of the proposed Supremacy Clause, Art. VI, cl. 2, and state officers's oath requirement, Art. VI, cl. 3, and he states that "the Legislatures, Courts and Magistrates of the respective members will be incorporated into the operations of the national government, as far as its just and constitutional authority extends; and will be rendered auxiliary to the enforcement of its laws." The natural reading of this language is not merely that the officers of the various branches of state governments may be employed in the performance of national functions; Hamilton says that the state governmental machinery "will be incorporated" into the Nation's operation, and because the "auxiliary" status of the state officials will occur because they are "bound by the sanctity of an oath," I take him to mean that their auxiliary functions will be the products of their obligations thus undertaken to support federal law, not of their own, or the States', unfettered choices. Madison in No. 44 supports this reading. [He] asks why state magistrates should have to swear to support the National Constitution, when national officials will not be required to oblige themselves to support the state counterparts. His answer is that national officials "will have no agency in carrying the State Constitutions into effect. The members and officers of the State Governments, on the contrary, will have an essential agency in giving effect to the Federal Constitution."

[Contrary to the majority's argument,] Federalist No. 27 [is not] incompatible with our decision in New York v. United States. [The notion that] all state officials who take the oath are "incorporated" or are "auxiliaries" operates on officers of the three branches in accordance with the quite different powers of their respective branches. The core power of an executive officer is to enforce a law in accordance with its terms; that is why a state executive "auxiliary" may be told what result to bring about. The core power of a legislator acting within the legislature's subject-matter jurisdiction is to make a discretionary decision on what the law should be; that is why a legislator may not be legally ordered to exercise discretion a particular way without damaging the legislative power as such. The discretionary nature of the authorized legislative Act is probably why Madison's two examples of legislative "auxiliary" obligation address the elections of the President and Senators, not the passage of legislation to please Congress. [Accordingly, I] cannot persuade myself that the statements from No. 27 speak of anything less than the authority of the National Government, when exercising an otherwise legitimate power (the commerce power, say), to require state "auxiliaries" to take appropriate action. To be sure, it does not follow that any conceivable requirement may be imposed on any state official. I continue to agree, for example, [that] New York v. United States was rightly decided.

Justice BREYER, with whom Justice STEVENS joins, dissenting.

[The] United States is not the only nation that seeks to reconcile the practical need for a central authority with the democratic virtues of more local control. At least some other countries, facing the same basic problem, have found that local control is better maintained through application of a principle that is the direct opposite of the principle the majority derives from the silence of our Constitution. The federal systems of Switzerland, Germany, and the European Union, for example, all provide that constituent states, not federal bureaucracies, will themselves implement many of the laws, rules, regulations, or decrees enacted by the central "federal" body. They do so in part because they believe that such a system interferes less, not more, with the independent authority of the "state," member nation, or other subsidiary government, and helps to safeguard individual liberty as well. Of course, we are interpreting our own Constitution, not those of other nations, and there may be relevant political and structural differences between their systems and our own. Cf. The Federalist No.20 (J. Madison and A. Hamilton) (rejecting certain aspects of European federalism). But their experience may nonetheless cast an empirical light on the consequences of different solutions to a common legal problem. [As] comparative experience suggests, there is no need to interpret the Constitution as containing an absolute principle—forbidding the assignment of virtually any federal duty to any state official.

In RENO v. CONDON, 120 S.Ct. 666 (2000), a unanimous Supreme Court held that New York v. United States and Printz had not limited Congress' ability to regulate the commercial vending of personal data by the states. At issue were amendments to the federal Driver's Privacy Protection Act of 1994 (DPPA), which regulated and restricted the ability of states to sell the personal information their motor vehicle departments (DMVs) collect on drivers and car owners. As amended, the DPPA prohibited state DMVs from "knowingly disclos[ing] or otherwise mak[ing] available to any person or entity personal information about any individual obtained by the department in connection with a motor vehicle record," without that individual's consent. The DPPA also imposed extensive regulations on the resale or disclosure of DMV-derived information by private persons and entities. Because South Carolina's own laws explicitly required its DMV to sell this personal information to requesting parties, the state filed suit alleging that the DPPA violated principles of federalism. The Supreme Court upheld the constitutionality of the DPPA as a valid exercise of the Commerce Power.

Speaking for the unanimous Court, Chief Justice REHNQUIST agreed with the United States' contention that, because "the personal, identifying information [regulated by] the DPPA [is] a 'thin[g] in interstate commerce'" within the meaning of United States v. Lopez [1995; 13th Ed., p. 142], "the sale or release of that information is therefore a proper subject of congressional regulation. [The] motor vehicle information which the States have historically sold is used by insurers, manufacturers, [marketers], and others engaged in interstate commerce to contact drivers with customized solicitations. The information is also used in the stream of interstate commerce [for] matters related to interstate motoring. Because drivers' information is, in this context, an article of commerce, its sale or release into the interstate stream of business is sufficient to support congressional regulation."

The Chief Justice then addressed South Carolina's federalism claims: "In New York [1992; 13th ed., p. 212] and Printz, we held federal statutes invalid not because Congress lacked legislative authority over the subject matter, but because [of] principles of federalism contained in the Tenth Amendment. South Carolina contends that the DPPA violates the Tenth Amendment because it 'thrusts upon the States all of the day-to-day responsibility for administering its complex provisions' [making] 'state officials the unwilling implements of federal policy.'

"[We] agree with South Carolina's assertion that the DPPA's provisions will require time and effort on the part of state employees, but reject the State's argument that the DPPA violates the principles laid down in either New York or Printz. We think, instead, that this case is governed by our decision in South Carolina v. Baker [1988; 13th ed., p. 212]. In Baker, we upheld a statute that prohibited States from issuing unregistered bonds because the law 'regulate[d] state activities,' rather than 'seek[ing] to control or influence the manner in which States regulate private parties.'

"Like the statute at issue in Baker, the DPPA does not require the States in their sovereign capacity to regulate their own citizens. The DPPA regulates the States as the owners of databases. It does not require the South Carolina Legislature to enact any laws or regulations, and it does not require state officials to assist in the enforcement of federal statutes regulating private individuals. We accordingly conclude that the DPPA is consistent with the constitutional principles enunciated in New York and Printz.

"As a final matter, we turn to South Carolina's argument that the DPPA is unconstitutional because it regulates the States exclusively. The essence of South Carolina's argument is that Congress may only regulate the States by means of 'generally applicable' laws, or laws that apply to individuals as well as States. But we need not address the question whether general applicability is a constitutional requirement for federal regulation of the States, because the

DPPA is generally applicable. The DPPA regulates the universe of entities that participate as suppliers to the market for motor vehicle information—the States as initial suppliers of the information in interstate commerce and private resellers or redisclosers of that information in commerce."

Page 227. Add after Note, "The Eleventh Amendment as a protector of state sovereignty":

In ALDEN v. MAINE, 119 S. Ct. 2240 (1999), the Court extended the state sovereignty immunity bar announced in Seminole Tribe from lawsuits against states in federal court to lawsuits against states in state court. The sharply divided 5–4 decision affirmed the dismissal of a suit filed in a Maine state court by state probation officers seeking damages for the state's failure to pay them overtime compensation required by the federal Fair Labor Standards Act. The suit had been filed in state court after the plaintiffs' case in federal court had been dismissed under the authority of Seminole Tribe. In an opinion by Justice KENNEDY, the Court held that Congress, in exercising its Article I powers, may not abrogate state sovereign immunity by authorizing private actions for money damages against nonconsenting states in their own courts. Justice Kennedy acknowledged that this limitation on congressional power could not be derived from the text of the Eleventh Amendment, which merely limits the exercise of federal judicial power. He rooted it instead in "the Constitution's structure, and its history, [which] make clear [that] the States' immunity from suit is a fundamental aspect of the sovereignty which the States enjoyed before the ratification of the Constitution, and which they retain today."

Justice Kennedy explained: "Although the Constitution establishes a National Government with broad, often plenary authority over matters within its recognized competence, the founding document 'specifically recognizes the States as sovereign entities.' [Any] doubt regarding the constitutional role of the States as sovereign entities is removed by the Tenth Amendment, which, like the other provisions of the Bill of Rights, was enacted to allay lingering concerns about the extent of the national power. [The] federal system established by our Constitution preserves the sovereign status of the States, [together] with the dignity and essential attributes inhering in that status. [The] generation that designed and adopted our federal system considered immunity from private suits central to sovereign dignity. When the Constitution was ratified, it was well established in English law that the Crown could not be sued without consent in its own courts. [Although] the American people had rejected other aspects of English political theory, the doctrine that a sovereign could not be sued without its consent was universal in the States when the Constitution was drafted and ratified." Interpreting Chisholm v. Georgia (13th ed., p.225) as a sharp deviation from this original understanding, Justice Kennedy read the Eleventh Amendment "not to change but to restore the original constitutional design." And noting that decisions such as Hans v. Louisiana (13th ed., p.225) had declined to "conform the principle of sovereign immunity to the strict language of the Eleventh Amendment," he concluded that "sovereign immunity derives not from the Eleventh Amendment but from the structure of the original Constitution itself."

Turning to the specific question whether Congress may under Article I subject nonconsenting states to private suits in their own courts, which he labeled one "of first impression," Justice Kennedy relied principally on "the structure of the Constitution": "Although the Constitution grants broad powers to Congress, our federalism requires that Congress treat the States in a manner consistent with their status as residuary sovereigns and joint participants in the governance of the Nation. [Private] suits against nonconsenting States [present] 'the indignity of subjecting a State to the coercive process of judicial tribunals at the instance of private parties,' regardless of the forum. [A] power to press a State's own courts into federal service to coerce the other branches of the State [is] the power [ultimately] to commandeer the entire political machinery of the State against its will. [Private] suits against nonconsenting States—especially suits for money damages—may threaten the financial integrity of the States. [An] unlimited congressional power to authorize suits in state court to levy upon the treasuries of the States for compensatory damages, attorney's fees, and even punitive damages could create staggering burdens, giving Congress a power and a leverage over the States that is not contemplated by our constitutional design. [A] congressional power to strip the States of their immunity from private suits in their own courts would [also interfere with the] allocation of scarce resources among competing needs and interests [that] lies at the heart of [a] State's most fundamental political processes." Justice Kennedy concluded that a decision the other way would be anomalous: "Congress cannot abrogate the States' sovereign immunity in federal court; were the rule to be different here, the National Government would wield greater power in the state courts than in its own judicial instrumentalities."

Justice Kennedy took pains to insist that federal laws such as FLSA remained binding on the states: "The constitutional privilege of a State to assert its sovereign immunity in its own courts does not confer upon the State a concomitant right to disregard the Constitution or valid federal law." He also noted a number of alternative routes to enforcement of federal law against the states. He observed that state sovereign immunity does not bar suits to enforce Article I legislation when they are brought by the federal government itself: "Suits brought by the United States itself require the exercise of political responsibility for each suit prosecuted against a State, a control which is absent from a broad delegation to private persons to sue nonconsenting States." Reaffirming Fitzpatrick v. Bitzer (13th ed., p. 225), he noted that state sovereign immunity does not bar suits brought even by private individuals under federal statutes authorized by § 5 of the Fourteenth Amendment: "By imposing explicit limits on the powers of the States and granting Congress the power to enforce them, the Amendment 'fundamentally altered the balance of state and federal power struck by the Constitution,' [allowing] Congress [to] assert an authority over the States which would be otherwise unauthorized by the Constitution." And, reaffirming Ex Parte Young (13th ed., p. 225), he noted that state sovereign immunity does not bar "certain actions against state officers for injunctive or declaratory relief." After finding that Maine had not consented to FLSA suits in its own courts so as to lift the presumptive sovereign immunity bar, Justice Kennedy concluded: "Congress has vast power but not all power. When Congress legislates in matters affecting the States, it may not treat these sovereign entities as mere prefectures or corporations. Congress must accord States the esteem due to them as joint participants in a federal system, one beginning with the premise of sovereignty in both the central Government and the separate States. Congress has ample means to ensure compliance with valid federal laws, but it must respect the sovereignty of the States."

Justice SOUTER, joined by Justices Stevens, Ginsburg and Breyer, filed a lengthy dissent. All four had dissented in Seminole Tribe. Justice Souter began by seeking to refute the majority's arguments from history: "[C]onfront[ing] the fact that the state forum renders the Eleventh Amendment beside the point, [the Court] has responded by discerning a simpler and more straightforward theory of state sovereign immunity than it found in Seminole Tribe: a State's sovereign immunity from all individual suits is a 'fundamental aspect' of state sovereignty 'confirmed' by the Tenth Amendment. [Thus], Seminole Tribe's contorted reliance on the Eleventh Amendment and its background was presumably unnecessary. [But there] is no evidence that the Tenth Amendment constitutionalized a concept of sovereign immunity as inherent in the notion of statehood, and no evidence that any concept of inherent sovereign immunity was understood historically to apply when the sovereign sued was not the font of the law. [The] American Colonies did not enjoy sovereign immunity, that being a privilege understood in English law to be reserved for the Crown alone. [Despite] a tendency among the state constitutions to announce and declare certain inalienable and natural rights of men and even of the collective people of a State, no State declared that sovereign immunity was one of those rights. To the extent that States were thought to possess immunity, it was perceived as a prerogative of the sovereign under common law, [from] which it follows that it was subject to abrogation by Congress as to a matter within Congress's Article I authority. [Even if] a natural law conception of state sovereign immunity in a State's own courts were implicit in the Constitution, [the] Court fails to realize that under the natural law theory, sovereign immunity may be invoked only by the sovereign that is the source of the right upon which suit is brought. [Since] the law in this case proceeds from the national source, whose laws authorized by Article I are binding in state courts, sovereign immunity cannot be a defense."

Justice Souter also disputed the majority's arguments from the Constitution's federalist structure: "The State of Maine is not sovereign with respect to the national objective of the FLSA. It is not the authority that promulgated the FLSA, on which the right of action in this case depends. That authority is the United States acting through the Congress, whose legislative power under Article I of the Constitution to extend FLSA coverage to state employees has already been decided, see Garcia v. San Antonio Metropolitan Transit Authority [1985; 13th ed., p.209] and is not contested here. [The] Court calls 'immunity from private suits central to sovereign dignity,' [but dignity is not] a quality easily translated from the person of the King to the participatory abstraction of a republican State. [It] would be hard to imagine anything more inimical to the republican conception, which rests on the understanding of its citizens precisely that the government is not above them, but of them, its actions being governed by law just like their own." Justice Souter concluded by stressing the practical difficulties the decision imposed upon FLSA enforcement: given that there are 4.7 million state employees, he suggested, the majority's "allusion to enforcement of private rights by the National Government is probably not much more than whimsy. [There] is much irony in the Court's profession that it grounds its opinion on a deeply rooted historical tradition of sovereign immunity, when the Court abandons a principle nearly as inveterate, and much closer to the hearts of the Framers: that where there is a right, there must be a remedy."

On the same day as Alden, the Court invalidated two federal statutes enacted to expressly abrogate state sovereign immunity against patent and trademark actions brought against states in federal court. It found these statutes forbidden by Seminole Tribe if construed as exercises of Article I powers, and inadequately justified as exercises of Congress's powers under § 5 of the Fourteenth Amendment, under which state sovereign immunity might still be abrogated notwithstanding Seminole Tribe. See FLORIDA PREPAID POSTSECONDARY EDUCATION EXPENSE BOARD v. COLLEGE SAVINGS BANK, 119 S. Ct. 2199 (1999), and COLLEGE SAVINGS BANK v. FLORIDA PREPAID POSTSECONDARY EDUCATION EXPENSE BOARD, 119 S. Ct. 2219 (1999), reported below at p. 105. Dissenting in the latter case, Justice BREYER, joined by Justices Stevens, Souter and Ginsburg, argued that the Court's protection of state sovereign immunity paradoxically disserved the values underlying federalism, especially when viewed in light of the circumstances of a world that had changed greatly since the founding: "[Seminole Tribe and progeny] deprive Congress of necessary legislative flexibility. Their rules will make it more difficult for Congress to create [decentralized] regulatory systems that deliberately take account of local differences by assigning roles, powers, or responsibility, not just to federal administrators, but to citizens, at least if such a regime must incorporate a private remedy against a State [to] work effectively. Yet, ironically, Congress needs this kind of flexibility if it is to achieve one of federalism's basic objectives.

"That basic objective should not be confused with the details of any particular federalist doctrine, for the contours of federalist doctrine have changed over the course of our Nation's history. Thomas Jefferson's purchase of Louisiana, for example, reshaped the great debate about the need for a broad, rather than a literal, interpretation of federal powers; the Civil War effectively ended the claim of a State's right to 'nullify' a federal law; the Second New Deal, and its ultimate judicial ratification, showed that federal and state legislative authority were not mutually exclusive; this Court's 'civil rights' decisions clarified the protection against state infringement that the Fourteenth Amendment offers to basic human liberty. In each instance the content of specific federalist doctrines had to change to reflect the Nation's changing needs (territorial expansion, the end of slavery, the Great Depression, and desegregation).

"But those changing doctrines reflect at least one unchanging goal: the protection of liberty. Federalism helps to protect liberty not simply in our modern sense of helping the individual remain free of restraints imposed by a distant government, but more directly by promoting the sharing among citizens of governmental decisionmaking authority. [In] today's world, legislative flexibility is necessary if we are to protect this kind of liberty. Modern commerce and the technology upon which it rests needs large markets and seeks government large enough to secure trading rules that permit industry to compete in the global market place, to prevent pollution that crosses borders, and to assure adequate protection of health and safety by discouraging a regulatory 'race to the bottom.' Yet local control over local decisions remains necessary. Uniform regulatory decisions about, for example, chemical waste disposal, pesticides, or food labeling, will directly affect daily life in every locality. But they may reflect differing views among localities about the relative importance of the wage levels or environmental preferences that underlie them. Local control can take account of such concerns and help to maintain a sense of community despite global forces that threaten it. Federalism matters to ordinary citizens seeking to maintain a degree of control, a sense of community, in an increasingly interrelated and complex world.

"Courts [cannot] easily draw the proper basic lines of authority. The proper local/national/international balance is often highly context specific. And judicial rules that would allocate power are often far too broad. Legislatures, however, can write laws that more specifically embody that balance. [The] modern substantive federalist problem demands a flexible, context-specific legislative response (and it does not help to constitutionalize an ahistoric view of sovereign immunity that, by freezing its remedial limitations, tends to place the State beyond the reach of law). [By] making [sovereign immunity] doctrine immune from congressional Article I modification, the Court makes it more difficult for Congress to decentralize governmental decisionmaking and to provide individual citizens, or local communities, with a variety of enforcement powers. By diminishing congressional flexibility to do so, the Court makes it somewhat more difficult to satisfy modern federalism's more important liberty-protecting needs."

In KIMEL v. FLORIDA BOARD OF REGENTS, 120 S.Ct. 631 (2000), the Court once again invalidated a Congressional attempt to abrogate sovereign immunity—this time under the Age Discrimination in Employment Act of 1967 (ADEA). The ADEA, which originally regulated only private employers, had later been amended to give most state employees the right to sue in federal court for employers' violations of the Act. When several employees at state universities and prisons in Alabama and Florida sued their employers alleging violations of the ADEA, Alabama and Florida raised the defense of sovereign immunity. Before reaching the Fourteenth Amendment issue on which the sovereign immunity decision ultimately hinged (see page 110 below), the Court addressed questions of statutory construction and the Commerce Power.

In a section of the Court's opinion joined by Chief Justice Rehnquist and Justices Stevens, Scalia, Souter, Ginsburg, and Breyer, Justice O'CONNOR began by noting the "simple but stringent test" of statutory construction: " 'Congress may abrogate the States' constitutionally secured immunity from suit in federal court only by making its intention unmistakably clear in the language of the statute' [quoting Atascadero State Hospital v. Scanlon, 473 U.S. 234, 242 (1985)]. [Read] as a whole, the plain language of [the amended statute] clearly demonstrates Congress' intent to subject the States to suit for money damages at the hands of individual employees."

Continuing, in a part of the opinion joined by Chief Justice Rehnquist and Justices Scalia, Kennedy, and Thomas, Justice O'Connor noted that the regulation of age discrimination among employers in general, including the States, was a valid exercise of Congress' Commerce Power. However, she continued, the Commerce Power did not include the power to abrogate sovereign immunity: "[Congress'] powers under Article I [do] not include the power to subject States to suit at the hands of private individuals. [Accordingly], the private petitioners in these cases may maintain their [suits] against the States of

Alabama and Florida if, and only if, the ADEA is appropriate under § 5 [of the 14th Amendment]."

Justice THOMAS, joined by Justice Kennedy, agreed with the majority's constitutional analysis, but maintained that "Congress [had] not made its intention to abrogate 'unmistakably clear' in the text of the ADEA."

Justice STEVENS, joined by Justices Souter, Ginsburg, and Breyer, concurred with the majority's statutory construction analysis, but dissented from the Court's judgment because of disagreement with Justice O'CONNOR's sovereign immunity analysis. Contending that the Eleventh Amendment "only places a textual limitation on [diversity suits in] federal courts," not a limitation on federal courts' power to entertain suits against a state by that state's own citizens, Justice Stevens argued that Seminole Tribe's understanding of sovereign immunity "is so profoundly mistaken and so fundamentally inconsistent with the Framers' conception of the constitutional order that it has forsaken any claim to the usual deference or respect owed to decisions of this Court."

CHAPTER 5

FEDERAL LIMITS ON STATE POWER TO REGULATE THE NATIONAL ECONOMY

SECTION 1. STATE REGULATION AND THE DORMANT COMMERCE CLAUSE

B. THE MODERN COURT'S APPROACH

Page 279. Add at the end of Note, "Facially discriminatory taxes and fees":

In GENERAL MOTORS CORP. v. TRACY, 519 U.S. 278 (1997), the Court rejected a claim that a state sales and use tax exemption scheme was facially discriminatory in violation of the dormant commerce clause. Ohio imposed general sales and use taxes on natural gas purchases from all sellers, whether in-state or out-of-state, that did not meet its statutory definition of a "natural gas company." Ohio's state-regulated local utilities were deemed to satisfy the statutory definition, but producers and independent marketers of natural gas were not. General Motors bought virtually all the gas for its plants from out-of-state independent marketers rather than from local utilities. GM challenged the Ohio tax scheme, arguing that, although it did not distinguish expressly between in-state and out-of-state gas sellers, it was in fact discriminatory because the favored entities by definition were all located within the State. The Court, by a vote of 8–1, rejected the claim, holding that the differential tax treatment of natural gas sales by public utilities and independent marketers was constitutional because the two types of entities effectively competed in separate markets.

Justice SOUTER wrote for the Court: "Conceptually, of course, any notion of discrimination assumes a comparison of substantially similar entities. [In] the absence of actual or prospective competition between the supposedly favored and disfavored entities in a single market there can be no local preference, whether by express discrimination against interstate commerce or undue burden upon it, to which the dormant Commerce Clause may apply." Here, he reasoned, there were two separate markets at issue: the in-state market for gas bundled with various services and protections mandated by state regulators, and the interstate market for unbundled gas. The "natural gas marketers did not serve the [local utilities'] core market of small, captive users, typified by residential consumers who want and need the bundled product. [So] far as this market is concerned, competition would not be served by eliminating any tax differential as between sellers, and the dormant Commerce Clause has no job to do." Justice Stevens was the lone dissenter.

In contrast, in CAMPS NEWFOUND/OWATONNA, INC. v. TOWN OF HARRISON, 520 U.S. 564 (1997), the Court again applied a virtually per se rule of invalidity to a state law that it found facially discriminatory against interstate commerce. A Maine statute provided a property tax exemption to "benevolent and charitable institutions incorporated" in the State, but denied the full exemption to any institution "conducted or operated principally for the benefit of persons who are not residents of Maine." Petitioner, operator of a religious summer camp that had been denied the exemption because 95% of its campers were not Maine residents, challenged this denial as a violation of the dormant commerce clause. The Court invalidated the law by a vote of 5–4. Justice STEVENS wrote for the Court:

"[There] is no question that were this statute targeted at profit-making entities, it would violate the dormant Commerce Clause. 'State laws discriminating against interstate commerce on their face are "virtually per se invalid." ' [The] Maine law expressly distinguishes between entities that serve a principally interstate clientele and those that primarily serve an intrastate market, singling out camps that serve mostly in-staters for beneficial tax treatment, and penalizing those camps that do a principally interstate business. [If] such a policy were implemented by a statutory prohibition against providing camp services to nonresidents, the statute would almost certainly be invalid. [See, e.g.,] Philadelphia v. New Jersey [1978; 13th ed., p. 271.] [Of] course, this case does not involve a total prohibition. [But] discriminatory burdens on interstate commerce imposed by regulation or taxation may also violate the Commerce Clause. See, e.g., Chemical Waste [1996; 13th ed., p. 277.] [It] matters little that it is the camp that is taxed rather than the campers. The record demonstrates that the economic incidence of the tax falls at least in part on the campers. [With] respect to those businesses—like petitioner's—that continue to engage in a primarily interstate trade, the Maine statute therefore functionally serves as an export tariff that targets out-of-state consumers by taxing the businesses that principally serve them. As our cases make clear, this sort of discrimination is at the very core of activities forbidden by the dormant commerce clause."

Justice Stevens went on to reject the argument that different rules should apply to tax exemptions for charitable and commercial entities: "For purposes of Commerce Clause analysis, any categorical distinction between the activities of profit-making enterprises and not-for-profit entities is [wholly] illusory. Entities in both categories are major participants in interstate markets. And, although the summer camp involved in this case may have a relatively insignificant impact on the commerce of the entire Nation, the interstate commercial activities of nonprofit entities as a class are unquestionably significant. [Protectionism,] whether targeted at for-profit entities or serving, as here, to encourage nonprofits to keep their efforts close to home, is forbidden under the dormant Commerce Clause. If there is need for a special exception for nonprofits, Congress not only has the power to create it, but also is in a far better position than we to determine its dimensions." Justice Stevens also rejected the town's argument for application of the "market participant" exception to dormant commerce clause scrutiny. (For this aspect of the case, see p. 21 below.)

Justice SCALIA filed a dissent joined by Chief Justice Rehnquist and Justices Thomas and Ginsburg. He argued first that the Maine tax law did not constitute "facial discrimination" against interstate commerce: "The provision at issue here is a narrow tax exemption, designed merely to compensate or subsidize those organizations that contribute to the public fisc by dispensing public benefits the State might otherwise provide. [Disparate] treatment constitutes discrimination only if the objects of the disparate treatment are, for the relevant purposes, similarly situated. And for purposes of entitlement to a tax subsidy from the State, it is certainly reasonable to think that property gratuitously devoted to relieving the State of some of its welfare burden is not similarly situated to property used 'principally for the benefit of persons who are not residents of [the State].' "In his view, the law ought therefore to have been subject at most to Pike balancing review, which it easily survived.

He argued, second, that even if the law was facially discriminatory, it was supported by such traditional and important state interests that it should survive scrutiny even under the "virtually per se rule of invalidity": "[States] have restricted public assistance to their own bona fide residents since colonial times, and such self-interested behavior (or, put more benignly, application of the principle that charity begins at home) is inherent in the very structure of our federal system. We have [upheld] against equal protection challenge continuing residency requirements for municipal employment and bona fide residency requirements for free primary and secondary schooling. [If] a State that provides social services directly may limit its largesse to its own residents, I see no reason why a State that chooses to provide some of its social services indirectly—by compensating or subsidizing private charitable providers—cannot be similarly restrictive." Finally, he argued that, if the statute was otherwise deemed unconstitutional, the Court should carve out a "domestic charity" exception to the dormant commerce clause, because "the provision by a State of free public schooling, public assistance, and other forms of social welfare to only (or principally) its own residents implicates none of the concerns underlying our negative-commerce-clause jurisprudence."

Justice THOMAS filed a separate dissent, joined by Justice Scalia and in part by Chief Justice Rehnquist, setting forth a general critique of dormant commerce clause jurisprudence: "The negative Commerce Clause has no basis in the text of the Constitution, makes little sense, and has proved virtually unworkable in application. [The] theory [that] the Commerce Clause itself constituted an exclusive grant of power to Congress [has] long since [been] 'repudiated.' [The] theory [that] Congress, by its silence, pre-empts state legislation [has] long since been rejected by this Court in virtually every analogous area of the law. [See, e.g., Erie R. Co. v. Tompkins, 304 U.S. 64 (1938).] [We] have [also] used the Clause to make policy-laden judgments that we are ill-equipped and arguably unauthorized to make."

In a portion of his dissent not joined by Chief Justice Rehnquist, Justice Thomas urged reinterpretation of the Import–Export Clause of Art. I, § 10, cl. 2, which provides that "no State shall, without the Consent of the Congress, lay any Imposts or Duties on Imports or Exports." While the Clause has long been interpreted to prohibit States only from levying taxes on goods imported from or exported to foreign nations, see Woodruff v. Parham, 75 U.S. (8 Wall.) 123 (1869), Justice Thomas urged that the original understanding of the terms "imports" and "exports" might have "encompassed not just trade with foreign nations, but trade with other States as well." He suggested that, "were we to revisit Woodruff," which he exhaustively reviewed and found wrongly decided, "we might find that the Constitution already affords us a textual mechanism with which to address the more egregious of State actions discriminating against interstate commerce." But he would not have found the Maine statute a violation of the Import–Export Clause, if that clause were applied, because the tax involved was neither an "impost" nor a "duty" on goods.

In SOUTH CENTRAL BELL TELEPHONE CO. v. ALABAMA, 119 S. Ct. 1180 (1999), the Court unanimously invalidated an Alabama franchise tax that gave "domestic corporations the ability to reduce their franchise tax liability simply by reducing the par value of their stock, while den[ying] foreign corporations that same ability." The Court deemed the tax rule impermissibly discriminatory against interstate commerce, and rejected the claim that the foreign franchise tax was a " 'compensatory' tax that offsets the tax burden that the domestic shares tax imposes upon domestic corporations," finding insufficient evidence that the special burden that the franchise tax imposed upon foreign corporations was equivalent to any burden on domestic corporations.

C. THE "MARKET PARTICIPANT" EXCEPTION TO THE DORMANT COMMERCE CLAUSE

Page 328. Add after South–Central Timber Devel. v. Wunnicke:

In CAMPS NEWFOUND/OWATONNA, INC. v. TOWN OF HARRISON, 520 U.S. 564 (1997), whose principal holding is set forth above at p. 19, the Court rejected a state's attempt to defend a discriminatory property tax exemption provision on market participant grounds. Maine granted property tax exemptions to charitable corporations but limited the amount of such benefits available to charitable enterprises that, like petitioner's, were operated principally for the benefit of out-of-state residents. Justice STEVENS, writing for the Court, rejected the town's argument that the selective exemption statute amounted to "a governmental 'purchase' of charitable services": "[Maine's] tax exemption statute cannot be characterized as a proprietary activity falling within the market-participant exception. [That a] tax program [has] 'the purpose and effect of subsidizing a particular industry, as do many dispositions of the tax laws, [does] not transform it into a form of state participation in the free market.' [New Energy Co. v. Limbach, 486 U.S. 269 (1988).] 'Assessment and computation of taxes [is] a primeval governmental activity.' [A] tax exemption is not the sort of direct state involvement in the market that falls within the market-participation doctrine.

"Even if we were prepared to expand the exception in the manner suggested by the Town, the Maine tax statute at issue here would be a poor candidate. Alexandria Scrap [see 13th ed., p. 324] involved Maryland's entry into the market for automobile hulks, a discrete activity focused on a single industry. Similarly, South Dakota's participation in the market for cement [in Reeves, Inc. v. Stake, see 13th ed., p. 324] was—in part because of its narrow scope—readily conceived as a proprietary action of the State. In contrast, Maine's tax exemption—which sweeps to cover broad swathes of the nonprofit sector—must be viewed as action taken in the State's sovereign capacity rather than a proprietary decision to make an entry into all of the markets in which the exempted charities function. The Town's version of the 'market participant' exception would swallow the rule against discriminatory tax schemes. [The] notion that whenever a State provides a discriminatory tax abatement it is 'purchasing' some service in its proprietary capacity is not readily confined to the charitable context. A special tax concession for liquors indigenous to Hawaii, for example, might be conceived as a 'purchase' of the jobs produced by local industry, or an investment in the unique local cultural value provided by these beverages. Cf. Bacchus [13th ed., p. 289]. Discriminatory schemes favoring local farmers might be seen as the 'purchase' of agricultural services in order to ensure that the State's citizens will have a steady local supply of the product. Cf. West Lynn [13th ed., p. 278]. Our cases provide no support for the Town's radical effort to expand the market-participant doctrine."

SECTION 2. THE PRIVILEGES AND IMMUNITIES CLAUSE OF ARTICLE IV

Page 336. Add after Edwards v. California:

In SAENZ v. ROE, 119 S. Ct. 1518 (1999), the Court invalidated, by a vote of 7–2, a state durational residency requirement that limited new state residents to the same level of welfare benefits they would have received in their prior states of residence, reasoning that such discrimination between new and old state residents violated the Citizenship Clause of the Fourteenth Amendment, which provides: "All persons born or naturalized in the United States, and subject to the jurisdiction thereof, are citizens of the United States and of the State wherein they reside. No State shall make or enforce any law which shall abridge the privileges or immunities of citizens of the United States;. . . ." In the course of the opinion, Justice STEVENS, writing for the Court, reaffirmed in dicta the right of federal citizens to cross state borders freely, as set forth in Edwards. But because the law at issue in Saenz did not directly implicate that right, he wrote that "we need not identify the source of that particular right in the text of the Constitution. The right of 'free ingress and regress to and from' neighboring States, which was expressly mentioned in the text of the Articles of Confederation, may simply have been 'conceived from the beginning to be a necessary concomitant of the stronger Union the Constitution created.' "

SECTION 3. CONGRESSIONAL ORDERING OF FEDERAL-STATE RELATIONSHIPS BY PREEMPTION AND CONSENT

A. PREEMPTION OF STATE AUTHORITY

Page 344. Add after Gade v. National Solid Wastes Management Ass'n:

In CROSBY v. NATIONAL FOREIGN TRADE COUNCIL, 120 S.Ct. 2288 (2000), the Court unanimously struck down a Massachusetts law barring state entities from buying goods or services from companies doing business with Burma (Myanmar). Delivering the opinion of the Court, Justice SOUTER held that Congress's passage of a federal law imposing mandatory and conditional sanctions on Burma preempted the earlier Massachusetts law, since Massachusetts' more stringent and inflexible provisions presented "an obstacle to the accomplishment of Congress's full objectives under the federal Act."

Justice Souter examined the legislative history of the congressional act in great detail, and concluded that "the state law undermines the intended purpose and 'natural effect' of at least three provisions of the federal Act, that is, its delegation of effective discretion to the President to control economic sanctions against Burma, its limitation of sanctions solely to United States persons and new investment, and its directive to the President to proceed diplomatically in developing a comprehensive, multilateral strategy towards Burma."

He continued: "Congress manifestly intended to limit economic pressure against the Burmese Government to a specific range. [The] State [statute] conflicts with federal law at a number of points by penalizing individuals and conduct that Congress has explicitly exempted or excluded from sanctions. [The] conflicts are not rendered irrelevant by the State's argument that there is no real conflict between the statutes because they share the same goals and because some companies may comply with both sets of restrictions. The fact of a common end hardly neutralizes conflicting means, and the fact that some companies may be able to comply with both sets of sanctions does not mean that the state Act is not at odds with achievement of the federal decision. [Sanctions] are drawn not only to bar what they prohibit but to allow what they permit, and the inconsistency of sanctions here undermines the congressional calibration of force.

"[In addition], the state Act is at odds with the President's intended authority to speak for the United States among the world's nations in developing a 'comprehensive, multilateral strategy to bring democracy to and improve human rights practices [in] Burma.' Congress called for Presidential cooperation with [other] countries in developing such a strategy, directed the President to encourage a dialogue between the government of Burma and the democratic opposition, and required him to report to the Congress on the progress of his diplomatic efforts. [Congress's] express command to the President to take the initiative for the United States among the international community invested him with the maximum authority of the National Government, [citing the Steel Seizure Case (1952; 13th ed., p. 356)], in harmony with the President's own constitutional powers. [This] clear mandate and invocation of exclusively national power belies any suggestion that Congress intended the President's effective voice to be obscured by state or local action.

"[T]he state Act undermines the President's capacity, in this instance for effective diplomacy. It is not merely that the differences between the state and federal Acts in scope and type of sanctions threaten to complicate discussions; they compromise the very capacity of the President to speak for the Nation with one voice in dealing with other governments. [The] President's maximum power to persuade rests on his capacity to bargain for the benefits of access to the entire national economy without exception for enclaves fenced off willy-nilly by inconsistent political tactics."

Justice Souter noted that the Massachusetts law had caused the European Union and Japan to lodge formal complaints against the United States at the World Trade Organization: "[The] consequence has been to embroil the National Government for some time now in international dispute proceedings. [Indeed, the] Executive has consistently represented that the state Act has complicated its dealings with foreign sovereigns and proven an impediment to accomplishing objectives assigned it by Congress. [This] evidence in combination is more than sufficient to show that the state Act stands as an obstacle in addressing the congressional obligation to devise a comprehensive, multilateral strategy."

Justice Souter rejected the state's arguments that it should be free to act given Congress's failure to preempt the state law expressly: "A failure to provide for preemption expressly may reflect nothing more than the settled character of implied preemption doctrine, [and] in any event, the existence of conflict [under] the Supremacy Clause does not depend on express congressional recognition that federal and state law [conflict]." He concluded: "Because the state Act's provisions conflict with Congress's specific delegation to the President of flexible discretion, with limitation of sanctions to a limited scope of actions and actors, and with direction to develop a comprehensive, multilateral strategy under the federal Act, it is preempted, and its application is unconstitutional, under the Supremacy Clause."

Justice SCALIA, joined by Justice Thomas, concurred in a separate opinion objecting to the Court's reliance on "unreliable legislative history" to construe a statute whose meaning and effects were "perfectly obvious": "[E]ven if all of the Court's invocations of legislative history were not utterly irrelevant, I would still object to them, since neither the statements of individual Members of Congress (ordinarily addressed to a virtually empty floor), nor Executive statements and letters addressed to congressional committees, nor the nonenactment of other proposed legislation, is a reliable indication of what a majority of both Houses of Congress intended when they voted. [The] only reliable indication of that intent [is] the words of the bill that they voted to make law. [The] portion of the Court's opinion that I consider irrelevant is quite extensive. [I] consider that to be not just wasteful [but] harmful, since it tells future litigants that, even when a statute is clear on its face, and its effects clear upon the record, statements from the legislative history may help [or harm] the case. If so, they must be researched and discussed by counsel—which makes appellate litigation considerably more time consuming [and] expensive. This to my mind outweighs the arguable good that may come of such persistent irrelevancy, at least when it is indulged in the margins: that it may encourage readers to ignore our footnotes."

CHAPTER 6

SEPARATION OF POWERS

SECTION 2. CONGRESSIONAL ENCROACHMENTS ON THE EXECUTIVE'S DOMAIN

Page 385. Add after Notes on Chadha and the Impoundment Controversy:

Clinton v. New York

524 U.S. 417, 118 S. Ct. 2091, 141 L.Ed.2d 393 (1998).

Justice STEVENS delivered the opinion of the Court.

[Shortly after the decision in Raines v. Byrd, p. 3 above, President Clinton exercised his authority under the Line Item Veto Act of 1996 by canceling a provision of the Balanced Budget Act of 1997 allowing New York to keep certain funds it would otherwise have had to repay to the federal government under the Medicaid program, and a provision of the Taxpayer Relief Act of 1997 giving a tax benefit to food processors acquired by farmers' cooperatives. Claiming that they would be adversely affected by two of these cancellations, New York City and several private organizations challenged the constitutionality of the Medicaid cancellation, and the Snake River Potato Growers, a farmers' cooperative, challenged the constitutionality of the food processors provision. The majority opinion began by finding that, unlike the Members of Congress who filed suit in Raines, these challengers met both prudential and Article III standing requirements (see p. 3 above).]

The Line Item Veto Act gives the President the power to "cancel in whole" three types of provisions that have been signed into law: "(1) any dollar amount of discretionary budget authority; (2) any item of new direct spending; or (3) any limited tax benefit." [In] identifying items for cancellation he must consider the legislative history, the purposes, and other relevant information about the items. He must determine, with respect to each cancellation, that it will "(i) reduce the Federal budget deficit; (ii) not impair any essential Government functions; and (iii) not harm the national interest." Moreover, he must transmit a special message to Congress notifying it of each cancellation within five calendar days (excluding Sundays) after the enactment of the canceled provision. [A] cancellation takes effect upon receipt by Congress of the special message from the President. If, however, a "disapproval bill" pertaining to a special message is enacted into law, the cancellations set forth in that message become "null and void." [A] majority vote of both Houses is sufficient to enact a disapproval bill. The Act does not grant the President the authority to cancel a disapproval bill, but he does, of course, retain his constitutional authority to veto such a bill.

[In] both legal and practical effect, the President has amended two Acts of Congress by repealing a portion of each. "Repeal of statutes, no less than enactment, must conform with Art. I." INS v. Chadha, [1983; 13th ed., p. 375]. There is no provision in the Constitution that authorizes the President to enact, to amend, or to repeal statutes [although] he may initiate and influence legislative proposals. Moreover, after a bill has passed both Houses of Congress, but "before it becomes a Law," it must be presented to the President. If he approves it, "he shall sign it, but if not he shall return it, with his Objections to that House in which it shall have originated, who shall enter the Objections at large on their Journal, and proceed to reconsider it." Art. I, § 7, cl. 2. His "return" of a bill, which is usually described as a "veto," is subject to being overridden by a two-thirds vote in each House.

There are important differences between the President's "return" of a bill pursuant to Article I, § 7, and the exercise of the President's cancellation authority pursuant to the Line Item Veto Act. The constitutional return takes place before the bill becomes law; the statutory cancellation occurs after the bill becomes law. The constitutional return is of the entire bill; the statutory cancellation is of only a part. Although the Constitution expressly authorizes the President to play a role in the process of enacting statutes, it is silent on the subject of unilateral Presidential action that either repeals or amends parts of duly enacted statutes.

There are powerful reasons for construing constitutional silence on this profoundly important issue as equivalent to an express prohibition. The procedures governing the enactment of statutes set forth in the text of Article I were the product of the great debates and compromises that produced the Constitution itself. Familiar historical materials provide abundant support for the conclusion that the power to enact statutes may only "be exercised in accord with a single, finely wrought and exhaustively considered, procedure." [Chadha.] Our first President understood the text of the Presentment Clause as requiring that he either "approve all the parts of a Bill, or reject it in toto." What has emerged in these cases from the President's exercise of his statutory cancellation powers, however, are truncated versions of two bills that passed both Houses of Congress. They are not the product of the "finely wrought" procedure that the Framers designed.

[The] Government [argues that] cancellations do not amend or repeal properly enacted statutes in violation of the Presentment Clause [because] the cancellations were merely exercises of discretionary authority [granted by Congress. But unlike the President's power to suspend exemptions from import duties under provisions of the Tariff Act of 1890 upheld in Field v. Clark, 143 U.S. 649 (1892), the] power to cancel portions of a duly enacted statute [involves greater presidential discretion. Whenever] the President suspended an exemption under the Tariff Act, he was executing the policy that Congress had embodied in the statute. In contrast, whenever the President cancels an item of new direct spending or a limited tax benefit he is rejecting the policy judgment made by Congress and relying on his own policy judgment. Thus, the conclusion in Field v. Clark that the suspensions mandated by the Tariff Act were not exercises of legislative power does not undermine our opinion that cancellations pursuant to the Line Item Veto Act are the functional equivalent of partial repeals of Acts of Congress that fail to satisfy Article I, § 7.

[Neither] are we persuaded by the Government's contention that the President's authority to cancel new direct spending and tax benefit items is no greater than his traditional authority to decline to spend appropriated funds. The Government has reviewed in some detail the series of statutes in which Congress has given the Executive broad discretion over the expenditure of appropriated funds. For example, the First Congress appropriated "sums not exceeding" specified amounts to be spent on various Government operations. In those statutes, as in later years, the President was given wide discretion with respect to both the amounts to be spent and how the money would be allocated among different functions. It is argued that the Line Item Veto Act merely confers comparable discretionary authority over the expenditure of appropriated funds. The critical difference between this statute and all of its predecessors, however, is that unlike any of them, this Act gives the President the unilateral power to change the text of duly enacted statutes. None of the Act's predecessors could even arguably have been construed to authorize such a change.

[We] emphasize [that] we express no opinion about the wisdom of the procedures authorized by the Line Item Veto Act, [that] because we conclude that the Act's cancellation provisions violate Article I, § 7, of the Constitution, we find it unnecessary to consider the District Court's alternative holding that the Act "impermissibly disrupts the balance of powers among the three branches of government," [and that] our decision rests on the narrow ground that the procedures authorized by the Line Item Veto Act are not authorized by the Constitution. [If] the Line Item Veto Act were valid, it would authorize the President to create a different law—one whose text was not voted on by either House of Congress or presented to the President for signature. Something that might be known as "Public Law 105–33 as modified by the President" may or may not be desirable, but it is surely not a document that may "become a law" pursuant to the procedures designed by the Framers of Article I, § 7, of the Constitution. If there is to be a new procedure in which the President will play a different role in determining the final text of what may "become a law," such change must come not by legislation but through the amendment procedures set forth in Article V of the Constitution.

[Affirmed.]

Justice KENNEDY, concurring.

A nation cannot plunder its own treasury without putting its Constitution and its survival in peril. The statute before us, then, is of first importance, for it seems undeniable the Act will tend to restrain persistent excessive spending. Nevertheless, for the reasons given by Justice Stevens in the opinion for the Court, the statute must be found invalid. Failure of political will does not justify unconstitutional remedies. [I disagree with] Justice Breyer, who observes that the statute does not threaten the liberties of individual citizens. [Liberty] is always at stake when one or more of the branches seek to transgress the separation of powers. Separation of powers was designed to implement a fundamental insight: concentration of power in the hands of a single branch is a threat to liberty. [It] follows that if a citizen who is taxed has the measure of the tax or the decision to spend determined by the Executive alone, without adequate control by the citizen's Representatives in Congress, liberty is threatened.

Justice SCALIA, with whom Justice O'CONNOR joins, and with whom Justice BREYER joins as to Part III, concurring in part and dissenting in part.

[III. The] Presentment Clause requires, in relevant part, that "every Bill which shall have passed the House of Representatives and the Senate, shall, before it becomes a Law, be presented to the President of the United States; If he approve he shall sign it, but if not he shall return it," U.S. Const., Art. I, § 7, cl. 2. There is no question that enactment of the Balanced Budget Act complied with these requirements: the House and Senate passed the bill, and the President signed it into law. It was only after the requirements of the Presentment Clause had been satisfied that the President exercised his authority under the Line Item Veto Act to cancel the [New York] spending item. Thus, the Court's problem with the Act is not that it authorizes the President to veto parts of a bill and sign others into law, but rather that it authorizes him to "cancel"—prevent from "having legal force or effect"—certain parts of duly enacted statutes.

Article I, § 7 of the Constitution obviously prevents the President from cancelling a law that Congress has not authorized him to cancel. [But] that is not this case. It was certainly arguable, as an original matter, that Art. I, § 7 also prevents the President from cancelling a law which itself authorizes the President to cancel it. But as the Court acknowledges, that argument has long since been made and rejected. In 1809, Congress passed a law authorizing the President to cancel trade restrictions against Great Britain and France if either revoked edicts directed at the United States. Joseph Story regarded the conferral of that authority as entirely unremarkable in The Orono (CCD Mass. 1812). The Tariff Act of 1890 authorized the President to "suspend, by proclamation to that effect" certain of its provisions if he determined that other countries were imposing "reciprocally unequal and unreasonable" duties. This Court upheld the constitutionality of that Act in Field v. Clark.

[Art. I, § 7] no more categorically prohibits the Executive reduction of congressional dispositions in the course of implementing statutes that authorize such reduction, than it categorically prohibits the Executive augmentation of congressional dispositions in the course of implementing statutes that authorize such augmentation—generally known as substantive rulemaking. There are, to be sure, limits upon the former just as there are limits upon the latter—and I am prepared to acknowledge that the limits upon the former may be much more severe. Those limits are established, however, not by some categorical prohibition of Art. I, § 7, which our cases conclusively disprove, but by what has come to be known as the doctrine of unconstitutional delegation of legislative authority: When authorized Executive reduction or augmentation is allowed to go too far, it usurps the nondelegable function of Congress and violates the separation of powers.

[I] turn, then, to the crux of the matter: whether Congress's authorizing the President to cancel an item of spending gives him a power that our history and traditions show must reside exclusively in the Legislative Branch. [The] President's discretion under the Line Item Veto [is] no broader than the discretion traditionally granted the President in his execution of spending laws. Insofar as the degree of political, "law-making" power conferred upon the Executive is concerned, there is not a dime's worth of difference between Congress's authorizing the President to cancel a spending item, and Congress's authorizing money to be spent on a particular item at the President's discretion. And the latter has been done since the Founding of the Nation. From 1789–1791, the First Congress made lump-sum appropriations for the entire Government—"sums not exceeding" specified amounts for broad purposes. From a very early date Congress also made permissive individual appropriations, leaving the decision whether to spend the money to the President's unfettered discretion. [Examples] of appropriations committed to the discretion of the President abound in our history. [The] constitutionality of such appropriations has never seriously been questioned.

[Certain] Presidents [including Grant, Franklin Roosevelt, and Truman] have claimed Executive authority to withhold appropriated funds even absent an express conferral of discretion to do so. [President] Nixon, the Mahatma Ghandi of all impounders, asserted at a press conference in 1973 that his "constitutional right" to impound appropriated funds was "absolutely clear." Our decision two years later in Train v. City of New York, 420 U.S. 35 (1975), proved him wrong, but it implicitly confirmed that Congress may confer discretion upon the executive to withhold appropriated funds, even funds appropriated for a specific purpose. [The] short of the matter is this: Had the Line Item Veto Act authorized the President to "decline to spend" any item of spending contained in the Balanced Budget Act of 1997, there is not the slightest doubt that authorization would have been constitutional. What the Line Item Veto Act does instead—authorizing the President to "cancel" an item of spending—is technically different. But the technical difference does not relate to the technicalities of the Presentment Clause, which have been fully complied with; and the doctrine of unconstitutional delegation, which is at issue here, is preeminently not a doctrine of technicalities. The title of the Line Item Veto Act, which was perhaps designed to simplify for public comprehension, or perhaps merely to comply with the terms of a campaign pledge, has succeeded in faking out the Supreme Court. The President's action it authorizes in fact is not a line-item veto and thus does not offend Art. I, § 7; and insofar as the substance of that action is concerned, it is no different from what Congress has permitted the President to do since the formation of the Union.

Justice BREYER, with whom Justice O'CONNOR and Justice SCALIA join as to Part III, dissenting.

I. I agree with the Court that the parties have standing, but I do not agree with its ultimate conclusion. In my view the Line Item Veto Act does not violate any specific textual constitutional command, nor does it violate any implicit Separation of Powers principle. Consequently, I believe that the Act is constitutional.

II. I approach the constitutional question before us with three general considerations in mind. First, the Act represents a legislative effort to provide the President with the power to give effect to some, but not to all, of the expenditure and revenue-diminishing provisions contained in a single massive appropriations bill. And this objective is constitutionally proper. When our Nation was founded, Congress could easily have provided the President with this kind of power. In that time period, our population was less than four million, federal employees numbered fewer than 5,000, annual federal budget outlays totaled approximately $4 million. [At] that time, a Congress, wishing to give a President the power to select among appropriations, could simply have embodied each appropriation in a separate bill, each bill subject to a separate Presidential veto. Today, however, our population is about 250 million, the Federal Government employs more than four million people, the annual federal budget is $1.5 trillion, and a typical budget appropriations bill may have a dozen titles, hundreds of sections, and spread across more than 500 pages of the Statutes at Large. Congress cannot divide such a bill into thousands, or tens of thousands, of separate appropriations bills, each one of which the President would have to sign, or to veto, separately. Thus, the question is whether the Constitution permits Congress to choose a particular novel means to achieve this same, constitutionally legitimate, end.

Second, the case in part requires us to focus upon the Constitution's generally phrased structural provisions, provisions that delegate all "legislative" power to Congress and vest all "executive" power in the President. The Court, when applying these provisions, has interpreted them generously in terms of the institutional arrangements that they permit. [McCulloch v. Maryland (1819); 13th ed., p. 89.] [This Court has long recognized] the genius of the Framers' pragmatic vision [in] cases that find constitutional room for necessary institutional innovation. Third, we need not here referee a dispute among the other two branches [but rather review an Act] "approved by both Houses of the Congress and signed by the President." [If] we [interpret] nonliteral Separation of Powers principles in light of the need for "workable government," [Youngstown (Jackson, J., concurring), the] Act is constitutional.

III. The Court believes that the Act violates the literal text of the Constitution. A simple syllogism captures its basic reasoning: Major Premise: The Constitution sets forth an exclusive method for enacting, repealing, or amending laws. Minor Premise: The Act authorizes the President to "repeal or amend" laws in a different way, namely by announcing a cancellation of a portion of a previously enacted law. Conclusion: The Act is inconsistent with the Constitution. I find this syllogism unconvincing, however, because its Minor Premise is faulty. When the President "canceled" the two appropriation measures now before us, he did not repeal any law nor did he amend any law. He simply followed the law, leaving the statutes, as they are literally written, intact.

[Imagine] that the canceled New York health care tax provision at issue here had [specifically provided] "that the President may prevent the just-mentioned provision from having legal force or effect if he determines x, y and z." [One] could not say that a President who "prevents" the [law] from "having legal force or effect," has either repealed or amended [it. He] has executed the law, not repealed it. It could make no significant difference to this linguistic point were the [proviso] to appear [at] the bottom of the statute page, say referenced by an asterisk, with a statement that it applies to every spending provision in the act next to which a similar asterisk appears. And that being so, it could make no difference if that proviso appeared, instead, in a different, earlier-enacted law, along with legal language that makes it applicable to every future spending provision picked out according to a specified formula. But, of course, this last-mentioned possibility is this very case.

[For] that reason, one cannot dispose of this case through a purely literal analysis as the majority does. Literally speaking, the President has not "repealed" or "amended" anything. He has simply executed a power conferred upon him by Congress, which power is contained in laws that were enacted in compliance with the exclusive method set forth in the Constitution. [Because] one cannot say that the President's exercise of the power the Act grants is, literally speaking, a "repeal" or "amendment," the fact that the Act's procedures differ from the Constitution's exclusive procedures for enacting (or repealing) legislation is beside the point. The Act itself was enacted in accordance with these procedures, and its failure to require the President to satisfy those procedures does not make the Act unconstitutional.

IV. Because I disagree with the Court's holding of literal violation, I must consider whether the Act nonetheless violates Separation of Powers principles. [There] are three relevant Separation of Powers questions here: (1) Has Congress given the President the wrong kind of power, i.e., "non-Executive" power? (2) Has Congress given the President the power to "encroach" upon Congress' own constitutionally reserved territory? (3) Has Congress given the President too much power, violating the doctrine of "nondelegation?" [The] answer to all these questions is "no."

[The] power the Act conveys [is] "executive." [It] closely resembles the kind of delegated authority—to spend or not to spend appropriations, to change or not to change tariff rates—that Congress has frequently granted the President, any differences being differences in degree, not kind. The fact that one could also characterize this kind of power as "legislative," say, if Congress itself (by amending the appropriations bill) prevented a provision from taking effect, is beside the point. This Court has frequently found that the exercise of a particular power, [can] fall within the constitutional purview of more than one branch of Government, [for] the Constitution "blends" as well as "separates" powers in order to create a workable government.

[One] cannot say that the Act "encroaches" upon Congress' power, when Congress retained the power to insert, by simple majority, into any future appropriations bill, into any section of any such bill, or into any phrase of any section, a provision that says the Act will not apply. Congress also retained the power to "disapprove," and thereby reinstate, any of the President's cancellations. And it is Congress that drafts and enacts the appropriations statutes that are subject to the Act in the first place—and thereby defines the outer limits of the President's cancellation authority. [Nor] can one say the Act's grant of power "aggrandizes" the Presidential office. The grant is limited to the context of the budget. It is limited to the power to spend, or not to spend, particular appropriated items, and the power to permit, or not to permit, specific limited exemptions from generally applicable tax law from taking effect. The delegation of those powers to the President may strengthen the Presidency, but any such change in Executive Branch authority seems minute when compared with the changes worked by delegations of other kinds of authority that the Court in the past has upheld.

[While the] Constitution permits only those delegations where Congress "shall lay down by legislative act an intelligible principle to which the person or body authorized to [act] is directed to conform," [the] Court has only twice in its history found that a congressional delegation of power violated the "nondelegation" doctrine. [Panama Refining, Schechter Poultry; see 13th ed., p. 400.] [Unlike those cases,] the case before us does not involve [any] "roving commission," [or delegation] to private parties, nor does it bring all of American industry within its scope. It is limited to one area of government, the budget, and it seeks to give the President the power, in one portion of that budget, to tailor spending and special tax relief to what he concludes are the demands of fiscal responsibility. [The] broadly phrased limitations in the Act, together with its evident deficit reduction purpose, and a procedure that guarantees Presidential awareness of the reasons for including a particular provision in a budget bill, [guide] the President's exercise of his discretionary powers. [While, unlike administrative agencies to whom broad power is delegated, the President] has not narrowed his discretionary power through rule, [the] President, unlike most agency decisionmakers, is an elected official. He is responsible to the voters, who, in principle, will judge the manner in which he exercises his delegated authority. [Thus] I believe that the power the Act grants the President to prevent spending items from taking effect does not violate the "nondelegation" doctrine.

[In] sum, I recognize that the Act before us is novel. In a sense, it skirts a constitutional edge. But that edge has to do with means, not ends. The means chosen do not amount literally to the enactment, repeal, or amendment of a law [nor] violate any basic Separation of Powers principle. They do not improperly shift the constitutionally foreseen balance of power from Congress to the President. Nor, since they comply with Separation of Powers principles, do they threaten the liberties of individual citizens. They represent an experiment that may, or may not, help representative government work better. The Constitution, in my view, authorizes Congress and the President to try novel methods in this way.

SECTION 3. EXECUTIVE PRIVILEGE AND IMMUNITIES

Page 410. Add to Note 1 after Nixon v. Fitzgerald:

Clinton v. Jones

520 U.S. 681, 117 S.Ct. 1636, 137 L.Ed.2d 945 (1997).

Justice STEVENS delivered the opinion of the Court.

This case raises a constitutional and a prudential question concerning the Office of the President of the United States. Respondent, a private citizen, seeks to recover damages from the current occupant of that office based on actions allegedly taken before his term began. The President submits that in all but the most exceptional cases the Constitution requires federal courts to defer such litigation until his term ends and that, in any event, respect for the office warrants such a stay. Despite the force of the arguments supporting the President's submissions, we conclude that they must be rejected.

Petitioner, William Jefferson Clinton, was elected to the Presidency in 1992, and re-elected in 1996. His term of office expires on January 20, 2001. In 1991 he was the Governor of the State of Arkansas. On May 6, 1994, [respondent Paula Corbin Jones] commenced this action in the United States District Court for the Eastern District of Arkansas by filing a complaint naming petitioner as [a] defendant. [As] the case comes to us, we are required to assume the truth of the detailed—but as yet untested—factual allegations in the complaint.

Those allegations principally describe events that are said to have occurred on the afternoon of May 8, 1991, during an official conference held at the Excelsior Hotel in Little Rock, Arkansas. The Governor delivered a speech at the conference; respondent—working as a state employee—staffed the registration desk. She alleges that [a state trooper also named in the complaint] persuaded her to leave her desk and to visit the Governor in a business suite at the hotel, where he made "abhorrent" sexual advances that she vehemently rejected. She further claims that her superiors at work subsequently dealt with her in a hostile and rude manner, and changed her duties to punish her for rejecting those advances. Respondent seeks actual damages of $75,000, and punitive damages of $100,000. Her complaint [alleges deprivation and conspiracy to deprive her of federal civil rights under color of state law, and state-law torts of intentional infliction of emotional distress and defamation.] Inasmuch as the legal sufficiency of the claims has not yet been challenged, we assume, without deciding, that each [count] states a cause of action as a matter of law. [Excepting defamation, the] alleged misconduct of petitioner was unrelated to any of his official duties as President of the United States and, indeed, occurred before he was elected to that office.

In response to the complaint, petitioner [filed] a motion to dismiss on grounds of Presidential immunity, and requested the court to defer all other pleadings and motions until after the immunity issue was resolved. [The] District Judge denied the motion to dismiss on immunity grounds and ruled that discovery in the case could go forward, but ordered any trial stayed until the end of petitioner's Presidency. [Both] parties appealed. A divided panel of the Court of Appeals affirmed the denial of the motion to dismiss, but because it regarded the order postponing the trial until the President leaves office as the "functional equivalent" of a grant of temporary immunity, it reversed that order.

P.H.

[The President's] principal submission—that "in all but the most exceptional cases," the Constitution affords the President temporary immunity from civil damages litigation arising out of events that occurred before he took office—cannot be sustained on the basis of precedent. [The] principal rationale for affording certain public servants immunity from suits for money damages arising out of their official acts is inapplicable to unofficial conduct. In cases involving prosecutors, legislators, and judges we have repeatedly explained that the immunity serves the public interest in enabling such officials to perform their designated functions effectively without fear that a particular decision may give rise to personal liability. [That] rationale provided the principal basis for our holding that a former President of the United States was "entitled to absolute immunity from damages liability predicated on his official acts," Nixon v. Fitzgerald, [1982; 13th ed., p. 408.] Our central concern was to avoid rendering the President "unduly cautious in the discharge of his official duties."[1]

precedent

1. [In] Fitzgerald [we noted] that "because of the singular importance of the President's duties, diversion of his energies by concern with private lawsuits would raise unique risks to the effective functioning of government," and suggested further that

This reasoning provides no support for an immunity for unofficial conduct. As we explained in Fitzgerald, "the sphere of protected action must be related closely to the immunity's justifying purposes." Because of the President's broad responsibilities, we recognized in that case an immunity from damages claims arising out of official acts extending to the "outer perimeter of his authority." But we have never suggested that the President, or any other official, has an immunity that extends beyond the scope of any action taken in an official capacity. [As] our opinions have made clear, immunities are grounded in "the nature of the function performed, not the identity of the actor who performed it."

We are also unpersuaded by the evidence from the historical record to which petitioner has called our attention. He points to a comment by Thomas Jefferson protesting the subpoena duces tecum Chief Justice Marshall directed to him in the Burr trial,[2] a statement in the diaries kept by Senator William Maclay of the first Senate debates, in which then Vice-President John Adams and Senator Oliver Ellsworth are recorded as having said that "the President personally [is] not . . . subject to any process whatever," lest it be "put . . . in the power of a common Justice to exercise any Authority over him and Stop the Whole Machine of Government," and to [Justice] Story's comments in his constitutional law treatise [that,] because the President's "incidental powers" must include "the power to perform [his duties], without any obstruction," he "cannot, therefore, be liable to arrest, imprisonment, or detention, while he is in the discharge of the duties of his office; and for this purpose his person must be deemed, in civil cases at least, to possess an official inviolability." Story said only that "an official inviolability" was necessary to preserve the President's ability to perform the functions of the office; [it] does not follow that the broad immunity from all civil damages suits that petitioner seeks is also necessary.

Respondent, in turn, has called our attention to conflicting historical evidence. Speaking in favor of the Constitution's adoption at the Pennsylvania Convention, James Wilson—who had participated in the Philadelphia Convention at which the document was drafted—explained that, although the President "is placed [on] high," "not a single privilege is annexed to his character; far from being above the laws, he is amenable to them in his private character as a citizen, and in his public character by impeachment." 2 J. Elliot, Debates

"cognizance of . . . personal vulnerability frequently could distract a President from his public duties." [The President] argues that in this aspect the Court's concern was parallel to the issue he suggests is of great importance in this case, the possibility that a sitting President might be distracted by the need to participate in litigation during the pendency of his office. In context, however, it is clear that our dominant concern was with the diversion of the President's attention during the decisionmaking process caused by needless worry as to the possibility of damages actions stemming from any particular official decision. [Footnote by Justice Stevens.]

2. The statement by Jefferson to which Justice Stevens alludes here was as follows: "The leading principle of our Constitution is the independence of the Legislature, executive and judiciary of each other, and none are more jealous of this than the judiciary. But would the executive be independent of the judiciary, if he were subject to the commands of the latter, & to imprisonment for disobedience; if the several courts could bandy him from pillar to post, keep him constantly trudging from north to south & east to west, and withdraw him entirely from his constitutional duties?" 10 Works of Thomas Jefferson 404, n. (P. Ford ed. 1905) (letter of June 20, 1807, from President Thomas Jefferson to United States Attorney George Hay).

on the Federal Constitution 480 (2d ed. 1863). This description is consistent with both the doctrine of presidential immunity as set forth in Fitzgerald, and rejection of the immunity claim in this case. [In] the end, as applied to the particular question before us, we reach the same conclusion about these historical materials that Justice Jackson described when confronted with an issue concerning the dimensions of the President's power. "Just what our forefathers did envision, or would have envisioned had they foreseen modern conditions, must be divined from materials almost as enigmatic as the dreams Joseph was called upon to interpret for Pharaoh. A century and a half of partisan debate and scholarly speculation yields no net result but only supplies more or less apt quotations from respected sources on each side.... They largely cancel each other." Youngstown Sheet & Tube Co. v. Sawyer [1952; 13th ed., p. 356.]

[The President's] strongest argument supporting his immunity claim is based on the text and structure of the Constitution. He does not contend that the occupant of the Office of the President is "above the law," in the sense that his conduct is entirely immune from judicial scrutiny. The President argues merely for a postponement of the judicial proceedings that will determine whether he violated any law. His argument is grounded in the character of the office that was created by Article II of the Constitution, and relies on separation of powers principles that have structured our constitutional arrangement since the founding. [The President] contends that he occupies a unique office with powers and responsibilities so vast and important that the public interest demands that he devote his undivided time and attention to his public duties. He submits that—given the nature of the office—the doctrine of separation of powers places limits on the authority of the Federal Judiciary to interfere with the Executive Branch that would be transgressed by allowing this action to proceed.

We have no dispute with the initial premise of the argument. Former presidents, from George Washington to George Bush, have consistently endorsed petitioner's characterization of the office. After serving his term, Lyndon Johnson observed: "Of all the 1,886 nights I was President, there were not many when I got to sleep before 1 or 2 A.M., and there were few mornings when I didn't wake up by 6 or 6:30." In 1967, the Twenty-fifth Amendment to the Constitution was adopted to ensure continuity in the performance of the powers and duties of the office; one of the sponsors of that Amendment stressed the importance of providing that "at all times" there be a President "who has complete control and will be able to perform" those duties. As Justice Jackson has pointed out, the Presidency concentrates executive authority "in a single head in whose choice the whole Nation has a part, making him the focus of public hopes and expectations. In drama, magnitude and finality his decisions so far overshadow any others that almost alone he fills the public eye and ear." Youngstown. We have, in short, long recognized the "unique position in the constitutional scheme" that this office occupies. Fitzgerald.

[It] does not follow, however, that separation of powers principles would be violated by allowing this action to proceed. [There] is no suggestion that the Federal Judiciary is being asked to perform any function that might in some way be described as "executive." [Nor is there any] possibility that the decision will curtail the scope of the official powers of the Executive Branch. Rather [petitioner] contends that—as a by-product of an otherwise traditional exercise of judicial power—[this case] as well as the potential additional litigation that an affirmance [here] might spawn may impose an unacceptable burden on the President's time and energy, and thereby impair the effective performance of his office.

Petitioner's predictive judgment finds little support in either history or the relatively narrow compass of the issues raised in this particular case. [In] the more than 200-year history of the Republic, only three sitting Presidents have been subjected to suits for their private actions.[3] If the past is any indicator, it seems unlikely that a deluge of such litigation will ever engulf the Presidency. As for the case at hand, if properly managed by the District Court, it appears to us highly unlikely to occupy any substantial amount of petitioner's time.

[The] fact that a federal court's exercise of its traditional Article III jurisdiction may significantly burden the time and attention of the Chief Executive is not sufficient to establish a violation of the Constitution. [We] have long held that when the President takes official action, the Court has the authority to determine whether he has acted within the law. Perhaps the most dramatic example of such a case is our holding that President Truman exceeded his constitutional authority when he issued an order directing the Secretary of Commerce to take possession of and operate most of the Nation's steel mills in order to avert a national catastrophe. Youngstown. [It] is also settled that the President is subject to judicial process in appropriate circumstances. Although Thomas Jefferson apparently thought otherwise, Chief Justice Marshall, when presiding in the treason trial of Aaron Burr, ruled that a subpoena duces tecum could be directed to the President. United States v. Burr, 25 F. Cas. 30 (No. 14,692d) (CC Va. 1807). We unequivocally and emphatically endorsed Marshall's position when we held that President Nixon was obligated to comply with a subpoena commanding him to produce certain tape recordings of his conversations with his aides. United States v. Nixon [1974; 13th ed., p. 404.]

[In] sum, "it is settled law that the separation-of-powers doctrine does not bar every exercise of jurisdiction over the President of the United States." Fitzgerald. If the Judiciary may severely burden the Executive Branch by reviewing the legality of the President's official conduct, and if it may direct appropriate process to the President himself, it must follow that the federal courts have power to determine the legality of his unofficial conduct. The burden on the President's time and energy that is a mere by-product of such review surely cannot be considered as onerous as the direct burden imposed by judicial review and the occasional invalidation of his official actions. We therefore hold that the doctrine of separation of powers does not require federal courts to stay all private actions against the President until he leaves office.

We add a final comment on [the] risk that our decision will generate a large volume of politically motivated harassing and frivolous litigation, and the danger that national security concerns might prevent the President from explaining a legitimate need for a continuance. We are not persuaded that either of these risks is serious. Most frivolous and vexatious litigation is

3. Complaints against the pre-presidential conduct of Theodore Roosevelt and Harry Truman were dismissed before they took office, and two cases against John F. Kennedy involving an auto accident during the 1960 Presidential campaign were settled after he took office.

terminated at the pleading stage or on summary judgment, with little if any personal involvement by the defendant. Moreover, the availability of sanctions provides a significant deterrent to litigation directed at the President in his unofficial capacity for purposes of political gain or harassment. History indicates that the likelihood that a significant number of such cases will be filed is remote. Although scheduling problems may arise, there is no reason to assume that the District Courts will be either unable to accommodate the President's needs or unfaithful to the tradition—especially in matters involving national security—of giving "the utmost deference to Presidential responsibilities." Several Presidents, including petitioner, have given testimony without jeopardizing the Nation's security. In short, we have confidence in the ability of our federal judges to deal with both of these concerns. If Congress deems it appropriate to afford the President stronger protection, it may respond with appropriate legislation.

[The] Federal District Court has jurisdiction to decide this case. Like every other citizen who properly invokes that jurisdiction, respondent has a right to an orderly disposition of her claims. [Affirmed.]

Justice BREYER, concurring in the judgment.

I agree with the majority that the Constitution does not automatically grant the President an immunity from civil lawsuits based upon his private conduct. Nor does the "doctrine of separation of powers ... require federal courts to stay" virtually "all private actions against the President until he leaves office." [To] obtain a postponement the President must "bear the burden of establishing its need." In my view, however, once the President sets forth and explains a conflict between judicial proceeding and public duties, [the] Constitution permits a judge to schedule a trial in an ordinary civil damages action [only] within the constraints of a constitutional principle [that] forbids a federal judge in such a case to interfere with the President's discharge of his public duties. I have no doubt that the Constitution contains such a principle applicable to civil suits, based upon Article II's vesting of the entire "executive Power" in a single individual, implemented through the Constitution's structural separation of powers, and revealed both by history and case precedent.

[The] Constitution states that the "executive Power shall be vested in a President." Art. II, § 1. This constitutional delegation means that a sitting President is unusually busy, that his activities have an unusually important impact upon the lives of others, and that his conduct embodies an authority bestowed by the entire American electorate. He (along with his constitutionally subordinate Vice President) is the only official for whom the entire Nation votes, and is the only elected officer to represent the entire Nation both domestically and abroad. [Article] II makes a single President responsible for the actions of the Executive Branch in much the same way that the entire Congress is responsible for the actions of the Legislative Branch, or the entire Judiciary for those of the Judicial Branch. [The Founders decided] to vest Executive authority in one person rather than several [in order] to focus, rather than to spread, Executive responsibility thereby facilitating accountability. They also sought to encourage energetic, vigorous, decisive, and speedy execution of the laws by placing in the hands of a single, constitutionally indispensable, individual the ultimate authority that, in respect to the other branches, the Constitution divides among many.

[For] present purposes, this constitutional structure means that the President is not like Congress, for Congress can function as if it were whole, even when up to half of its members are absent, [and] that the President is not like the Judiciary, for judges often can designate other judges [to] sit even should an entire court be detained by personal litigation. It means that, unlike Congress, which is regularly out of session, the President never adjourns. More importantly, these constitutional objectives explain why a President, though able to delegate duties to others, cannot delegate ultimate responsibility or the active obligation to supervise that goes with it. And the related constitutional equivalence between President, Congress, and the Judiciary, means that judicial scheduling orders in a private civil case must not only take reasonable account of, say, a particularly busy schedule, or a job on which others critically depend, or an underlying electoral mandate. They must also reflect the fact that interference with a President's ability to carry out his public responsibilities is constitutionally equivalent to interference with the ability of the entirety of Congress, or the Judicial Branch, to carry out their public obligations.

[It is true that in] several instances sitting Presidents have given depositions or testified at criminal trials, and [this] Court has twice authorized the enforcement of subpoenas seeking documents from a sitting President for use in a criminal case. I agree with the majority that these precedents reject any absolute Presidential immunity from all court process. But they do not cast doubt upon Justice Story's basic conclusion that "in civil cases," a sitting President "possesses an official inviolability" as necessary to permit him to "perform" the duties of his office without "obstruction or impediment." The first set of precedents tells us little about what the Constitution commands, for they amount to voluntary actions on the part of a sitting President. The second set of precedents amounts to a search for documents, rather than a direct call upon Presidential time. More important, both sets of precedents involve criminal proceedings in which the President participated as a witness. Criminal proceedings, unlike private civil proceedings, are public acts initiated and controlled by the Executive Branch, they are not normally subject to postponement, and ordinarily they put at risk, not a private citizen's hope for monetary compensation, but a private citizen's freedom from enforced confinement.

The remaining precedent to which the majority refers does not seem relevant in this case. That precedent, Youngstown Sheet & Tube Co. v. Sawyer, concerns official action. And any Presidential time spent dealing with, or action taken in response to, that kind of case is part of a President's official duties. Hence court review in such circumstances could not interfere with, or distract from, official duties. Insofar as a court orders a President, in any such a proceeding, to act or to refrain from action, it defines, or determines, or clarifies, the legal scope of an official duty. By definition (if the order itself is lawful), it cannot impede, or obstruct, or interfere with, the President's basic task—the lawful exercise of his Executive authority.

not relevant

[Nixon v. Fitzgerald] strongly supports the principle that judges hearing a private civil damages action against a sitting President may not issue orders that could significantly distract a President from his official duties. [The] Court rested its conclusion in important part upon the fact that civil lawsuits "could distract a President from his public duties, to the detriment of not only the President and his office but also the Nation that the Presidency was designed to serve." [Fitzgerald's] key paragraph, explaining why the President enjoys an absolute immunity rather than a qualified immunity, contains seven sentences, four of which focus primarily upon time and energy distraction and three of which focus primarily upon official decision distortion. Indeed, that key paragraph begins by stating: "Because of the singular importance of the President's duties, diversion of his energies by concern with private lawsuits would raise unique risks to the effective functioning of government." Moreover, the Court, in numerous other cases, has found the problem of time and energy distraction a critically important consideration militating in favor of a grant of immunity.

[The] majority points to the fact that private plaintiffs have brought civil damage lawsuits against a sitting President only three times in our Nation's history; and it relies upon the threat of sanctions to discourage, and "the court's discretion" to manage, such actions so that "interference with the President's duties would not occur." I am less sanguine. Since 1960, when the last such suit was filed, the number of civil lawsuits filed annually in Federal District Courts has increased from under 60,000 to about 240,000; the number of federal district judges has increased from 233 to about 650; the time and expense associated with both discovery and trial have increased; an increasingly complex economy has led to increasingly complex sets of statutes, rules and regulations, that often create potential liability, with or without fault. And this Court has now made clear that such lawsuits may proceed against a sitting President. The consequence, as the Court warned in Fitzgerald, is that a sitting President, given "the visibility of his office," could well become "an easily identifiable target for suits for civil damages."

I concede the possibility that district courts [might] prove able to manage private civil damage actions against sitting Presidents without significantly interfering with the discharge of Presidential duties. [But] ordinary case-management principles are unlikely to prove sufficient to deal with private civil lawsuits for damages unless supplemented with a constitutionally based requirement that district courts schedule proceedings so as to avoid significant interference with the President's ongoing discharge of his official responsibilities. [It] may well be that the trial of this case cannot take place without significantly interfering with the President's ability to carry out his official duties. Yet, I agree with the majority that there is no automatic temporary immunity and that the President should have to provide the District Court with a reasoned explanation of why the immunity is needed; and I also agree that, in the absence of that explanation, the court's postponement of the trial date was premature. For those reasons, I concur in the result.

CHAPTER 8

SUBSTANTIVE DUE PROCESS: RISE, DECLINE, REVIVAL

SECTION 1. SUBSTANTIVE DUE PROCESS AND ECONOMIC REGULATION: THE RISE AND DECLINE OF JUDICIAL INTERVENTION

C. THE MODERN ERA: THE DECLINE—AND DISAPPEARANCE?—OF JUDICIAL SCRUTINY OF ECONOMIC REGULATION

Page 483. Add at the end of Note 1, "The possibility of more substantial scrutiny of economic regulation":

In EASTERN ENTERPRISES v. APFEL, 524 U.S. 498 (1998), the Court, by a vote of 5–4, invalidated provisions of the Coal Industry Retiree Health Benefit Act of 1992 that required companies that had previously employed coal miners to bear a certain portion of the miners' health care costs in retirement, even if they had long since left the business and even if they had not been signatories to the most recent federally brokered labor-management agreements for covering such costs. Four justices, expressing "concerns about using the Due Process Clause to invalidate economic legislation," found the provision imposing this retroactive liability to be a regulatory taking subject to the Just Compensation Clause of the Fifth Amendment. See p. 58 below. Supplying the crucial fifth vote, Justice KENNEDY found takings analysis inapposite, but concurred in the judgment, finding that the Act violated the substantive implications of the Due Process Clause: "Although we have been hesitant to subject economic legislation to due process scrutiny as a general matter, the Court has given careful consideration to due process challenges to legislation with retroactive effects. [For] centuries our law has harbored a singular distrust of retroactive statutes. [Retroactive] lawmaking is a particular concern for the courts because of the legislative 'temptation to use retroactive legislation as a means of retribution against unpopular groups or individuals.' [If] retroactive laws change the legal consequences of transactions long closed, the change can destroy the reasonable certainty and security which are the very objects of property ownership. As a consequence, due process protection for property must be understood to incorporate our settled tradition against retroactive laws of great severity. [The] case before us represents one of the rare instances where the Legislature has exceeded the limits imposed by due process. [In] creating liability for events which occurred 35 years ago the Coal Act has a retroactive effect of unprecedented scope. While we have upheld the imposition of liability on former employers based on past employment relationships, the statutes at issue were remedial, designed to impose an 'actual, measurable cost of [the employer's] business' which the employer had been able to avoid in the past. [The] Coal Act, however, does not serve this purpose. Eastern was once in the coal business and employed many of the beneficiaries, but [their] expectation of lifetime health benefits [was] created by promises and agreements made long after Eastern left the coal business. [This] case is far outside the bounds of retroactivity permissible under our law."

Justice BREYER, joined by Justices Stevens, Souter and Ginsburg in dissent, agreed with Justice Kennedy that the statute did not implicate the Takings Clause, but disagreed that the statute had worked any fundamental unfairness violating due process. He emphasized several factors: "the liability that the statute imposes upon Eastern extends only to miners whom Eastern itself employed," Eastern had earlier "contributed to the making of an important 'promise' to the miners" that their health care costs would be paid in retirement, and "Eastern continued to obtain profits from the coal mining industry" through a subsidiary long after it left the business. These circumstances convinced the dissenters "that Eastern cannot show a sufficiently reasonable expectation that it would remain free of future health care cost liability for the workers whom it employed. Eastern has therefore failed to show that the law unfairly upset its legitimately settled expectations." Justice STEVENS also filed a dissent joined by the other three dissenters, stating that the presumption of constitutionality that should be accorded an act of Congress in the economic area under either the Takings or the Due Process Clause had not been overcome.

SECTION 2. OTHER CONSTITUTIONAL SAFEGUARDS OF ECONOMIC RIGHTS: THE "TAKING–REGULATION" DISTINCTION; THE CONTRACTS CLAUSE

C. EMINENT DOMAIN AND THE "TAKING–REGULATION" DISTINCTION

Page 503. Add after Note 5:

6. *Regulatory "taking" through the imposition of liability.* In EASTERN ENTERPRISES v. APFEL, 524 U.S. 498 (1998), the Court, by a vote of 5–4, invalidated provisions of the Coal Industry Retiree Health Benefit Act of 1992 that required companies formerly in the coal business to bear a significant share of retired miners' health care costs. Justice O'CONNOR, writing for a plurality that also included Chief Justice Rehnquist and Justices Scalia and Thomas, would have treated the law as effecting a compensable taking. Conceding that "[t]his case does not present the 'classic taking' in which the government directly appropriates private property for its own use," Justice O'Connor wrote that it nonetheless interfered with Eastern's property rights: "Our decisions [have] left open the possibility that legislation might be unconstitutional if it imposes severe retroactive liability on a limited class of parties that could not have anticipated the liability, and the extent of that liability is substantially disproportionate to the parties' experience. We believe that the Coal Act's allocation scheme, as applied to Eastern, presents such a case. [There] is no doubt that the Coal Act has forced a considerable financial burden upon Eastern. [The] fact that the Federal Government has not specified the

assets that Eastern must use to satisfy its obligation does not negate that impact. [The] Act's beneficiary allocation scheme reaches back 30 to 50 years to impose liability against Eastern based on the company's activities between 1946 and 1965. [Retroactivity] is generally disfavored in the law, in accordance with 'fundamental notions of justice' that have been recognized throughout history. [The] distance into the past that the Act reaches back to impose a liability on Eastern and the magnitude of that liability raise substantial questions of fairness. [The] Constitution does not permit a solution to the problem of funding miners' benefits that imposes such a disproportionate and severely retroactive burden upon Eastern." Justice THOMAS filed a concurrence stating that he would be willing to reexamine the assumption since Calder v. Bull that the Ex Post Facto Clause applies solely to punishments, and to derive the prohibition on retroactive economic legislation directly from that textual source.

Justice KENNEDY concurred in the judgment on the ground that the law violated substantive due process, see p. 57 above, but dissented vigorously from the plurality's takings analysis: "Until today, [one] constant limitation has been that in all of the cases where the regulatory taking analysis has been employed, a specific property right or interest has been at stake. [The] plurality's opinion disregards this requirement and, by removing this constant characteristic from takings analysis, would expand an already difficult and uncertain rule to a vast category of cases not deemed, in our law, to implicate the Takings Clause. [True,] the burden imposed by the Coal Act may be just as great if the Government had appropriated one of Eastern's plants, but the mechanism by which the Government injures Eastern is so unlike the act of taking specific property that it is incongruous to call the Coal Act a taking, even as that concept has been expanded by the regulatory takings principle." Justices STEVENS and BREYER, each joined by the other and also by Justices Souter and Ginsburg, dissented from both the plurality's takings analysis and Justice Kennedy's due process ruling. Justice Breyer, like Justice Kennedy, emphasized that the general liability imposed by the Act did not apply to any "specific, separately identifiable fund of money," and "runs not to the Government, but to third parties."

7. *Takings of intangible property.* The Court has long regarded the Takings Clause as applying to property other than real property, including intellectual property, see Ruckelshaus v. Monsanto Co., 467 U.S. 986 (1984) (trade secrets), and monetary interest generated from a fund into which a private individual has paid money, see Webb's Fabulous Pharmacies, Inc. v. Beckwith, 449 U.S. 155 (1980) (interest accruing on an interpleader fund deposited in the registry of the court). In PHILLIPS v. WASHINGTON LEGAL FOUNDATION, 524 U.S. 156 (1998), the Court, by a vote of 5–4, considered a takings challenge to a Texas law that, like the laws of many other states, required lawyers to keep clients' funds in escrow in so-called IOLTA accounts—accounts that were permitted to accrue interest if the interest was transferred to charitable purposes such as the provision of legal services for the poor. The challengers contended that the transfer of this interest to legal aid organizations constituted a taking of the clients' property. Chief Justice REHNQUIST, writing for the Court, held that the interest was, under state law, the property of the clients, relying essentially on the ancient adage that "interest follows principal." The Court remanded the case without resolving the further issue

whether the transfer was in fact a taking requiring just compensation. The dissenters, in opinions by Justices SOUTER and BREYER, joined by each other and by Justices Stevens and Ginsburg, objected that the IOLTA program did not in fact "take" interest from clients, because clients would not have been able to obtain any net interest on funds subject to IOLTA if IOLTA did not exist, given background regulatory restrictions on the accrual of interest on individual accounts. In other words, any interest that accrued on IOLTA accounts was government-created property, the government's use of which could not constitute a taking. The majority opinion replied: "While the interest income at issue here may have no economically realizable value to its owner, possession, control, and disposition are nonetheless valuable rights that inhere in the property."

SECTION 3. THE REVIVAL OF SUBSTANTIVE DUE PROCESS, FOR NONECONOMIC RIGHTS: PRIVACY; AUTONOMY; FAMILY RELATIONS; SEXUALITY; THE RIGHT TO DIE

Page 584. Add after Note 3, "The 'undue burden' standard":

4. *Casey and purpose to restrict abortion.* The lead opinion in Casey stated that "unnecessary health regulations that have the *purpose or effect* of presenting a substantial obstacle to a woman seeking an abortion impose an undue burden on the right." What if a law has the purpose of discouraging abortion but does not impose what would otherwise be considered a substantial obstacle? Consider a state that for a period of time permits licensed physicians' assistants to perform various medical procedures including abortions, but that then passes a law restricting the performance of abortions to licensed physicians.

In MAZUREK v. ARMSTRONG, 520 U.S. 968 (1997), the Court held, per curiam, that a Montana law passed under such circumstances did not impose an "undue burden" within the meaning of Casey. It recalled the Court's previous rulings, beginning with Roe, that the performance of abortions may be restricted to physicians. But challengers to the law argued that the law here was nonetheless invalid because drafted specifically to prevent Susan Cahill, a physician's assistant who was the only nonphysician licensed to perform abortions in Montana under the preexisting law, from performing abortions. The Court held that, "even assuming that a legislative purpose to interfere with the constitutionally protected right to abortion without the effect of interfering with that right (here it is uncontested that there was insufficient evidence of a 'substantial obstacle' to abortion) could render the Montana law invalid, there is no basis for finding a vitiating legislative purpose here. [It] is true that the law 'targeted' Cahill in the sense that she was the only nonphysician performing abortions at the time it was passed. But it is difficult to see how that helps rather than harms respondents' case. [Any] claim that this was an unconstitutional bill of attainder [would] be implausible as applied to a provision so commonplace as to exist in 40 other States. And [any view that] the purpose of the law may have been to create a 'substantial obstacle' to abortion is positively contradicted by the fact that only a single practitioner is affected. [There] is simply no evidence that the legislature intended the law to do what it plainly did not do."

In a dissent joined by Justices Ginsburg and Breyer, Justice STEVENS objected to the Court's decision to review the case at all given its preliminary posture in the lower courts, but noted that "there is substantial evidence indicating that the sole purpose of the statute was to target a particular licensed professional" despite the lack of any proven health risk from her practice, and thus that "there is evidence from which one could conclude that the legislature's predominant motive was to make abortions more difficult" in violation of Casey.

5. *"Partial birth" abortion.* In STENBERG v. CARHART, 120 S.Ct. 2597 (2000), the Court struck down a Nebraska law that banned so-called "partial birth abortions" (otherwise known as "dilation and extraction" abortions, or D & X) without providing for exceptions to preserve the mother's health.

Justice BREYER's majority opinion, joined by Justices Stevens, O'Connor, Souter, and Ginsburg, contained a lengthy analysis of the several procedures used in abortion, and analyzed conflicting expert opinions on the relative safety of each option. Although Nebraska contended that a health exception to the ban was unnecessary since D & X was never itself necessary to maternal health, the Court relied on the District Court's finding that "D & X significantly obviates health risks in certain circumstances" in concluding that "a statute that altogether forbids D & X creates a significant health risk. [Where] substantial medical authority supports the proposition that banning a particular abortion procedure could endanger women's health, Casey requires the statute to include a health exception when the procedure is 'necessary, in appropriate medical judgment, for the preservation of the life or health of the mother.' [1992; 13th ed., p. 557] Requiring such an exception in this case is no departure from Casey, but simply a straightforward application of its holding." Justice Breyer further stated that the statute's language could be reasonably interpreted to ban activities commonly occurring during the main type of non-D & X abortion procedures; hence, the statute violated Casey: "[U]sing this law some present prosecutors and future Attorneys General may choose to pursue physicians who use [dilation and extraction, or] D & E procedures, the most commonly used method for performing previability second trimester abortions. All those who perform abortion procedures using that method must fear prosecution, conviction, and imprisonment. The result is an undue burden upon a woman's right to make an abortion decision."

Justice STEVENS, joined by Justice Ginsburg, concurred: "[D]uring the past 27 years, the central holding of Roe v. Wade [1973; 13th ed., p. 530] has been endorsed by all but 4 of the 17 Justices who have addressed the issue. That holding—that the word 'liberty' in the Fourteenth Amendment includes a woman's right to make this difficult and extremely personal decision—makes it impossible for me to understand how a State has any legitimate interest in requiring a doctor to follow any procedure other than the one that he or she reasonably believes will best protect the woman in her exercise of this constitutional liberty. Justice GINSBURG also wrote a concurrence, joined by Justice Stevens, which saw the Nebraska law as an attempt 'to chip away at the private choice shielded by Roe v. Wade, even as modified by Casey.' "

Justice O'CONNOR concurred: "[If] Nebraska's statute limited its application to the D & X procedure and included an exception for the life and health of the mother, the question presented would be quite different than the one we face today. [If] there were adequate alternative methods for a woman safely to obtain an abortion before viability, it is unlikely that prohibiting the D & X procedure alone would 'amount in practical terms to a substantial obstacle to a woman seeking an abortion.' Thus, a ban on partial-birth abortion that only proscribed the D & X method of abortion and that included an exception to preserve the life and health of the mother would be constitutional in my view."

Justice KENNEDY (one of the Casey plurality's joint authors) dissented, joined by Chief Justice Rehnquist. "The Court's failure to accord any weight to Nebraska's interest in prohibiting partial-birth abortion is erroneous and undermines its discussion and holding. [Casey] is premised on the States having an important constitutional role in defining their interests in the abortion debate. [States] may take sides in the abortion debate and come down on the side of [life] in the unborn. [States] also have an interest in forbidding medical procedures which, [might] cause the medical profession or society as a whole to become insensitive [to] life. [A] State may take measures to ensure the medical profession and its members are viewed as healers [cognizant] of the dignity and value of human life. Washington v. Glucksberg. [The] issue is not whether members of the judiciary can see a difference between [various abortion] procedures. [Nebraska] was entitled to find the existence of a consequential moral difference between the procedures. [Demonstrating] a further and basic misunderstanding of Casey, the Court holds the ban on the D & X procedure fails because it does not include an exception permitting an abortionist to perform a D & X whenever he believes it will best preserve the health of the woman. [The] holding of Casey, allowing a woman to elect abortion in defined circumstances, is not in question here. Nebraska, however, was entitled to conclude that its ban, while advancing important interests regarding the sanctity of life, deprived no woman of a safe abortion and therefore did not impose a substantial obstacle on the rights of any woman."

Justice THOMAS's vigorous dissent, joined by Chief Justice Rehnquist and Justice Scalia, contained a graphic description of the "partial birth" procedure, rejected the Court's interpretation that the statute could be read to extend to non-D & X procedures, and criticized the majority's analysis of the maternal-health issue. "In Roe and Casey, the Court stated that the State may 'regulate, and even proscribe, abortion except where it is necessary, in appropriate medical judgment, for the preservation of the life or health of the mother.' Casey said that a health exception must be available if 'continuing her pregnancy would constitute a threat' to the woman. [These] cases addressed only the situation in which a woman must obtain an abortion because of some threat to her health from continued pregnancy. [The] majority [fails] to distinguish between cases in which health concerns require a woman to obtain an abortion and cases in which health concerns cause a woman who desires an abortion (for whatever reason) to prefer one method over another. [As] if this state of affairs were not bad enough, the majority expands the health exception rule [in] one additional and equally pernicious way. [According] to the majority, so long as a doctor can point to support in the profession for his (or the woman's) preferred procedure, it is 'necessary' and the physician is entitled to perform it. But such a health exception requirement eviscerates Casey's undue burden standard and imposes unfettered abortion-on-demand. [In] effect, no regulation of abortion procedures is permitted because there will always be some support for a procedure and there will always be some doctors who conclude that the procedure is preferable. [The] Casey joint opinion makes clear that the Court should not strike down state regulations of abortion based on the fact that some women might face a marginally higher health risk from the regulation.

"[We] were reassured repeatedly in Casey that not all regulations of abortion are unwarranted. [Under] Casey, the regulation before us today should easily pass constitutional muster. But [today] we are told that 30 States are prohibited from banning one rarely used form of abortion that they believe to border on infanticide. It is clear that the Constitution does not compel this result." Chief Justice REHNQUIST and Justice SCALIA each wrote separate dissents, as well.

Page 587. Add at end of Note 1 on Moore v. East Cleveland:

In a 6–3 decision in TROXEL v. GRANVILLE, 120 S. Ct. 2054 (2000), the Court concluded that a state court decision granting grandparents visiting rights to their grandchildren over the objections of the sole surviving parent—a "fit, custodial mother"—had violated the mother's substantive due process rights.

Writing for herself, Chief Justice Rehnquist and Justices Ginsburg and Breyer, Justice O'CONNOR stated that "it cannot now be doubted that the Due Process Clause of the Fourteenth Amendment protects the fundamental right of parents to make decisions concerning the care, custody, and control of their children. [So] long as a parent adequately cares for his or her children, [there] will normally be no reason for the State to inject itself into the private realm of the family [to contradict a parent's] decisions concerning [childrearing]. [If] a fit parent's decision of the kind at issue here becomes subject to judicial review, the court must accord at least some special weight to the parent's own determination. [The] Due Process Clause does not permit a State to infringe on the fundamental right of parents to make childrearing decisions simply because a state judge believes a 'better' decision could be made." Justice O'Connor declined to define "the precise scope" of parents' right to control their children's visitation, but concluded that, because the trial judge in this case had granted the visitation rights without according special weight to the mother's decision, the visitation order was an infringement on her due process right.[1]

Justice THOMAS's concurrence reluctantly saw the case as controlled by substantive due process precedent: "[N]either party has argued that our substantive due process cases were wrongly decided and that the original understanding of the Due Process Clause precludes judicial enforcement of unenumerated rights. [As] a result, I express no view on the merits of this matter, and [understand] the plurality [to] leave the resolution of that issue for another day. Consequently, I agree with the plurality that this Court's recognition of [the fundamental parental right] resolves this case."

1. Concurring in the judgment, Justice SOUTER found the State Supreme Court's judgment that the statute was unconstitutional controlling in this case.

Justice STEVENS dissented: "[T]here are plainly any number of cases—indeed, one suspects, the most common to arise—in which the 'person' [seeking] visitation is a once-custodial caregiver, an intimate relation, or even a genetic parent. Even the Court would seem to agree that in many circumstances, it would be constitutionally permissible for a court to award some visitation of a child to a parent or previous caregiver. [While the Constitution] certainly protects the parent-child relationship from arbitrary impairment by the State, we have never held that the parent's liberty interest in this relationship is so inflexible as to establish a rigid constitutional shield, protecting every arbitrary parental decision from any challenge absent a threshold finding of harm. [Cases] like this do not present a bipolar struggle between the parents and the State over who has final authority to determine what is in a child's best interests. There is at a minimum a third individual, whose interests are implicated in every case to which the statute applies—the child. [It] seems clear to me that the Due Process Clause of the Fourteenth Amendment leaves room for States to consider the impact on a child of possibly arbitrary parental decisions that neither serve nor are motivated by the best interests of the child."

Justice SCALIA likewise dissented: "[W]hile I would think it entirely compatible with [representative] democracy [to] argue, in legislative chambers or in electoral campaigns, that the state has no power to interfere with parents' authority over the rearing of their children, I do not believe that the power which the Constitution confers upon me as a judge entitles me to deny legal effect to laws that (in my view) infringe upon what is (in my view) [an] unenumerated right."

Justice KENNEDY's dissent echoed Justice Stevens: "[T]he constitutionality of the application of the best interests standard depends on [specific] factors. [A] fit parent's right vis-a-vis a complete stranger is one thing; her right vis-a-vis another parent or a de facto parent may be another. [Family] courts in the 50 States confront these factual variations each day, and are best situated to consider the [issues] that arise."

Page 601. Add after Note 2, "Substantive Due Process and the Mentally Retarded":

2a. *Substantive due process and civil confinement of the dangerous and mentally ill.* In KANSAS v. HENDRICKS, 521 U.S. 346 (1997), the Court considered the constitutionality of a statute that provided for the involuntary civil commitment, upon release from prison, of any person who had been convicted of a sexually violent offense and "who suffers from a mental abnormality or personality disorder which makes [him] likely to engage in the predatory acts of sexual violence." Hendricks was ordered confined on a diagnosis of the "mental abnormality" of pedophilia. The Court sustained the statute against Hendricks' substantive due process challenge. In an opinion by Justice THOMAS, the Court noted that "an individual's constitutionally protected interest in avoiding physical restraint" may be overridden by "civil commitment statutes when they have coupled proof of dangerousness with the proof of some additional factor, such as a 'mental illness' or 'mental abnormality.'" Justice Thomas rejected Hendricks' claim that the Kansas statute was deficient because its terms "mental abnormality" and "personality disorder" ranged more broadly than the concept of "mental illness" as defined by the psychiatric profession. He noted that "we have traditionally left to legislators the task of defining terms of a medical nature that have legal significance" and that these terms "need not mirror those advanced by the medical profession." The Court also rejected Hendricks' double jeopardy and ex post facto claims on the ground that his term of civil confinement was not punitive in nature, but rather intended to prevent his dangerous behavior.

Justice BREYER, joined by Justices Stevens and Souter, agreed that "the Due Process Clause permits Kansas to classify Hendricks as a mentally ill and dangerous person for civil commitment purposes." He suggested, though, that there was a serious question whether Kansas had violated substantive due process by deeming Hendricks treatable but failing to provide certain available treatment. But he did not reach that question, finding instead, here joined as well by Justice Ginsburg, that the state's failure to provide treatment helped to render the confinement punitive and therefore a violation of the Ex Post Facto Clause (because the civil confinement law was enacted after the crime for which Hendricks had been punished).

Page 610. Replace Note 2, "A right to physician-assisted suicide," with:

Washington v. Glucksberg

521 U.S. 702, 117 S.Ct. 2258, 138 L.Ed.2d 772 (1997).

Chief Justice REHNQUIST delivered the opinion of the Court.

The question presented in this case is whether Washington's prohibition against "causing" or "aiding" a suicide offends the Fourteenth Amendment to the United States Constitution. We hold that it does not.

It has always been a crime to assist a suicide in the State of Washington. In 1854, Washington's first Territorial Legislature outlawed "assisting another in the commission of self-murder." Today, Washington law provides: "A person is guilty of promoting a suicide attempt when he knowingly causes or aids another person to attempt suicide." "Promoting a suicide attempt" is a felony, punishable by up to five years' imprisonment and up to a $10,000 fine. At the same time, Washington's Natural Death Act, enacted in 1979, states that the "withholding or withdrawal of life-sustaining treatment" at a patient's direction "shall not, for any purpose, constitute a suicide."

Petitioners in this case are the State of Washington and its Attorney General. Respondents [are] physicians who practice in Washington. These doctors occasionally treat terminally ill, suffering patients, and declare that they would assist these patients in ending their lives if not for Washington's assisted-suicide ban. In January 1994, respondents, along with three gravely ill, pseudonymous plaintiffs who have since died and Compassion in Dying, a nonprofit organization that counsels people considering physician-assisted suicide, sued in the United States District Court, seeking a declaration that [the assisted-suicide ban] is, on its face, unconstitutional. [The district court invalidated the statute and the Court of Appeals reversed, but then reversed itself en banc and affirmed the district court. The en banc decision held that] "the Constitution encompasses a due process liberty interest in controlling the time and manner of one's death" [and] that the State's assisted-suicide ban was unconstitutional "as applied to terminally ill competent adults who wish to hasten their deaths with medication prescribed by their physicians."[1] [We] now reverse.

We begin, as we do in all due-process cases, by examining our Nation's history, legal traditions, and practices. In almost every State—indeed, in almost every western democracy—it is a crime to assist a suicide. The States' assisted-suicide bans are not innovations. Rather, they are longstanding expressions of the States' commitment to the protection and preservation of all human life. Indeed, opposition to and condemnation of suicide—and, therefore, of assisting suicide—are consistent and enduring themes of our philosophical, legal, and cultural heritages. [For] over 700 years, the Anglo–American common-law tradition has punished or otherwise disapproved of both suicide and assisting suicide. In the 13th century, Henry de Bracton, one of the first legal-treatise writers, observed that "just as a man may commit felony by slaying another so may he do so by slaying himself." [The criminal sanction for suicide was forfeiture of property to the king.] [Centuries] later, Sir William Blackstone, whose Commentaries on the Laws of England not only provided a definitive summary of the common law but was also a primary legal authority for 18th and 19th century American lawyers, [emphasized] that "the law has . . . ranked [suicide] among the highest crimes."

For the most part, the early American colonies adopted the common-law approach. [Over] time, however, the American colonies abolished [the] criminal-forfeiture sanction. [The] movement away from the common law's harsh sanctions did not represent an acceptance of suicide; rather, [it] reflected the growing consensus that it was unfair to punish the suicide's family for his wrongdoing. [Courts] continued to condemn it as a [grievous,] though nonfelonious, wrong. [Colonial] and early state legislatures and courts did not retreat from prohibiting assisting suicide. [And] the prohibitions against assisting suicide never contained exceptions for those who were near death. The earliest American statute explicitly to outlaw assisting suicide was enacted in New York in 1828, and many of the new States and Territories followed New York's example. [By] the time the Fourteenth Amendment was ratified, it was a crime in most States to assist a suicide. [In] this century, the Model Penal Code also prohibited "aiding" suicide, prompting many States to enact or revise their assisted-suicide bans.

[Though] deeply rooted, the States' assisted-suicide bans have in recent years been reexamined and, generally, reaffirmed. Because of advances in medicine and technology, Americans today are increasingly likely to die in institutions, from chronic illnesses. Public concern and democratic action are therefore sharply focused on how best to protect dignity and independence at the end of life, with the result that there have been many significant changes in state laws and in the attitudes these laws reflect. Many States, for example, now permit "living wills," surrogate health-care decisionmaking, and the withdrawal or refusal of life-sustaining medical treatment. At the same time, however, voters and legislators continue for the most part to reaffirm their States' prohibitions on assisting suicide.

1. [It] is the court [of appeals'] holding that Washington's physician-assisted suicide statute is unconstitutional as applied to the "class of terminally ill, mentally competent patients" that is before us today. [Footnote by Chief Justice Rehnquist.]

[In] 1991, Washington voters rejected a ballot initiative which, had it passed, would have permitted a form of physician-assisted suicide. [California] voters rejected an assisted-suicide initiative similar to Washington's in 1993. On the other hand, in 1994, voters in Oregon enacted, also through ballot initiative, that State's "Death With Dignity Act," which legalized physician-assisted suicide for competent, terminally ill adults. Since the Oregon vote, many proposals to legalize assisted-suicide have been and continue to be introduced in the States' legislatures, but none has been enacted. [Last] year, Iowa and Rhode Island joined the overwhelming majority of States explicitly prohibiting assisted suicide. [On] April 30, 1997, President Clinton signed the Federal Assisted Suicide Funding Restriction Act of 1997, which prohibits the use of federal funds in support of physician-assisted suicide. [Attitudes] toward suicide itself have changed since Bracton, but our laws have consistently condemned, and continue to prohibit, assisting suicide.

The Due Process Clause guarantees more than fair process, and the "liberty" it protects includes more than the absence of physical restraint. [We] have also assumed, and strongly suggested, that the Due Process Clause protects the traditional right to refuse unwanted lifesaving medical treatment. Cruzan [v. Director, Mo. Dept. Health (1990); 13th ed., p. 602.] But we "have always been reluctant to expand the concept of substantive due process because guideposts for responsible decisionmaking in this unchartered area are scarce and open-ended." By extending constitutional protection to an asserted right or liberty interest, we, to a great extent, place the matter outside the arena of public debate and legislative action. We must therefore "exercise the utmost care whenever we are asked to break new ground in this field," lest the liberty protected by the Due Process Clause be subtly transformed into the policy preferences of the members of this Court,

Our established method of substantive-due-process analysis has two primary features: First, we have regularly observed that the Due Process Clause specially protects those fundamental rights and liberties which are, objectively, "deeply rooted in this Nation's history and tradition," Moore v. East Cleveland (plurality opinion) and "implicit in the concept of ordered liberty," such that "neither liberty nor justice would exist if they were sacrificed," Palko v. Connecticut. Second, we have required in substantive-due-process cases a "careful description" of the asserted fundamental liberty interest. Our Nation's history, legal traditions, and practices thus provide the crucial "guideposts for responsible decisionmaking" that direct and restrain our exposition of the Due Process Clause. Justice Souter, relying on Justice Harlan's dissenting opinion in Poe v. Ullman, would largely abandon this restrained methodology, and instead ask "whether [Washington's] statute sets up one of those 'arbitrary impositions' or 'purposeless restraints' at odds with the Due Process Clause of the Fourteenth Amendment." In our view, however, the development of this Court's substantive-due-process jurisprudence has been a process whereby the outlines of the "liberty" specially protected by the Fourteenth Amendment—never fully clarified, to be sure, and perhaps not capable of being fully clarified—have at least been carefully refined by concrete examples involving fundamental rights found to be deeply rooted in our legal tradition. This approach tends to rein in the subjective elements that are necessarily present in due-process judicial review.

[The] question before us is whether the "liberty" specially protected by the Due Process Clause includes a right to commit suicide which itself includes a right to assistance in doing so. We now inquire whether this asserted right has any place in our Nation's traditions. Here [we] are confronted with a consistent and almost universal tradition that has long rejected the asserted right, and continues explicitly to reject it today, even for terminally ill, mentally competent adults. To hold for respondents, we would have to reverse centuries of legal doctrine and practice, and strike down the considered policy choice of almost every State. Respondents contend, however, that the liberty interest they assert is consistent with this Court's substantive-due-process line of cases, if not with this Nation's history and practice.

[Respondents] contend that in Cruzan we "acknowledged that competent, dying persons have the right to direct the removal of life-sustaining medical treatment and thus hasten death," and that "the constitutional principle behind recognizing the patient's liberty to direct the withdrawal of artificial life support applies at least as strongly to the choice to hasten impending death by consuming lethal medication." [The] right assumed in Cruzan, however, was not simply deduced from abstract concepts of personal autonomy. Given the common-law rule that forced medication was a battery, and the long legal tradition protecting the decision to refuse unwanted medical treatment, our assumption was entirely consistent with this Nation's history and constitutional traditions. The decision to commit suicide with the assistance of another may be just as personal and profound as the decision to refuse unwanted medical treatment, but it has never enjoyed similar legal protection. Respondents also rely on Casey. [The] Court of Appeals, like the District Court, found Casey "'highly instructive'" and "'almost prescriptive'" for determining "'what liberty interest may inhere in a terminally ill person's choice to commit suicide.'" [But language in Casey suggesting that] many of the rights and liberties protected by the Due Process Clause sound in personal autonomy does not warrant the sweeping conclusion that any and all important, intimate, and personal decisions are so protected, and Casey did not suggest otherwise.

The history of the law's treatment of assisted suicide in this country has been and continues to be one of the rejection of nearly all efforts to permit it. That being the case, our decisions lead us to conclude that the asserted "right" to assistance in committing suicide is not a fundamental liberty interest protected by the Due Process Clause. The Constitution also requires, however, that Washington's assisted-suicide ban be rationally related to legitimate government interests. This requirement is unquestionably met here. Washington's assisted-suicide ban implicates a number of state interests.

First, Washington has an "unqualified interest in the preservation of human life." Cruzan. The State's prohibition on assisted suicide, like all homicide laws, both reflects and advances its commitment to this interest. This interest is symbolic and aspirational as well as practical. [The] Court of Appeals [held] that the "weight" of this interest depends on the "medical condition and the wishes of the person whose life is at stake." [But] the States "may properly decline to make judgments about the 'quality' of life that a particular individual may enjoy," Cruzan, [even] for those who are near death.

Relatedly, all admit that suicide is a serious public-health problem, especially among persons in otherwise vulnerable groups. [The] State has an interest in preventing suicide, and in studying, identifying, and treating its causes. Those who attempt suicide—terminally ill or not—often suffer from depression or other mental disorders. Research indicates, however, that many people who request physician-assisted suicide withdraw that request if their depression and pain are treated. [Thus,] legal physician-assisted suicide could make it more difficult for the State to protect depressed or mentally ill persons, or those who are suffering from untreated pain, from suicidal impulses.

The State also has an interest in protecting the integrity and ethics of the medical profession. [The] American Medical Association, like many other medical and physicians' groups, has concluded that "physician-assisted suicide is fundamentally incompatible with the physician's role as healer." And physician-assisted suicide could, it is argued, undermine the trust that is essential to the doctor-patient relationship by blurring the time-honored line between healing and harming.

Next, the State has an interest in protecting vulnerable groups—including the poor, the elderly, and disabled persons—from abuse, neglect, and mistakes. We have recognized [the] real risk of subtle coercion and undue influence in end-of-life situations. Cruzan. The [blue-ribbon] New York Task Force [on Life and the Law] warned that "legalizing physician-assisted suicide would pose profound risks to many individuals who are ill and vulnerable.... The risk of harm is greatest for the many individuals in our society whose autonomy and well-being are already compromised by poverty, lack of access to good medical care, advanced age, or membership in a stigmatized social group." If physician-assisted suicide were permitted, many might resort to it to spare their families the substantial financial burden of end-of-life health-care costs. The State's interest here goes beyond protecting the vulnerable from coercion; it extends to protecting disabled and terminally ill people from prejudice, negative and inaccurate stereotypes, and "societal indifference."

Finally, the State may fear that permitting assisted suicide will start it down the path to voluntary and perhaps even involuntary euthanasia. [What] is couched as a limited right to "physician-assisted suicide" is likely, in effect, a much broader license, which could prove extremely difficult to police and contain. [This] concern is supported by evidence about the practice of euthanasia in the Netherlands. The Dutch government's own study [suggests] that [euthanasia] in the Netherlands has not been limited to competent, terminally ill adults who are enduring physical suffering, and that regulation of the practice may not have prevented abuses in cases involving vulnerable persons, including severely disabled neonates and elderly persons suffering from dementia. Washington, like most other States, reasonably ensures against this risk by banning, rather than regulating, assisting suicide.

We need not weigh exactingly the relative strengths of these various interests. They are unquestionably important and legitimate, and Washington's ban on assisted suicide is at least reasonably related to their promotion and protection. We therefore hold that [the Washington statute] does not violate the Fourteenth Amendment, either on its face or "as applied to competent, terminally ill adults who wish to hasten their deaths by obtaining medication prescribed by their doctors."[2]

2. [We] emphasize that we today reject the Court of Appeals' specific holding that the statute is unconstitutional "as applied" to a particular class. Justice Stevens agrees

Throughout the Nation, Americans are engaged in an earnest and profound debate about the morality, legality, and practicality of physician-assisted suicide. Our holding permits this debate to continue, as it should in a democratic society. [Reversed.]

Justice O'CONNOR, concurring.[3]

[I] join the Court's opinions because I agree that there is no generalized right to "commit suicide." But respondents urge us to address the narrower question whether a mentally competent person who is experiencing great suffering has a constitutionally cognizable interest in controlling the circumstances of his or her imminent death. I see no need to reach that question in the context of the facial challenges to the New York and Washington laws at issue here. The parties and amici agree that in these States a patient who is suffering from a terminal illness and who is experiencing great pain has no legal barriers to obtaining medication, from qualified physicians, to alleviate that suffering, even to the point of causing unconsciousness and hastening death. In this light, even assuming that we would recognize such an interest, I agree that the State's interests in protecting those who are not truly competent or facing imminent death, or those whose decisions to hasten death would not truly be voluntary, are sufficiently weighty to justify a prohibition against physician-assisted suicide.

Justice STEVENS, concurring in the judgments.

[Today,] the Court decides that Washington's statute prohibiting assisted suicide is not invalid "on its face," that is to say, in all or most cases in which it might be applied. That holding, however, does not foreclose the possibility that some applications of the statute might well be invalid. [History] and tradition provide ample support for refusing to recognize an open-ended constitutional right to commit suicide. [The] State has an interest in preserving and fostering the benefits that every human being may provide to the community. [The] value to others of a person's life is far too precious to allow the individual to claim a constitutional entitlement to complete autonomy in making a decision to end that life. Thus, I fully agree with the Court that the "liberty" protected by the Due Process Clause does not include a categorical "right to commit suicide which itself includes a right to assistance in doing so." But just as our conclusion that capital punishment is not always unconstitutional did not preclude later decisions holding that it is sometimes impermissibly cruel, so is it equally clear that a decision upholding a general statutory prohibition of assisted suicide does not mean that every possible application of the statute would be valid.

with this holding, but would not "foreclose the possibility that an individual plaintiff seeking to hasten her death, or a doctor whose assistance was sought, could prevail in a more particularized challenge." Our opinion does not absolutely foreclose such a claim. However, given our holding that the Due Process Clause of the Fourteenth Amendment does not provide heightened protection to the asserted liberty interest in ending one's life with a physician's assistance, such a claim would have to be quite different from the ones advanced by respondents here. [Footnote by Chief Justice Rehnquist.]

3. Justice GINSBURG concurs in the Court's judgments substantially for the reasons stated in this Opinion. Justice BREYER joins this opinion except insofar as it joins the opinions of the Court. [Footnote by the Court. The other judgment and opinion referred to here is that in Vacco v. Quill, see p. 76 below.]

[In] Cruzan, the Court assumed that the interest in liberty protected by the Fourteenth Amendment encompassed the right of a terminally ill patient to direct the withdrawal of life-sustaining treatment. [Cruzan's] interest in refusing medical care was incidental to her more basic interest in controlling the manner and timing of her death. [The] source of [her] right to refuse treatment was not just a common-law rule. Rather, this right is an aspect of a far broader and more basic concept of freedom that is even older than the common law. This freedom embraces, not merely a person's right to refuse a particular kind of unwanted treatment, but also her interest in dignity, and in determining the character of the memories that will survive long after her death. [Avoiding] intolerable pain and the indignity of living one's final days incapacitated and in agony is certainly "at the heart of [the] liberty . . . to define one's own concept of existence, of meaning, of the universe, and of the mystery of human life." Casey. While I agree with the Court that Cruzan does not decide the issue presented by these cases, Cruzan did give recognition, not just to vague, unbridled notions of autonomy, but to the more specific interest in making decisions about how to confront an imminent death. Although there is no absolute right to physician-assisted suicide, Cruzan makes it clear that some individuals who no longer have the option of deciding whether to live or to die because they are already on the threshold of death have a constitutionally protected interest that may outweigh the State's interest in preserving life at all costs. The liberty interest at stake in a case like this differs from, and is stronger than, both the common-law right to refuse medical treatment and the unbridled interest in deciding whether to live or die. It is an interest in deciding how, rather than whether, a critical threshold shall be crossed.

The state interests supporting a general rule banning the practice of physician-assisted suicide do not have the same force in all cases. First and foremost of these interests is the " 'unqualified interest in the preservation of human life.' " [Although] as a general matter the State's interest in the contributions each person may make to society outweighs the person's interest in ending her life, this interest does not have the same force for a terminally ill patient faced not with the choice of whether to live, only of how to die. Allowing the individual, rather than the State, to make judgments " 'about the "quality" of life that a particular individual may enjoy' " does not mean that the lives of terminally-ill, disabled people have less value than the lives of those who are healthy. Rather, it gives proper recognition to the individual's interest in choosing a final chapter that accords with her life story, rather than one that demeans her values and poisons memories of her. Similarly, the State's legitimate interests in preventing suicide, protecting the vulnerable from coercion and abuse, and preventing euthanasia are less significant in this context. [The] State's legitimate interest in preventing abuse does not apply to an individual who is not victimized by abuse, who is not suffering from depression, and who makes a rational and voluntary decision to seek assistance in dying. [As to] the concern that patients whose physical pain is inadequately treated will be more likely to request assisted suicide, [palliative care] cannot alleviate all pain and suffering [and an] individual adequately informed of the care alternatives thus might make a rational choice for assisted suicide. For such an individual, the State's interest in preventing potential abuse and mistake is only minimally implicated.

The final major interest asserted by the State is its interest in preserving the traditional integrity of the medical profession. [But] for some patients, it would be a physician's refusal to dispense medication to ease their suffering and make their death tolerable and dignified that would be inconsistent with the healing role. [And] because physicians are already involved in making decisions that hasten the death of terminally ill patients—through termination of life support, withholding of medical treatment, and terminal sedation—there is in fact significant tension between the traditional view of the physician's role and the actual practice in a growing number of cases.

Although, as the Court concludes today, these potential harms are sufficient to support the State's general public policy against assisted suicide, they will not always outweigh the individual liberty interest of a particular patient. [While] I would not say as a categorical matter that these state interests are invalid as to the entire class of terminally ill, mentally competent patients, I do not [foreclose] the possibility that an individual plaintiff seeking to hasten her death, or a doctor whose assistance was sought, could prevail in a more particularized challenge. Future cases will determine whether such a challenge may succeed.

Justice SOUTER, concurring in the judgment.

[The] question [here] is whether the [Washington] statute sets up one of those "arbitrary impositions" or "purposeless restraints" at odds with the Due Process Clause of the Fourteenth Amendment. Poe v. Ullman, 367 U.S. 497, 543 (1961) (Harlan, J., dissenting) [13th ed., p. 522]. [For] two centuries American courts, and for much of that time this Court, have thought it necessary to provide some degree of review over the substantive content of legislation under constitutional standards of textual breadth. The obligation was understood before Dred Scott and has continued after the repudiation of Lochner's progeny. This enduring tradition of American constitutional practice is, in Justice Harlan's view, nothing more than what is required by the judicial authority and obligation to construe constitutional text and review legislation for conformity to that text. Like many judges who preceded him and many who followed, he found it impossible to construe the text of due process without recognizing substantive, and not merely procedural, limitations. [The] business of such review is not the identification of extratextual absolutes but scrutiny of a legislative resolution (perhaps unconscious) of clashing principles, each quite possibly worthy in and of itself, but each to be weighed within the history of our values as a people. It is a comparison of the relative strengths of opposing claims that informs the judicial task, not a deduction from some first premise. Thus informed, judicial review still has no warrant to substitute one reasonable resolution of the contending positions for another, but authority to supplant the balance already struck between the contenders only when it falls outside the realm of the reasonable.

[My] understanding of unenumerated rights in the wake of the Poe dissent [begins] with a concept of "ordered liberty" comprising a continuum of rights to be free from "arbitrary impositions and purposeless restraints." Poe (Harlan, J., dissenting). [The] claims of arbitrariness that mark almost all instances of unenumerated substantive rights are those resting on interests in liberty sufficiently important to be judged "fundamental." In the face of an interest this powerful a State may not rest on threshold rationality or a presumption of constitutionality, but may prevail only on the ground of an interest sufficiently compelling to place within the realm of the reasonable a refusal to recognize the individual right asserted.

This approach calls for a court to assess the relative "weights" or dignities of the contending interests, and to this extent the judicial method is familiar to the common law. Common law method is subject, however, to two important constraints in the hands of a court engaged in substantive due process review. First, such a court is bound to confine the values that it recognizes to those truly deserving constitutional stature, either to those expressed in constitutional text, or those exemplified by "the traditions from which [the Nation] developed," or revealed by contrast with "the traditions from which it broke." Poe (Harlan, J., dissenting). [Second, it] is only when the legislation's justifying principle, critically valued, is so far from being commensurate with the individual interest as to be arbitrarily or pointlessly applied that the statute must give way. [Common-law] method tends to pay respect [to] detail, seeking to understand old principles afresh by new examples and new counterexamples. The "tradition is a living thing," id., albeit one that moves by moderate steps carefully taken. "The decision of an apparently novel claim must depend on grounds which follow closely on well-accepted principles and criteria. The new decision must take its place in relation to what went before and further [cut] a channel for what is to come." Exact analysis and characterization of any due process claim is critical to the method and to the result.

[The] argument supporting respondents' position [progresses] through three steps of increasing forcefulness. First, it emphasizes the decriminalization of suicide. Reliance on this fact is sanctioned under the standard that looks not only to the tradition retained, but to society's occasional choices to reject traditions of the legal past. [The] second step in the argument is to emphasize that the State's own act of decriminalization gives a freedom of choice much like the individual's option in recognized instances of bodily autonomy. One of these, abortion, is a legal right to choose in spite of the interest a State may legitimately invoke in discouraging the practice, just as suicide is now subject to choice, despite a state interest in discouraging it. The third step is to emphasize that respondents [base] their claim on the traditional right to medical care and counsel, subject to the limiting conditions of informed, responsible choice when death is imminent, conditions that support a strong analogy to rights of care in other situations in which medical counsel and assistance have been available as a matter of course. There can be no stronger claim to a physician's assistance than at the time when death is imminent, a moral judgment implied by the State's own recognition of the legitimacy of medical procedures [such as the withdrawal of life-support or the administration of medication to alleviate pain] necessarily hastening the moment of impending death.

In my judgment, the importance of the individual interest here, as within that class of "certain interests" demanding careful scrutiny of the State's contrary claim, cannot be gainsaid. Whether that interest might in some circumstances, or at some time, be seen as "fundamental" to the degree entitled to prevail is not, however, a conclusion that I need draw here, for I am satisfied that the State's interests [are] sufficiently serious to defeat the present claim that its law is arbitrary or purposeless.

The State has put forward [interests] protecting life generally, discouraging suicide even if knowing and voluntary, and protecting terminally ill patients from involuntary suicide and euthanasia, both voluntary and nonvoluntary. [The] third is dispositive for me. [It] is different from the first two, for it addresses specific features of respondents' claim, and it opposes that claim not with a moral judgment contrary to respondents', but with a recognized state interest in the protection of nonresponsible individuals and those who do not stand in relation either to death or to their physicians as do the patients whom respondents describe. [The] argument is that a progression would occur, obscuring the line between the ill and the dying, and between the responsible and the unduly influenced, until ultimately doctors and perhaps others would abuse a limited freedom to aid suicides by yielding to the impulse to end another's suffering under conditions going beyond the narrow limits the respondents propose.

The mere assertion that the terminally sick might be pressured into suicide decisions by close friends and family members would not alone be very telling. [The] State, however, goes further, to argue that dependence on the vigilance of physicians will not be enough. First, the lines proposed here (particularly the requirement of a knowing and voluntary decision by the patient) would be more difficult to draw than the lines that have limited other recently recognized due process rights. [Second,] this difficulty could become the greater by combining with another fact within the realm of plausibility, that physicians simply would not be assiduous to preserve the line. [Whether] acting from compassion or under some other influence, a physician who would provide a drug for a patient to administer might well go the further step of administering the drug himself; so, the barrier between assisted suicide and euthanasia could become porous, and the line between voluntary and involuntary euthanasia as well. The case for the slippery slope is fairly made out here, not because recognizing one due process right would leave a court with no principled basis to avoid recognizing another, but because there is a plausible case that the right claimed would not be readily containable by reference to facts about the mind that are matters of difficult judgment, or by gatekeepers who are subject to temptation, noble or not.

Respondents propose an answer to all this, the answer of state regulation with teeth. Legislation proposed in several States, for example, would authorize physician-assisted suicide but require two qualified physicians to confirm the patient's diagnosis, prognosis, and competence; and would mandate that the patient make repeated requests witnessed by at least two others over a specified time span; and would impose reporting requirements and criminal penalties for various acts of coercion. But at least at this moment there are reasons for caution in predicting the effectiveness of the teeth proposed. [Some] commentators marshall evidence that [similar] Dutch guidelines have in practice failed to protect patients from involuntary euthanasia and have been violated with impunity. This evidence is contested. The day might come when we can say with some assurance which side is right, but for now [the] substantiality of the factual disagreement, and the alternatives for resolving it [are,] for me, dispositive of the due process claim. [While] I do not decide for all time that respondents' claim should not be recognized, I acknowledge the legislative institutional competence as the better one to deal with that claim at this time.

Justice BREYER, concurring in the judgments.

I believe that Justice O'Connor's views, which I share, have greater legal significance than the Court's opinion suggests. I join her separate opinion, except insofar as it joins the majority. [I] do not agree [with] the Court's formulation of [the] claimed "liberty" interest. The Court describes it as a "right to commit suicide with another's assistance." But I would not reject the respondents' claim without considering a different formulation, for which our legal tradition may provide greater support. That formulation would use words roughly like a "right to die with dignity." But irrespective of the exact words used, at its core would lie personal control over the manner of death, professional medical assistance, and the avoidance of unnecessary and severe physical suffering—combined.

As Justice Souter points out, Justice Harlan's dissenting opinion in Poe offers some support for such a claim. In that opinion, Justice Harlan [recognized] that "certain interests require particularly careful scrutiny of the state needs asserted to justify their abridgment." [He] concluded that marital privacy was such a "special interest." He found in the Constitution a right of "privacy of the home"—with the home, the bedroom, and "intimate details of the marital relation" at its heart—by examining the protection that the law had earlier provided for related, but not identical, interests described by such words as "privacy," "home," and "family." The respondents here essentially ask us to do the same. They argue that one can find a "right to die with dignity" by examining the protection the law has provided for related, but not identical, interests relating to personal dignity, medical treatment, and freedom from state-inflicted pain. See [e.g., Cruzan; Casey.]

I do not believe, however, that this Court need or now should decide whether or a not such a right is "fundamental." That is because, in my view, the avoidance of severe physical pain (connected with death) would have to comprise an essential part of any successful claim and because, as Justice O'Connor points out, the laws before us do not force a dying person to undergo that kind of pain. [State law here does] not prohibit doctors from providing patients with drugs sufficient to control pain despite the risk that those drugs themselves will kill. [Medical] technology [makes] the administration of pain-relieving drugs sufficient, except for a very few individuals for whom the ineffectiveness of pain control medicines can mean, not pain, but the need for sedation which can end in a coma. [In] instances in which patients do not receive the palliative care that, in principle, is available, that is so for institutional reasons or inadequacies or obstacles, which would seem possible to overcome, and which do not include a prohibitive set of laws.

This legal circumstance means that the state laws before us do not infringe directly upon the (assumed) central interest (what I have called the core of the interest in dying with dignity). [Were] the legal circumstances different—for example, were state law to prevent the provision of palliative care, including the administration of drugs as needed to avoid pain at the end of life—then the law's impact upon serious and otherwise unavoidable physical pain (accompanying death) would be more directly at issue. And as Justice O'Connor suggests, the Court might have to revisit its conclusions in these cases.

In VACCO v. QUILL, 521 U.S. 793 (1997), decided together with Glucksberg, the Court held that New York did not violate the Equal Protection Clause by prohibiting assisted suicide while permitting patients to refuse lifesaving medical treatment. Chief Justice REHNQUIST again wrote for the Court: "The Equal Protection Clause [embodies] a general rule that States must treat like cases alike but may treat unlike cases accordingly. [On] their faces, neither New York's ban on assisting suicide nor its statutes permitting patients to refuse medical treatment treat anyone differently than anyone else or draw any distinctions between persons. Everyone, regardless of physical condition, is entitled, if competent, to refuse unwanted lifesaving medical treatment; no one is permitted to assist a suicide. [The] Court of Appeals, however, concluded that some terminally ill people—those who are on life-support systems—are treated differently than those who are not, in that the former may 'hasten death' by ending treatment, but the latter may not 'hasten death' through physician-assisted suicide. This conclusion depends on the submission that ending or refusing lifesaving medical treatment 'is nothing more nor less than assisted suicide.' Unlike the Court of Appeals, we think the distinction between assisting suicide and withdrawing life-sustaining treatment, a distinction widely recognized and endorsed in the medical profession and in our legal traditions, is both important and logical; it is certainly rational.

"The distinction comports with fundamental legal principles of causation and intent. First, when a patient refuses life-sustaining medical treatment, he dies from an underlying fatal disease or pathology; but if a patient ingests lethal medication prescribed by a physician, he is killed by that medication. Furthermore, a physician who withdraws, or honors a patient's refusal to begin, life-sustaining medical treatment purposefully intends, or may so intend, only to respect his patient's wishes and 'to cease doing useless and futile or degrading things to the patient when [the patient] no longer stands to benefit from them.' The same is true when a doctor provides aggressive palliative care; in some cases, painkilling drugs may hasten a patient's death, but the physician's purpose and intent is, or may be, only to ease his patient's pain. A doctor who assists a suicide, however, 'must, necessarily and indubitably, intend primarily that the patient be made dead.' Similarly, a patient who commits suicide with a doctor's aid necessarily has the specific intent to end his or her own life, while a patient who refuses or discontinues treatment might not. The law has long used actors' intent or purpose to distinguish between two acts that may have the same result.

"Given these general principles, it is not surprising that many courts, including New York courts, have carefully distinguished refusing life-sustaining treatment from suicide. [Similarly,] the overwhelming majority of state legislatures have drawn a clear line between assisting suicide and withdrawing or permitting the refusal of unwanted lifesaving medical treatment by prohibiting the former and permitting the latter. [This] Court has also recognized, at least implicitly, the distinction between letting a patient die and making that patient die. In Cruzan v. Director, Mo. Dept. of Health [1990; 13th ed., p. 602], we concluded that 'the principle that a competent person has a constitutionally protected liberty interest in refusing unwanted medical treatment may be inferred from our prior decisions,' and we assumed the existence of such a right for purposes of that case. But our assumption of a right to refuse treatment was grounded not, as the Court of Appeals supposed, on the proposition that patients have a general and abstract 'right to hasten death,' but on well established, traditional rights to bodily integrity and freedom from unwanted touching. In fact, we observed that 'the majority of States in this country have laws imposing criminal penalties on one who assists another to commit suicide.' Cruzan therefore provides no support for the notion that refusing life-sustaining medical treatment is 'nothing more nor less than suicide.'

"For all these reasons, we disagree with respondents' claim that the distinction between refusing lifesaving medical treatment and assisted suicide is 'arbitrary' and 'irrational.' Granted, in some cases, the line between the two may not be clear, but certainty is not required, even were it possible. Logic and contemporary practice support New York's judgment that the two acts are different, and New York may therefore, consistent with the Constitution, treat them differently. By permitting everyone to refuse unwanted medical treatment while prohibiting anyone from assisting a suicide, New York law follows a longstanding and rational distinction. [The] valid and important public interests [discussed in Glucksberg] easily satisfy the constitutional requirement that a legislative classification bear a rational relation to some legitimate end."

As they had in Glucksberg, Justice O'Connor concurred and Justices Stevens, Souter, Ginsburg and Breyer concurred in the judgment. Justice STEVENS noted: "I agree that the distinction between permitting death to ensue from an underlying fatal disease and causing it to occur by the administration of medication or other means provides a constitutionally sufficient basis for the State's classification. Unlike the Court, however, I am not persuaded that in all cases there will in fact be a significant difference between the intent of the physicians, the patients or the families in the two situations. [In] both situations, [they may be] seeking to hasten a certain, impending death. Thus, although the differences the majority notes in causation and intent between terminating life-support and assisting in suicide support the Court's rejection of the respondents' facial challenge, these distinctions may be inapplicable to particular terminally ill patients and their doctors. Our holding today does not foreclose the possibility that some applications of the New York statute may impose an intolerable intrusion on the patient's freedom."

In a potentially significant footnote to the majority opinion, Chief Justice REHNQUIST expressly agreed with Justice Stevens (as he had in Glucksberg) that the holding did not foreclose possible as-applied challenges, but stated that "a particular plaintiff hoping to show that New York's assisted-suicide ban was unconstitutional in his particular case would need to present different and considerably stronger arguments than those advanced by respondents here." What might those arguments be?

What is the significance of the concurring opinions in Glucksberg and Vacco? Only Justices Scalia, Kennedy and Thomas joined Chief Justice Rehnquist's opinion for the Court without qualification. Justice O'Connor concurred only on the understanding that these cases did not involve dying in untreatable pain because both Washington and New York allowed physicians to administer potentially lethal doses of painkilling medication under the doctrine of "double effect"—i.e., the view that action undertaken with the primary intent of stopping pain is permissible even if accompanied by the knowledge that it may cause death. Does Justice O'Connor's opinion, together with the separate concurrences of Justices Stevens, Souter, Ginsburg and Breyer, comprise a majority for the proposition that the states are constitutionally required to permit this practice? If so, what other forms of "active" assistance, if any, might be constitutionally protected?

CHAPTER 9

EQUAL PROTECTION

SECTION 2. SCRUTINY OF MEANS IN ECONOMIC REGULATIONS: THE RATIONALITY REQUIREMENT

Page 662. Add after FCC v. Beach Communications:

For a recent application of rationality review to uphold a challenged classification, see VACCO v. QUILL, 521 U.S. 793 (1997), reported at p. 76 above, in which the Court held that New York did not violate the Equal Protection Clause by prohibiting physician-assisted suicide while permitting patients to refuse lifesaving medical treatment.

But for a use of rationality review to strike down the government's arbitrarily unequal treatment of even a single individual, see the Court's per curiam opinion in VILLAGE OF WILLOWBROOK v. OLECH, 120 S.Ct. 1073 (2000). Olech, a homeowner, sued the Village of Willowbrook alleging a violation of Equal Protection: the Village had demanded a 33–foot easement as a condition of connecting her house to the municipal water supply, when the Village had only required a 15–foot easement from other property owners seeking similar access. Although the complainant had alleged that the Village's discriminatory treatment was "motivated by ill will resulting from the Olechs' previous filing of an unrelated, successful lawsuit against the Village," the Court addressed the Village's actions simply as an instance of irrationality, without regard to motive. The Court's opinion determined that "the number of individuals in a class is immaterial for equal protection analysis."

"Our cases have recognized successful equal protection claims brought by 'a class of one,' where the plaintiff alleges that she has been intentionally treated differently from others similarly situated and there is no rational basis for the difference in treatment. In doing so, we have explained that '[t]he purpose of the equal protection clause of the Fourteenth Amendment is to secure every person within the State's jurisdiction against intentional and arbitrary discrimination, whether occasioned by express terms of a statute or by its improper execution through duly constituted agents.'

"That reasoning is applicable to this case. Olech's complaint can fairly be construed as alleging that the Village intentionally demanded a 33–foot easement as a condition of connecting her property to the municipal water supply where the Village only required a 15–foot easement from other similarly situated property owners. The complaint also alleged that the Village's demand was 'irrational and wholly arbitrary' and that the Village ultimately connected her property after receiving a clearly adequate 15–foot easement. These allegations, quite apart from the Village's subjective motivation, are sufficient to state a claim for relief under traditional equal protection analysis."

Justice BREYER concurred separately to emphasize Olech's allegations about the Village's motive, and to allay concerns that the ruling would "transform [ordinary] violations of city or state law into violations of the Constitution. It might be thought that a rule that looks only to an intentional difference in treatment and a lack of a rational basis for that different treatment would work such a transformation. Zoning decisions, for example, will often, perhaps almost always, treat one landowner differently from another. [This] case, however, does not directly raise the question of whether the simple and common instance of a faulty zoning decision would violate the Equal Protection Clause. That is because [Olech has] alleged an extra factor as well—'[illegitimate] animus or ill will.' [In] my view, the presence of that added factor in this case is sufficient to minimize any concern about transforming run-of-the-mill zoning cases into cases of constitutional right."

SECTION 3. SUSPECT CLASSIFICATIONS AND THE PROBLEMS OF FORBIDDEN DISCRIMINATION

B. GENDER

Page 697. Add to Note 3, on "Discrimination against fathers of nonmarital children":

In MILLER v. ALBRIGHT, 523 U.S. 420 (1998), the Court, in a fragmented set of opinions, upheld portions of the Immigration and Nationality Act providing that the citizenship of a child of an alien father and a citizen mother is established at birth, while the citizenship of a child of an alien mother and a citizen father could be established only if and when the father acknowledged his paternity or was subject to an adjudication of paternity while the child was still a minor. This distinction was challenged as a denial of equal protection implicit in the Due Process Clause by a young woman born to a Philippine mother and an American father. Justice STEVENS, announcing the judgment of the Court and authoring an opinion joined only by Chief Justice Rehnquist, viewed the daughter as having standing to challenge the gender-based distinction among parents of nonmarital children born abroad, but on the merits found no equal protection violation. Even if the heightened scrutiny that normally attaches to gender discrimination claims were applied, Justice Stevens reasoned, the distinction between the requirements imposed on children of unmarried male and female citizens was substantially related to important governmental objectives: "ensur[ing] that a person born out of wedlock who claims citizenship by birth actually shares a blood relationship with an American citizen," "encouraging the development of a healthy relationship between the citizen parent and the child while the child is a minor," and "fostering ties between the foreign-born child and the United States." He found male and female parents differently situated with respect to these interests: "The blood relationship to the birth mother is immediately obvious and is typically established by hospital records and birth certificates; the relationship to the unmarried father may often be undisclosed and unrecorded in any contemporary public record," and "[w]hen a child is born out of wedlock outside of the United States, the citizen mother, unlike the citizen father, certainly knows of her child's existence and typically will have custody of the child immediately after the birth, [while] the unmarried father may not even know that his child exists."

Although five justices would have found the distinction invalid under heightened scrutiny, they did not produce a majority in the daughter's favor. Justice O'CONNOR, joined by Justice Kennedy, expressed doubt whether "any gender classifications based on stereotypes can survive heightened scrutiny," and disagreed with Justice Stevens that the provision here did so. Nonetheless, she found that the daughter lacked standing to raise her father's gender discrimination claim in the absence of some hindrance to the father's ability to assert his own rights. Accordingly, she found the daughter's claim subject only to rational basis scrutiny, under which "a statute may be defended based on generalized classifications unsupported by empirical evidence." Justice GINSBURG wrote a dissent, joined by Justices Souter and Breyer, and Justice BREYER wrote a dissent, joined by Justices Souter and Ginsburg, each reasoning that the daughter had standing to challenge the gender-discriminatory provision and that it could not be sustained under heightened scrutiny. Justice Ginsburg wrote: "[The INA] classifies unconstitutionally on the basis of gender in determining the capacity of a parent to qualify a child for citizenship. The section rests on familiar generalizations: mothers, as a rule, are responsible for a child born out of wedlock; fathers unmarried to the child's mother, ordinarily, are not. The law at issue might have made custody or support the relevant criterion. Instead, it treats mothers one way, fathers another, shaping government policy to fit and reinforce the stereotype or historic pattern. Characteristic of sex-based classifications, the stereotypes underlying this legislation may hold true for many, even most, individuals. But in prior decisions the Court has rejected official actions that classify unnecessarily and overbroadly by gender when more accurate and impartial functional lines can be drawn." Noting that the statute depended upon the impermissible "generalization that mothers are significantly more likely than fathers to care for their children, or to develop caring relationships with their children," Justice Breyer asked: "What sense does it make to apply [more demanding] conditions only to fathers and not to mothers in today's world—where paternity can readily be proved and where women and men both are likely to earn a living in the workplace?" Justice SCALIA, joined by Justice Thomas, concurred in the judgment, finding the complaint properly dismissed because the Court lacked power to confer citizenship on a basis other than that prescribed by Congress.

SECTION 4. THE "FUNDAMENTAL INTERESTS" STRAND OF EQUAL PROTECTION STRICT SCRUTINY

B. DENIAL AND "DILUTION" OF VOTING RIGHTS

Page 865. Add after Note 4, on Anti-"raiding" cutoff requirements:

5. *Race-based disenfranchisement and the Fifteenth Amendment.* In RICE v. CAYETANO, 120 S.Ct. 1044 (2000), the Court, by a vote of 7–2, invalidated under the Fifteenth Amendment a provision of the Hawaii Constitution that limited the vote for trustees of the state Office of Hawaiian Affairs (OHA) to "Hawaiians," defined by state statute as descendants of the peoples inhabiting the Hawaiian Islands in 1778, and "native Hawaiians," defined as descendants

in at least one-half part of such peoples. Writing for the Court, Justice KENNEDY detailed the difficulties that befell Hawaii's original inhabitants after the arrival of England's Captain Cook in 1778, including the decimation of the native population by diseases borne by settlers, the forced transfer of power from the Hawaiian monarchy to an American-led committee in 1893, and the cession of Hawaii to the United States as a territory in 1898. He likewise described various federal and state benefit programs, including OHA's programs, aimed at the betterment of conditions for native Hawaiians.

Without reaching the constitutionality of any such benefit programs under the Fourteenth Amendment, Justice Kennedy wrote that the restriction of the franchise in OHA elections was unconstitutional under the Fifteenth: "The purpose and command of the Fifteenth Amendment are set forth in language both explicit and comprehensive. The National Government and the States may not violate a fundamental principle: They may not deny or abridge the right to vote on account of race. [The] design of the Amendment is to reaffirm the equality of races at the most basic level of the democratic process, the exercise of the voting franchise. A resolve so absolute required language as simple in command as it was comprehensive in reach." He went on to find that the restriction of the vote to native Hawaiians and Hawaiians amounted to an impermissible denial of the vote on account of race: "Ancestry can be a proxy for race. It is that proxy here. Even if the residents of Hawaii in 1778 had been of more diverse ethnic backgrounds and cultures, it is far from clear that a voting test favoring their descendants would not be a race-based qualification. But that is not this case. For centuries Hawaii was isolated from migration. The inhabitants shared common physical characteristics, and by 1778 they had a common culture. [The] provisions before us reflect the State's effort to preserve that commonality of people to the present day. [The] State, in enacting the legislation before us, has used ancestry as a racial definition and for a racial purpose. [The] ancestral inquiry mandated by the State implicates the same grave concerns as a classification specifying a particular race by name. One of the principal reasons race is treated as a forbidden classification is that it demeans the dignity and worth of a person to be judged by ancestry instead of by his or her own merit and essential qualities. An inquiry into ancestral lines is not consistent with respect based on the unique personality each of us possesses, a respect the Constitution itself secures in its concern for persons and citizens."

Justice Kennedy rejected the state's attempt to analogize the voting restriction to various preferences the Court had previously upheld in favor of members of Indian tribes. Even assuming native Hawaiians were a tribe, he wrote, voting may not be limited by bloodlines in state as opposed to tribal elections, which are conducted by separate "quasi-sovereigns." He likewise rejected the state's attempt to draw an analogy to the special purpose district elections upheld against equal protection challenge in Salyer and Ball (see 13th ed., p. 862), reasoning that "the Fifteenth Amendment has independent meaning and force." Finally, he rejected the state's argument that the restriction reflected not race but rather the state's fiduciary relationship to native Hawaiians, reasoning that the "demeaning premise that citizens of a particular race are somehow more qualified than others to vote on certain matters [attacks] the central meaning of the Fifteenth Amendment."

Justice BREYER, joined by Justice Souter, concurred in the result, arguing that aboriginal Hawaiians are not an Indian tribe and therefore that tribal analogies "are too distant to save a race-based voting definition." In dissent, Justice STEVENS, joined by Justice Ginsburg, took the opposite view, arguing that "[t]he descendants of the native Hawaiians share with the descendants of the Native Americans on the mainland or in the Aleutian Islands not only a history of subjugation at the hands of colonial forces, but also a purposefully created and specialized 'guardian-ward' relationship with the Government of the United States," and therefore that legislation targeting native Hawaiians need only be tied rationally to that unique protective obligation.

Page 890. Add after Note 3, on Bush v. Vera:

4. *Further applications.* In ABRAMS v. JOHNSON, 521 U.S. 74 (1997), the Court rejected a challenge by black voters, joined by the United States, to the Georgia redistricting undertaken in the aftermath of Miller v. Johnson. On remand, the district court deferred to the legislature to redraw Georgia's congressional districts, but the legislature deadlocked, with the House adopting a plan with two majority-black districts while the Senate adopted a plan with one. The district court then devised its own redistricting plan, providing for only one majority-black district. The court reasoned that, even though the legislature would probably have preferred two majority-black districts, and that normally it was bound to defer to legislative preference, there was no area of black population of sufficient concentration to allow creation of a second majority-black district without "subordinat[ing] Georgia's traditional districting policies and consider[ing] race predominantly." In an opinion by Justice KENNEDY, the Court rejected arguments that the district court's redistricting plan exceeded its remedial authority, violated § 2 or § 5 of the Voting Rights Act, or created a population discrepancy violating the constitutional requirement of one person one vote. In reaching these conclusions, the Court found that "the trial court acted well within its discretion in deciding it could not draw two majority-black districts without itself engaging in racial gerrymandering," and that it correctly declined to use post–1990 districting plans that were tainted by the predominance of racial factors as benchmarks for measuring claimed retrogression in minority voting.

Justice BREYER, joined by Justices Stevens, Souter, and Ginsburg, dissented. In his view, the district court was not free to depart from the Georgia Legislature's preference for two majority-black districts if a two-district plan was not unconstitutional. And in his view, a two-district plan would not have been unconstitutional under Miller because the legislature had a "strong basis" after the 1990 census to believe that § 2 or § 5 of the Voting Rights Act would be violated unless a two-district plan were adopted. Under Justice O'Connor's concurrence in Miller, such a "strong basis" was sufficient to constitute "a compelling, hence redeeming interest" for the predominance of race in the drawing of the boundaries. Justice Breyer stressed that an actual finding of a § 2 or § 5 violation was not required: "A legal rule that permits legislatures to take account of race only when § 2 really requires them to do so is a rule that shifts the power to redistrict from legislatures to federal courts (for only the latter can say what § 2 really requires). A rule that rests upon a reasonable view of the evidence (i.e., that permits the legislature to use race if it has a 'strong basis' for believing it necessary to do so) is a rule that leaves at least a modicum of discretionary (race-related) redistricting authority in the hands of legislators." He also reiterated the four dissenters' concerns throughout the Shaw line of cases that the Court's "holdings [and] test—'predominant racial motive'—would prove unworkable, that they would improperly shift redistricting authority from legislatures to courts, and that they would prevent the legitimate use (among others the remedial use) of race as a political factor in redistricting, sometimes making unfair distinctions between racial minorities and others."

In LAWYER v. DEPARTMENT OF JUSTICE, 521 U.S. 567 (1997), a 5–4 majority of the Court upheld against equal protection challenge a Florida redistricting plan for state legislative districts. After the 1990 census, the Florida state legislature had devised a districting plan, the Justice Department had refused to preclear it under § 5 of the Voting Rights Act, the legislature reached an impasse in devising a new plan, and the Florida Supreme Court had devised its own plan. The state court's plan called for an irregularly shaped senate district with a voting-age population that was 45.8% black and that comprised portions of four counties in the Tampa Bay area. That plan was challenged in federal district court as violating the equal protection rights of white voters, and a different plan was fashioned in a settlement of that lawsuit joined by all parties except appellant, who was one of the several plaintiffs in the suit. The district court approved the plan in the settlement without formally adjudicating the state supreme court's earlier plan unconstitutional. In an opinion by Justice SOUTER joined by all the dissenters in the Shaw line of cases plus Chief Justice Rehnquist, the Court found no procedural problem in the settlement, and found no clear error (the appropriate standard of review after Miller) in the district court's finding that the plan reached in the settlement did not subordinate traditional districting principles to race:

"The District Court looked to the shape and composition of [the challenged state senate district] as redrawn in [the settlement plan] and found them 'demonstrably benign and satisfactorily tidy.' The district is located entirely in the Tampa Bay area, has an end-to-end distance no greater than that of most Florida Senate districts, and in shape does not stand out as different from numerous other Florida House and Senate districts. While [the redrawn district] crosses a body of water and encompasses portions of three counties, evidence submitted showed that both features are common characteristics of Florida legislative districts. Addressing composition, the District Court found that the residents of [the district] 'regard themselves as a community.' Evidence indicated that [the district] comprises a predominantly urban, low-income population, the poorest of the nine districts in the Tampa Bay region and among the poorest districts in the State, whose white and black members alike share a similarly depressed economic condition, and interests that reflect it. The fact that [the district] is not a majority black district, the black voting-age population being 36.2%, supports the District Court's finding that the district is not a 'safe' one for black-preferred candidates, but one that 'offers to any candidate, without regard to race, the opportunity' to seek and be elected to office."

In answer to appellant's objection that the percentage of black voters in the district was higher than that in any of the three counties it drew from, Justice Souter wrote: "[W]e have never suggested that the percentage of black residents in a district may not exceed the percentage of black residents in any of the counties from which the district is created, and have never recognized similar racial composition of different political districts as being necessary to avoid an inference of racial gerrymandering in any one of them. Since districting can be difficult, after all, just because racial composition varies from place to place, and counties and voting districts do not depend on common principles of size and location, facts about the one do not as such necessarily entail conclusions about the other."

Justice SCALIA dissented, joined by Justices O'Connor, Kennedy and Thomas. The dissent did not reach the constitutionality of the district but objected that the settlement was an "unprecedented intrusion upon state sovereignty." In the dissent's view, the district court should not have approved the settlement without first finding the state supreme court's plan unconstitutional and giving "the State an opportunity to do its own redrawing of the district to remedy whatever unconstitutional features it contained."

Page 895. Add after Note 7, on Burdick v. Takushi:

8. *Fusion tickets.* In TIMMONS v. TWIN CITIES AREA NEW PARTY, 520 U.S. 351 (1997), the Court, by a vote of 6–3, rejected a claim that a state ban on multiparty or "fusion" candidacies violated a party's or candidate's associational rights under the First and Fourteenth Amendments. Chief Justice REHNQUIST, writing for the Court, rejected the argument that such a ban was a "severe burden" on ballot access triggering strict scrutiny: "That a particular individual may not appear on the ballot as a particular party's candidate does not severely burden that party's association rights. [The fusion ticket] ban, which applies to major and minor parties alike, simply precludes one party's candidate from appearing on the ballot, as that party's candidate, if already nominated by another party. Respondent is free to try to convince [a candidate] to be [its], not [another party's], candidate." Nor did the ban prevent a minor party such as respondent "from developing consensual political alliances and thus broadening the base of public participation in and support for its activities. [Minnesota] has not directly precluded minor political parties from developing and organizing. [The] New Party remains free to endorse whom it likes, to ally itself with others, to nominate candidates for office, and to spread its message to all who will listen." And while "[i]t is true that Minnesota's fusion ban prevents the New Party from using the ballot to communicate to the public that it supports a particular candidate who is already another party's candidate," and in turn from using the parties' separately counted votes to inform the candidate "about the particular wishes and ideals of his constituency," the majority was "unpersuaded [by] the Party's contention that it has a right to use the ballot itself to send a particularized message, to its candidate and to the voters, about the nature of its support for the candidate. Ballots serve primarily to elect candidates, not as fora for political expression."

Accordingly, Chief Justice Rehnquist viewed that the fusion ban as among the "lesser burdens" or " 'reasonable, nondiscriminatory restrictions' "that, under Anderson and Burdick, "trigger less exacting review." Under this deferential standard, he concluded that "the burdens Minnesota's fusion ban imposes on the New Party's associational rights are justified by 'correspondingly weighty' valid state interests in ballot integrity and political stability."

Specifically, the state argued, fusion might be used "as a way of associating [party or candidate names] with popular slogans and catchphrases," undermining the ballot's purpose by "transforming it from a means of choosing candidates to a billboard for political advertising." Fusion also might undercut the state's ballot-access regime "by allowing minor parties to capitalize on the popularity of another party's candidate, rather than on their own appeal to the voters, in order to secure access to the ballot." Finally, it might undermine the state's "strong interest in the stability of [its] political system," an interest which permits it "to enact reasonable election regulations that may, in practice, favor the traditional two-party system, and that temper the destabilizing effects of party-splintering and excessive factionalism."

Justice STEVENS dissented, joined by Justice Ginsburg and for the most part by Justice Souter. He found the burden imposed by the fusion ban "significant" rather than minor: "[The] members of a recognized political party unquestionably have a constitutional right to select their nominees for public office and to communicate the identity of their nominees to the voting public. [The] Minnesota statutes place a significant burden on both of those rights. [The] fact that the Party may nominate its second choice surely does not diminish the significance of a restriction that denies it the right to have the name of its first choice appear on the ballot. Nor does the point that it may use some of its limited resources to publicize the fact that its first choice is the nominee of some other party provide an adequate substitute for the message that is conveyed to every person who actually votes when a party's nominees appear on the ballot. [In] this case [the] burden [is] imposed upon the members of a minor party, but its potential impact is much broader. Fiorello LaGuardia, Earl Warren, Ronald Reagan, and Franklin D. Roosevelt, are names that come readily to mind as candidates whose reputations and political careers were enhanced because they appeared on election ballots as fusion candidates. A statute that denied a political party the right to nominate any of those individuals for high office simply because he had already been nominated by another party would, in my opinion, place an intolerable burden on political expression and association."

Nor was Justice Stevens convinced that the fusion ban actually served asserted state interests in "avoiding voter confusion, preventing ballot clutter and manipulation, encouraging candidate competition, and minimizing intraparty factionalism." He described the state's arguments about possible ballot confusion as "imaginative" and "farfetched." and as "severely underestimat[ing] the intelligence of the typical voter." While recognizing that "States do certainly have an interest in maintaining a stable political system," he found that "the State has not convincingly articulated how the fusion ban will prevent the factionalism it fears." For example, it "would not prevent sore-loser candidates from defecting with a disaffected segment of a major party and running as an opposition candidate for a newly formed minor party." Nor would it "prevent the formation of numerous small parties. Indeed, the activity banned by Minnesota's law is the formation of coalitions, not the division and dissension of 'splintered parties and unrestrained factionalism.' "Finally, he found any interest in preserving the two-party system inadequate to sustain the fusion ban, both because the state had not shown that this was the actual purpose of the ban, as strict scrutiny requires, and because, even if it had, such an interest was at odds with fundamental notions of political competition: "The fact that the law was both intended to disadvantage minor parties and has had that effect is a matter that should weigh against, rather than in favor of, its constitutionality. [The] strength of the two-party system [is] the product of the power of the ideas, the traditions, the candidates, and the voters that constitute the parties. It demeans the strength of the two-party system to assume that the major parties need to rely on laws that discriminate against independent voters and minor parties in order to preserve their positions of power." In a brief additional dissent, Justice SOUTER explained that he agreed with Justice Stevens that the state was not entitled to raise the preservation-of-the-two-party-system defense ex post, but that he would not necessarily reject such a defense if properly made out.

9. *Open or blanket primaries*. In CALIFORNIA DEMOCRATIC PARTY v. JONES, 120 S.Ct. 2402 (2000), the Court, by a vote of 7–2, struck down a California initiative entitled Proposition 198, which had changed California's partisan primary from a closed primary to a blanket primary. Under the new system, any voter could vote for any candidate regardless of party affiliation, and the candidate of each party winning the largest number of votes became the party's nominee. The blanket primary was challenged by the California Democratic Party, the California Republican Party, the Libertarian Party of California, and the Peace and Freedom Party, each of which sought to restrict to its own members primary voting for its candidates.

Writing for the Court, Justice SCALIA rejected the argument that primaries "are wholly public affairs that States may regulate freely." He proceeded to invalidate the blanket primary system as a violation of parties' right of expressive association under the First Amendment: "Representative democracy in any populous unit of governance is unimaginable without the ability of citizens to band together in promoting among the electorate candidates who espouse their political views. The formation of national political parties was almost concurrent with the formation of the Republic itself. [A] corollary of the right to associate is the right not to associate. [In] no area is the political association's right to exclude more important than in the process of selecting its nominee. [Proposition 198] forces political parties to associate with—to have their nominees, and hence their positions, determined by—those who, at best, have refused to affiliate with the party, and, at worst, have expressly affiliated with a rival. [The] evidence in this case demonstrates that under California's blanket primary system, the prospect of having a party's nominee determined by adherents of an opposing party [through cross-over voting] is far from remote—indeed, it is a clear and present danger. [The] record also supports the obvious proposition that these substantial numbers of voters who help select the nominees of parties they have chosen not to join often have policy views that diverge from those of the party faithful. [Even] when the person favored by a majority of the party members prevails, he will have prevailed by taking somewhat different positions—and, should he be elected, will continue to take somewhat different positions in order to be renominated. [After all], the whole purpose of Proposition 198 was to favor nominees with 'moderate' positions. [In] sum, Proposition 198 forces petitioners to adulterate their candidate-selection process—the 'basic function of a political party'—by opening it up to persons wholly unaffiliated with the party. Such forced association has the likely outcome—indeed, in this case the intended outcome—of changing the parties' message. We can think of no heavier burden on a political party's associational freedom. Proposition 198 is therefore unconstitutional unless it is narrowly tailored to serve a compelling state interest."

Applying that standard, Justice Scalia found the state's proffered justifications wanting. He rejected as "inadmissible" any interest in "producing elected officials who better represent the electorate and expanding candidate debate beyond the scope of partisan concerns," or in drawing in "disenfranchised" voters, suggesting that such interests "reduce to nothing more than a stark repudiation of freedom of political association." And he found constitutionally inadequate any supposed government interest in promoting fairness, affording voters greater choice, increasing voter participation, or protecting privacy, by means of the blanket primary device. Even if such interests were compelling, he noted, the state could further them less restrictively by operating a nonpartisan blanket primary, in which voters could pick nominees regardless of party affiliation so long as those nominees did not advance to the general election as any party's nominees.

Justice STEVENS, joined by Justice Ginsburg, dissented, suggesting that "[a] State's power to determine how its officials are to be elected is a quintessential attribute of sovereignty," and that accordingly, "the associational rights of political parties are neither absolute nor as comprehensive as the rights enjoyed by wholly private associations." He insisted that the right not to associate "is simply inapplicable to participation in a state[-run and state-financed primary] election." He also would have given more deference to the state's proffered interests, ranking them "substantial, indeed compelling."

C. Access to Courts

Page 901. Add after Little v. Streater:

M. L. B. v. S. L. J.

519 U.S. 102, 117 S.Ct. 555, 136 L.Ed.2d 473 (1996).

Justice GINSBURG delivered the opinion of the Court.

By order of a Mississippi Chancery Court, petitioner M.L.B.'s parental rights to her two minor children were forever terminated. M.L.B. sought to appeal from the termination decree, but Mississippi required that she pay in advance record preparation fees estimated at $2,352.36. Because M.L.B. lacked funds to pay the fees, her appeal was dismissed. [We] agreed to hear and decide [the following question]: May a State, consistent with the Due Process and Equal Protection Clauses of the Fourteenth Amendment, condition appeals from trial court decrees terminating parental rights on the affected parent's ability to pay record preparation fees? We hold that [it may not.]

[Courts] have confronted, in diverse settings, the "age-old problem" of "providing equal justice for poor and rich, weak and powerful alike." Griffin v. Illinois [1956; 13th ed., p. 896]. Concerning access to appeal in general, and transcripts needed to pursue appeals in particular, Griffin is the foundation case. Griffin involved an Illinois rule that effectively conditioned thoroughgoing appeals from criminal convictions on the defendant's procurement of a transcript of trial proceedings. Indigent defendants, other than those sentenced to death, were not excepted from the rule, so in most cases, defendants without means to pay for a transcript had no access to appellate review at all. Although the Federal Constitution guarantees no right to appellate review, once a State affords that right, Griffin held, the State may not "bolt the door to equal justice."

[In] contrast to the "flat prohibition" of "bolted doors" that the Griffin line of cases securely established, the right to counsel at state expense, as delineated in our decisions, is less encompassing. A State must provide trial counsel for an indigent defendant charged with a felony, Gideon v. Wainwright, but that right does not extend to nonfelony trials if no term of imprisonment is actually imposed, Scott v. Illinois. A State's obligation to provide appellate counsel to poor defendants faced with incarceration applies to appeals of right. Douglas v. California. In Ross v. Moffitt, however, we held that neither the Due Process Clause nor the Equal Protection Clause requires a State to provide counsel at state expense to an indigent prisoner pursuing a discretionary appeal in the state system or petitioning for review in this Court.

We have also recognized a narrow category of civil cases in which the State must provide access to its judicial processes without regard to a party's ability to pay court fees. In Boddie v. Connecticut, we held that the State could not deny a divorce to a married couple based on their inability to pay approximately $60 in court costs. Crucial to our decision in Boddie was the fundamental interest at stake. "Given the basic position of the marriage relationship in this society's hierarchy of values and the concomitant state monopolization of the means for legally dissolving this relationship," we said, due process "prohibits a State from denying, solely because of inability to pay, access to its courts to individuals who seek judicial dissolution of their marriages." [In] United States v. Kras, the Court clarified that a constitutional requirement to waive court fees in civil cases is the exception, not the general rule. Kras concerned fees, totaling $50, required to secure a discharge in bankruptcy. The Court recalled in Kras that "on many occasions we have recognized the fundamental importance . . . under our Constitution" of "the associational interests that surround the establishment and dissolution of the [marital] relationship." But bankruptcy discharge entails no "fundamental interest," we said. Although "obtaining [a] desired new start in life [is] important," that interest, the Court explained, "does not rise to the same constitutional level" as the interest in establishing or dissolving a marriage. Nor is resort to court the sole path to securing debt forgiveness, we stressed; in contrast, termination of a marriage, we reiterated, requires access to the State's judicial machinery.

[In] sum, this Court has not extended Griffin to the broad array of civil cases. But tellingly, the Court has consistently set apart from the mine run of cases those involving state controls or intrusions on family relationships. In that domain, to guard against undue official intrusion, the Court has examined closely and contextually the importance of the governmental interest advanced in defense of the intrusion.

[Does] the Fourteenth Amendment require Mississippi to accord M.L.B. access to an appeal—available but for her inability to advance required costs—before she is forever branded unfit for affiliation with her children? Respondents urge us to classify M.L.B.'s case with the generality of civil cases, in which indigent persons have no constitutional right to proceed in forma pauperis. M.L.B., on the other hand, maintains that the accusatory state action she is trying to fend off is barely distinguishable from criminal condemnation in view of the magnitude and permanence of the loss she faces. [We] agree [with M.L.B.]

[We] observe first that the Court's decisions concerning access to judicial processes, commencing with Griffin, [reflect] both equal protection and due process concerns. [The] equal protection concern relates to the legitimacy of fencing out would-be appellants based solely on their inability to pay core costs. The due process concern homes in on the essential fairness of the state-ordered proceedings anterior to adverse state action. ["Most] decisions in this area," we have recognized, "rest on an equal protection framework," [because] due process does not independently require that the State provide a right to appeal.

[In Mayer v. Chicago, 404 U.S. 189 (1971), we] applied Griffin to a petty offender, fined a total of $500, who sought to appeal from the trial court's judgment. An "impecunious medical student," the defendant in Mayer could not pay for a transcript. We held that the State must afford him a record complete enough to allow fair appellate consideration of his claims. The defendant in Mayer faced no term of confinement, but the conviction, we observed, could affect his professional prospects and, possibly, even bar him from the practice of medicine. The State's pocketbook interest in advance payment for a transcript, we concluded, was unimpressive when measured against the stakes for the defendant.

Similarly here, the stakes for petitioner M.L.B.—forced dissolution of her parental rights—are large, " 'more substantial than mere loss of money.' "In contrast to loss of custody, which does not sever the parent-child bond, parental status termination is "irretrievably destructive" of the most fundamental family relationship. And the risk of error, Mississippi's experience shows, is considerable. [The] countervailing government interest, as in Mayer, is financial. Mississippi urges, as the justification for its appeal cost prepayment requirement, the State's legitimate interest in offsetting the costs of its court system. But in the tightly circumscribed category of parental status termination cases, appeals are few, and not likely to impose an undue burden on the State.

[In] aligning M.L.B.'s case and Mayer—parental status termination decrees and criminal convictions that carry no jail time—for appeal access purposes, we do not question the general rule, stated in Ortwein, that fee requirements ordinarily are examined only for rationality. The State's need for revenue to offset costs, in the mine run of cases, satisfies the rationality requirement; States are not forced by the Constitution to adjust all tolls to account for "disparity in material circumstances." But our cases solidly establish two exceptions to that general rule. The basic right to participate in political processes as voters and candidates cannot be limited to those who can pay for a license. Nor may access to judicial processes in cases criminal or "quasi criminal in nature," turn on ability to pay. [We] place decrees forever terminating parental rights in the category of cases in which the State may not "bolt the door to equal justice."

[In] numerous cases, respondents point out, the Court has held that government "need not provide funds so that people can exercise even fundamental rights." [See, e.g., Harris v. McRae (1980); 13th ed., p. 551.] A decision for M.L.B., respondents contend, would dishonor our cases recognizing that the

Constitution "generally confers no affirmative right to governmental aid, even where such aid may be necessary to secure life, liberty, or property interests of which the government itself may not deprive the individual." DeShaney v. Winnebago County Dept. of Social Servs. [1989; 13th ed., p. 960.] Complainants in the cases on which respondents rely sought state aid to subsidize their privately initiated action or to alleviate the consequences of differences in economic circumstances that existed apart from state action. M.L.B.'s complaint is of a different order. She is endeavoring to defend against the State's destruction of her family bonds, and to resist the brand associated with a parental unfitness adjudication. Like a defendant resisting criminal conviction, she seeks to be spared from the State's devastatingly adverse action.

[Respondents] and the dissenters urge that we will open floodgates if we do not rigidly restrict Griffin to cases typed "criminal." But [termination] decrees "work a unique kind of deprivation." In contrast to matters modifiable at the parties' will or based on changed circumstances, termination adjudications involve the awesome authority of the State "to destroy permanently all legal recognition of the parental relationship." [We] are therefore satisfied that the label "civil" should not entice us to leave undisturbed the Mississippi courts' disposition of this case. For the reasons stated, we hold that Mississippi may not withhold from M.L.B. "a 'record of sufficient completeness' to permit proper [appellate] consideration of [her] claims."

[Reversed.]

Justice KENNEDY, concurring in the judgment.

In my view the cases most on point, and the ones which persuade me we must reverse the judgment now reviewed, are the decisions addressing procedures involving the rights and privileges inherent in family and personal relations. [E.g., Boddie; Lassiter,] cases resting exclusively upon the Due Process Clause. Here, due process is quite a sufficient basis for our holding.

Justice THOMAS, with whom Justice SCALIA joins, and with whom Chief Justice REHNQUIST joins except as to Part II, dissenting.

Today the majority holds that the Fourteenth Amendment requires Mississippi to afford petitioner a free transcript because her civil case involves a "fundamental" right. The majority seeks to limit the reach of its holding to the type of case we confront here, one involving the termination of parental rights. I do not think, however, that the new-found constitutional right to free transcripts in civil appeals can be effectively restricted to this case. The inevitable consequence will be greater demands on the States to provide free assistance to would-be appellants in all manner of civil cases involving interests that cannot, based on the test established by the majority, be distinguished from the admittedly important interest at issue here. The cases on which the majority relies, primarily cases requiring appellate assistance for indigent criminal defendants, were questionable when decided, and have, in my view, been undermined since. Even accepting those cases, however, I am of the view that the majority takes them too far. I therefore dissent.

I. Petitioner requests relief under both the Due Process and Equal Protection Clauses, though she does not specify how either clause affords it. The majority accedes to petitioner's request. But, carrying forward the ambiguity in the cases on which it relies, the majority does not specify the source of the relief it grants.

[Assuming] that petitioner's interest may not be impinged without due process of law, I do not think that the Due Process Clause requires the result the majority reaches. Petitioner's largest obstacle to a due process appeal gratis is our oft-affirmed view that due process does not oblige States to provide for any appeal, even from a criminal conviction. [The] majority reaffirms that due process does not require an appeal. [Unlike in] Boddie, [where the concern] was that indigent persons were deprived of "fundamental rights" with no hearing whatsoever, [Petitioner] received not merely a hearing, but in fact enjoyed procedural protections above and beyond what our parental termination cases have required. She received both notice and a hearing before a neutral, legally trained decisionmaker. She was represented by counsel—even though due process does not in every case require the appointment of counsel. Through her attorney, petitioner was able to confront the evidence and witnesses against her. And [the] Chancery Court was required to find that petitioner's parental unfitness was proved by clear and convincing evidence. [There] seems, then, no place in the Due Process Clause—certainly as an original matter, and even as construed by this Court—for the constitutional "right" crafted by the majority today.

[I] do not think that the equal protection theory underlying the Griffin line of cases remains viable. [In] Griffin, the State of Illinois required all criminal appellants whose claims on appeal required review of a trial transcript to obtain it themselves. The plurality thought that this "discriminated against some convicted defendants on account of their poverty." Justice Harlan, in dissent, perceived a troubling shift in this Court's equal protection jurisprudence. Disputing [the Court's] early manifestation of the "disparate impact" theory of equal protection, Justice Harlan argued: "No economic burden attendant upon the exercise of a privilege bears equally upon all, and in other circumstances the resulting differentiation is not treated as an invidious classification by the State, even though discrimination against 'indigents' by name would be unconstitutional." Justice Harlan offered the example of a state university that conditions an education on the payment of tuition. If charging tuition did not create a discriminatory classification, then, Justice Harlan wondered, how did any other reasonable exaction by a State for a service it provides?

[Justice] Harlan's views were accepted by the Court in Washington v. Davis [1976; 13th ed., p. 755], in which we rejected a disparate impact theory of the Equal Protection Clause altogether. We spurned the claim that "a law, neutral on its face and serving ends otherwise within the power of government to pursue, is invalid under the Equal Protection Clause simply because it may affect a greater proportion of one race than of another." Absent proof of discriminatory purpose, official action did not violate the Fourteenth Amendment "solely because it has a racially disparate impact." [The] lesson of Davis is that the Equal Protection Clause shields only against purposeful discrimination: A disparate impact, even upon members of a racial minority, the classification of which we have been most suspect, does not violate equal protection. The Clause is not a panacea for perceived social or economic inequity; it seeks to "guarantee equal laws, not equal results." [I] see no principled difference between a facially neutral rule that serves in some cases to prevent persons from availing themselves of state employment, or a state-funded education, or a state-funded abortion—each of which the State may, but is not required to, provide—and a facially neutral rule that prevents a person from taking an appeal that is available only because the State chooses to provide it.

[The] Griffin line of cases ascribed to—one might say announced—an equalizing notion of the Equal Protection Clause that would, I think, have startled the Fourteenth Amendment's Framers. In those cases, the Court did not find, nor did it seek, any purposeful discrimination on the part of the state defendants. That their statutes had disproportionate effect on poor persons was sufficient for us to find a constitutional violation. In Davis, among other cases, we began to recognize the potential mischief of a disparate impact theory writ large, and endeavored to contain it. In this case, I would continue that enterprise. Mississippi's requirement of prepaid transcripts in civil appeals seeking to contest the sufficiency of the evidence adduced at trial is facially neutral; it creates no classification. The transcript rule reasonably obliges would-be appellants to bear the costs of availing themselves of a service that the State chooses, but is not constitutionally required, to provide. Any adverse impact that the transcript requirement has on any person seeking to appeal arises not out of the State's action, but out of factors entirely unrelated to it.

II. [If] this case squarely presented the question, I would be inclined to vote to overrule Griffin and its progeny. Even were I convinced that the cases on which the majority today relies ought to be retained, I could not agree with the majority's extension of them. The interest at stake in this case differs in several important respects from that at issue in cases such as Griffin. Petitioner's interest in maintaining a relationship with her children is the subject of a civil, not criminal, action. [Taking] the Griffin line as a given, [I] would restrict it to the criminal appeals to which its authors, see Boddie v. Connecticut (Black, J., dissenting), sought to limit it.

D. Durational Residence Requirements That "Penalize" the Right of Interstate Migration

Page 909. Add after Zobel v. Williams:

Saenz v. Roe

526 U.S. 489, 119 S. Ct. 1518, 143 L.Ed.2d 689 (1999).

Justice STEVENS delivered the opinion of the Court.

In 1992, California enacted a statute limiting the maximum welfare benefits available to newly arrived residents. The scheme limits the amount payable to a family that has resided in the State for less than 12 months to the amount payable by the State of the family's prior residence. [Thus, plaintiffs who were] former residents of Louisiana and Oklahoma would receive $190 and $341 respectively for a family of three even though the full California grant was $641; [and a plaintiff who was a] former resident of Colorado, who had just one child, was limited to $280 a month as opposed to the full California grant of $504 for a family of two. [Relying] primarily on our decisions in Shapiro v. Thompson [1969; 13th ed., p. 901] and Zobel v. Williams [1982; 13th ed., p.908], [the district court] concluded that the statute placed "a penalty on the decision of new residents to migrate to the State and be treated on an equal basis with existing residents." [In 1996,] Congress enacted the Personal Responsibility and Work Opportunity Reconciliation Act of 1996, [which] expressly authorizes any State that receives a block [federal welfare grant] to "apply to a family the rules (including benefit amounts) of the [welfare] program . . . of another State if the family has moved to the State from the other State and has resided in the State for less than 12 months." [The district court] concluded that the existence of the federal statute did not affect the legal analysis in his prior opinion. [The] Court of Appeals affirmed his issuance of a preliminary injunction. [We] now affirm.

The word "travel" is not found in the text of the Constitution. Yet the "constitutional right to travel from one State to another" is firmly embedded in our jurisprudence. [The] "right to travel" discussed in our cases embraces at least three different components. It protects the right of a citizen of one State to enter and to leave another State, the right to be treated as a welcome visitor rather than an unfriendly alien when temporarily present in the second State, and, for those travelers who elect to become permanent residents, the right to be treated like other citizens of that State. [The] right to go from one place to another, including the right to cross state borders while en route, [was] vindicated in Edwards v. California [1941; 13th ed., p.336], which invalidated a state law that impeded the free interstate passage of the indigent [and] reaffirmed [in] United States v. Guest [1966; 13th ed., p. 964], which afforded protection to the " 'right to travel freely to and from the State of Georgia and to use highway facilities and other instrumentalities of interstate commerce within the State of Georgia.' " The second component of the right to travel is [expressly] protected by the text of the Constitution. The first sentence of Article IV, § 2, provides: "The Citizens of each State shall be entitled to all Privileges and Immunities of Citizens in the several States." Thus, by virtue of a person's state citizenship, a citizen of one State who travels in other States, intending to return home at the end of his journey, is entitled to enjoy the "Privileges and Immunities of Citizens in the several States" that he visits. This provision removes "from the citizens of each State the disabilities of alienage in the other States." Paul v. Virginia, 75 U.S. 168 (1869).

What is at issue in this case [is] this third aspect of the right to travel—the right of the newly arrived citizen to the same privileges and immunities enjoyed by other citizens of the same State. That right is protected not only by the new arrival's status as a state citizen, but also by her status as a citizen of the United States. That additional source of protection is plainly identified in the opening words of the Fourteenth Amendment: "All persons born or naturalized in the United States, and subject to the jurisdiction thereof, are citizens of the United States and of the State wherein they reside. No State shall make or enforce any law which shall abridge the privileges or immunities of citizens of the United States;. . . ." Despite fundamentally differing views concerning the coverage of the Privileges or Immunities Clause of the Fourteenth Amendment, most notably expressed in the majority and dissenting opinions in the Slaughter–House Cases [1873; 13th ed., p. 421], it has always been common ground that this Clause protects the third component of the right to travel. Writing for the majority in the Slaughter–House Cases, Justice Miller explained that one of the privileges conferred by this Clause "is that a citizen of the United States can, of his own volition, become a citizen of any State of the Union by a bona fide residence therein, with the same rights as other citizens of that State." Justice Bradley, in dissent, used even stronger language to make the same point: "The states have not now, if they ever had, any power to restrict their citizenship to any classes or persons. A citizen of the United States has a perfect constitutional right to go to and reside in any State he chooses, and to claim citizenship therein, and an equality of rights with every other citizen; and the whole power of the nation is pledged to sustain him in that right. He is not bound to cringe to any superior, or to pray for any act of grace, as a means of enjoying all the rights and privileges enjoyed by other citizens."

[Neither] mere rationality nor some intermediate standard of review should be used to judge the constitutionality of a state rule that discriminates against some of its citizens because they have been domiciled in the State for less than a year. The appropriate standard may be more categorical than that articulated in Shapiro, but it is surely no less strict. Because this case involves discrimination against citizens who have completed their interstate travel, the State's argument that its welfare scheme affects the right to travel only "incidentally" is beside the point. Were we concerned solely with actual deterrence to migration, we might be persuaded that a partial withholding of benefits constitutes a lesser incursion on the right to travel than an outright denial of all benefits. But since the right to travel embraces the citizen's right to be treated equally in her new State of residence, the discriminatory classification is itself a penalty.

It is undisputed that respondents and the members of the class that they represent are citizens of California and that their need for welfare benefits is unrelated to the length of time that they have resided in California. We thus have no occasion to consider what weight might be given to a citizen's length of residence if the bona fides of her claim to state citizenship were questioned. Moreover, because whatever benefits they receive will be consumed while they remain in California, there is no danger that recognition of their claim will encourage citizens of other States to establish residency for just long enough to acquire some readily portable benefit, such as a divorce or a college education, that will be enjoyed after they return to their original domicile. See, e.g., Sosna v. Iowa, [1975; 13th ed., p. 907]; Vlandis v. Kline [1973; 13th ed., p. 908 n.2].

The classifications challenged in this case [may] not be justified by a purpose to deter welfare applicants from migrating to California. [As] we squarely held in Shapiro, such a purpose would be unequivocally impermissible. Disavowing any desire to fence out the indigent, California has instead advanced an entirely fiscal justification for its multi-tiered scheme. The enforcement of [the scheme] will save the State approximately $10.9 million a year. The question is not whether such saving is a legitimate purpose but whether the State may accomplish that end by the discriminatory means it has chosen. An evenhanded, across-the-board reduction of about 72 cents per month for every beneficiary would produce the same result. But our negative answer to the question does not rest on the weakness of the State's purported fiscal justification. It rests on the fact that the Citizenship Clause of the Fourteenth Amendment expressly equates citizenship with residence: "That Clause does not provide for, and does not allow for, degrees of citizenship based on length of residence." Zobel. It is equally clear that the Clause does not tolerate a hierarchy of 45 subclasses of similarly situated citizens based on the location of their prior residence.[1] [Neither] the duration of respondents' California residence, nor the identity of their prior States of residence, has any relevance to their need for benefits. [In] short, the State's legitimate interest in saving money provides no justification for its decision to discriminate among equally eligible citizens.

The question [remains] whether congressional approval of durational residency requirements in the 1996 [statute] somehow resuscitates the constitutionality of [the California law]. That question is readily answered, for we have consistently held that Congress may not authorize the States to violate the Fourteenth Amendment. Moreover, the protection afforded to the citizen by the Citizenship Clause of that Amendment is a limitation on the powers of the National Government as well as the States.

[Citizens] of the United States, whether rich or poor, have the right to choose to be citizens "of the State wherein they reside." U.S. Const., Amdt. 14, § 1. The States, however, do not have any right to select their citizens. The Fourteenth Amendment, like the Constitution itself, was, as Justice Cardozo put it, "framed upon the theory that the peoples of the several states must sink or swim together, and that in the long run prosperity and salvation are in union and not division." Baldwin v. G. A. F. Seelig, Inc. [1935; 13th ed., p. 287].

[Affirmed.]

Chief Justice REHNQUIST, with whom Justice Thomas joins, dissenting.

[The] right to travel clearly embraces the right to go from one place to another, and prohibits States from impeding the free interstate passage of citizens. [And] nonresident visitors of other States should not be subject to discrimination solely because they live out of State. [But] I cannot see how the right to become a citizen of another State is a necessary "component" of the right to travel, or why the Court tries to marry these separate and distinct rights. A person is no longer "traveling" in any sense of the word when he finishes his journey to a State which he plans to make his home. [No] doubt the Court has, in the past 30 years, essentially conflated the right to travel with the right to equal state citizenship in striking down durational residence requirements similar to the one challenged here. See, e.g., Shapiro, Dunn, Maricopa. [The] Court today tries to clear much of the underbrush created by these prior right-to-travel cases, abandoning its effort to define what residence requirements deprive individuals of "important rights and benefits" or "penalize" the right to travel. Under its new analytical framework, a State, outside certain ill-defined circumstances, cannot classify its citizens by the length of their residence in the State without offending the Privileges or Immunities Clause of the Fourteenth Amendment.

[In] unearthing from its tomb the right to become a state citizen and to be treated equally in the new State of residence, however, the Court ignores a State's need to assure that only persons who establish a bona fide residence receive the benefits provided to current residents of the State. [This] Court has

1. See Cohen, Discrimination Against New State Citizens: An Update, 11 Const. Comm. 73, 79 (1994) ("Just as it would violate the Constitution to deny these new arrivals state citizenship, it would violate the Constitution to concede their citizenship in name only while treating them as if they were still citizens of other states"). [Footnote by Justice Stevens.]

consistently recognized that while new citizens must have the same opportunity to enjoy the privileges of being a citizen of a State, the States retain the ability to use bona fide residence requirements to ferret out those who intend to take the privileges and run. [For example,] this Court has repeatedly sanctioned the State's use of durational residence requirements before new residents receive in-state tuition rates at state universities. The Court has done the same in upholding a 1–year residence requirement for eligibility to obtain a divorce in state courts, see Sosna. [If] States can require individuals to reside in-state for a year before exercising the right to educational benefits, [and] the right to terminate a marriage, then States may surely do the same for welfare benefits. [The] welfare payment here and in-state tuition rates are cash subsidies provided to a limited class of people, and California's standard of living and higher education system make both subsidies quite attractive. [The] Court tries to distinguish education and divorce benefits by contending that the welfare payment here will be consumed in California, while a college education or a divorce produces benefits that are "portable" and can be enjoyed after individuals return to their original domicile. But this "you can't take it with you" distinction is more apparent than real. [A] welfare subsidy is [as] much an investment in human capital as is a tuition subsidy, and their attendant benefits are just as "portable." [I] therefore believe that the durational residence requirement challenged here is a permissible exercise of the State's power to "assure that services provided for its residents are enjoyed only by residents."

[Congress'] express approval of durational residence requirements for welfare recipients only goes to show the reasonableness of [the California] law. The National Legislature, where people from Mississippi as well as California are represented, has recognized the need to protect state resources in a time of experimentation and welfare reform. As States like California revamp their total welfare packages, they should have the authority and flexibility to ensure that their new programs are not exploited. Congress has decided that it makes good welfare policy to give the States this power. California has reasonably exercised it through an objective, narrowly tailored residence requirement. I see nothing in the Constitution that should prevent the enforcement of that requirement.

Justice THOMAS, with whom the Chief Justice joins, dissenting.

[I] write separately to address the majority's conclusion that California has violated "the right of the newly arrived citizen to the same privileges and immunities enjoyed by other citizens of the same State." In my view, the majority attributes a meaning to the Privileges or Immunities Clause that likely was unintended when the Fourteenth Amendment was enacted and ratified. [At] the time the Fourteenth Amendment was adopted, people understood that "privileges or immunities of citizens" were fundamental rights, rather than every public benefit established by positive law. Accordingly, the majority's conclusion—that a State violates the Privileges or Immunities Clause when it "discriminates" against citizens who have been domiciled in the State for less than a year in the distribution of welfare benefits—appears contrary to the original understanding and is dubious at best. [Although] the majority appears to breathe new life into the [Privileges or Immunities] Clause today, it fails to address its historical underpinnings or its place in our constitutional jurisprudence. Because I believe that the demise of the Privileges or Immunities Clause has contributed in no small part to the current disarray of our Fourteenth Amendment jurisprudence, I would be open to reevaluating its meaning in an appropriate case. Before invoking the Clause, however, we should endeavor to understand what the framers of the Fourteenth Amendment thought that it meant.

CHAPTER 10

THE POST–CIVIL WAR AMENDMENTS AND CIVIL RIGHTS LEGISLATION: CONSTITUTIONAL RESTRAINTS ON PRIVATE CONDUCT; CONGRESSIONAL POWER TO IMPLEMENT THE AMENDMENTS

SECTION 4. CONGRESSIONAL POWER TO CHANGE THE CONTENT OF CONSTITUTIONAL RIGHTS?—"REMEDIAL" AND "SUBSTANTIVE" POWER UNDER § 5 OF THE 14TH AMENDMENT

Page 1014. Replace Note 3.d on the constitutionality of the Religious Freedom Restoration Act with:

City of Boerne v. Flores

521 U.S. 507, 117 S.Ct. 2157, 138 L.Ed.2d 624 (1997).

Justice KENNEDY delivered the opinion of the Court

A decision by local zoning authorities to deny a church a building permit was challenged under the Religious Freedom Restoration Act of 1993 (RFRA). The case calls into question the authority of Congress to enact RFRA. We conclude the statute exceeds Congress' power.

[Congress] enacted RFRA in direct response to the Court's decision in Employment Div., Dept. of Human Resources of Ore. v. Smith, 494 U.S. 872 (1990) [13th ed.; p. 1489]. There we considered a Free Exercise Clause claim brought by members of the Native American Church who were denied unemployment benefits when they lost their jobs because they had used peyote. Their practice was to ingest peyote for sacramental purposes, and they challenged an Oregon statute of general applicability which made use of the drug criminal. In evaluating the claim, we declined to apply the balancing test set forth in Sherbert v. Verner, 374 U.S. 398 (1963) [13th ed., p. 1479], under which we would have asked whether Oregon's prohibition substantially burdened a religious practice and, if it did, whether the burden was justified by a compelling government interest. [Smith] held that neutral, generally applicable laws may be applied to religious practices even when not supported by a compelling governmental interest.

[The Court's] constitutional interpretation [was] debated by Members of Congress in hearings and floor debates. Many criticized the Court's reasoning, and this disagreement resulted in the passage of RFRA. Congress announced: "(1) The framers of the Constitution, recognizing free exercise of religion as an unalienable right, secured its protection in the First Amendment to the Constitution; (2) laws 'neutral' toward religion may burden religious exercise as surely as laws intended to interfere with religious exercise; (3) governments should not substantially burden religious exercise without compelling justification; (4) in [Smith], the Supreme Court virtually eliminated the requirement that the government justify burdens on religious exercise imposed by laws neutral toward religion; and (5) the compelling interest test as set forth in prior Federal court rulings is a workable test for striking sensible balances between religious liberty and competing prior governmental interests."

The Act's stated purposes are: "(1) to restore the compelling interest test as set forth in [Sherbert] and to guarantee its application in all cases where free exercise of religion is substantially burdened; and (2) to provide a claim or defense to persons whose religious exercise is substantially burdened by government." RFRA prohibits "government" from "substantially burdening" a person's exercise of religion even if the burden results from a rule of general applicability unless the government can demonstrate the burden "(1) is in furtherance of a compelling governmental interest; and (2) is the least restrictive means of furthering that compelling governmental interest." The Act's mandate applies to any "branch, department, agency, instrumentality, and official (or other person acting under color of law) of the United States," as well as to any "State, or . . . subdivision of a State."

Congress relied on its Fourteenth Amendment enforcement power in enacting the most far reaching and substantial of RFRA's provisions, those which impose its requirements on the States. [The] parties disagree over whether RFRA is a proper exercise of Congress' § 5 power "to enforce" by "appropriate legislation" the constitutional guarantee that no State shall deprive any person of "life, liberty, or property, without due process of law" nor deny any person "equal protection of the laws." [All] must acknowledge that § 5 is "a positive grant of legislative power" to Congress. Katzenbach v. Morgan, [1966; 13th ed., p. 998]. [Legislation] which deters or remedies constitutional violations can fall within the sweep of Congress' enforcement power even if in the process it prohibits conduct which is not itself unconstitutional and intrudes into "legislative spheres of autonomy previously reserved to the States."

[It] is also true, however, that "as broad as the congressional enforcement power is, it is not unlimited." Oregon v. Mitchell [1970; 13th ed., p. 1004]. In assessing the breadth of § 5's enforcement power, we begin with its text. Congress has been given the power "to enforce" the "provisions of this article." We agree with respondent, of course, that Congress can enact legislation under § 5 enforcing the constitutional right to the free exercise of religion. The "provisions of this article" [include] the Due Process Clause of the Fourteenth Amendment. Congress' power to enforce the Free Exercise Clause follows from our holding in Cantwell v. Connecticut, 310 U.S. 296, 303 (1940), that the "fundamental concept of liberty embodied in [the Fourteenth Amendment's Due Process Clause] embraces the liberties guaranteed by the First Amendment."

Congress' power under § 5, however, extends only to "enforcing" the provisions of the Fourteenth Amendment. The Court has described this power as "remedial," South Carolina v. Katzenbach, [1966; 13th ed., p. 987]. The design of the Amendment and the text of § 5 are inconsistent with the suggestion that Congress has the power to decree the substance of the Fourteenth Amendment's restrictions on the States. Legislation which alters the meaning of the Free Exercise Clause cannot be said to be enforcing the Clause. Congress does not enforce a constitutional right by changing what the right is. It has been given the power "to enforce," not the power to determine what constitutes a constitutional violation. Were it not so, what Congress would be enforcing would no longer be, in any meaningful sense, the "provisions of [the Fourteenth Amendment]."

While the line between measures that remedy or prevent unconstitutional actions and measures that make a substantive change in the governing law is not easy to discern, and Congress must have wide latitude in determining where it lies, the distinction exists and must be observed. There must be a congruence and proportionality between the injury to be prevented or remedied and the means adopted to that end. Lacking such a connection, legislation may become substantive in operation and effect. History and our case law support drawing the distinction, one apparent from the text of the Amendment.

The Fourteenth Amendment's history[1] confirms the remedial, rather than substantive, nature of the Enforcement Clause. The Joint Committee on Reconstruction of the 39th Congress began drafting what would become the Fourteenth Amendment in January 1866. [In] February, Republican Representative John Bingham of Ohio reported the following draft amendment to the House of Representatives on behalf of the Joint Committee: "The Congress shall have power to make all laws which shall be necessary and proper to secure to the citizens of each State all privileges and immunities of citizens in the several States, and to all persons in the several States equal protection in the rights of life, liberty, and property."

The proposal encountered immediate opposition. [The] criticisms had a common theme: The proposed Amendment gave Congress too much legislative power at the expense of the existing constitutional structure. [The] Amendment in its early form was not again considered. Instead, the Joint Committee began drafting a new article of Amendment, which it reported to Congress on April 30, 1866. Section 1 of the new draft Amendment imposed self-executing limits on the States. Section 5 prescribed that "the Congress shall have power to enforce, by appropriate legislation, the provisions of this article." Under the revised Amendment, Congress' power was no longer plenary but remedial. Congress was granted the power to make the substantive constitutional prohibitions against the States effective. [The] revised Amendment proposal did not raise the concerns expressed earlier regarding broad congressional power to

1. Justice Scalia, while joining the rest of Justice Kennedy's opinion for the Court, did not join this account of 14th Amendment's history in the Reconstruction Congress.

prescribe uniform national laws with respect to life, liberty, and property. After revisions not relevant here, the new measure passed both Houses and was ratified in July 1868 as the Fourteenth Amendment.

The significance of the defeat of the Bingham proposal was apparent even then. During the debates over the Ku Klux Klan Act only a few years after the Amendment's ratification, Representative James Garfield argued there were limits on Congress' enforcement power, saying "unless we ignore both the history and the language of these clauses we cannot, by any reasonable interpretation, give to [§ 5] ... the force and effect of the rejected [Bingham] clause." Scholars of successive generations have agreed with this assessment.

The design of the Fourteenth Amendment has proved significant also in maintaining the traditional separation of powers between Congress and the Judiciary. The first eight Amendments to the Constitution set forth self-executing prohibitions on governmental action, and this Court has had primary authority to interpret those prohibitions. The Bingham draft, some thought, departed from that tradition by vesting in Congress primary power to interpret and elaborate on the meaning of the new Amendment through legislation. [While] this separation of powers aspect did not occasion the widespread resistance which was caused by the proposal's threat to the federal balance, it nonetheless attracted the attention of various Members. As enacted, the Fourteenth Amendment confers substantive rights against the States which, like the provisions of the Bill of Rights, are self-executing. The power to interpret the Constitution in a case or controversy remains in the Judiciary.

The remedial and preventive nature of Congress' enforcement power, and the limitation inherent in the power, were confirmed in our earliest cases on the Fourteenth Amendment. In the Civil Rights Cases, 109 U.S. 3 (1883), the Court invalidated sections of the Civil Rights Act of 1875 which prescribed criminal penalties for denying to any person "the full enjoyment of" public accommodations and conveyances, on the grounds that it exceeded Congress' power by seeking to regulate private conduct. The Enforcement Clause, the Court said, did not authorize Congress to pass "general legislation upon the rights of the citizen, but corrective legislation; that is, such as may be necessary and proper for counteracting such laws as the States may adopt or enforce, and which, by the amendment, they are prohibited from making or enforcing. . . ."

[Recent] cases have continued to revolve around the question of whether § 5 legislation can be considered remedial. In South Carolina v. Katzenbach [we] upheld various provisions of the Voting Rights Act of 1965, finding them to be "remedies aimed at areas where voting discrimination has been most flagrant," and necessary to "banish the blight of racial discrimination in voting, which has infected the electoral process in parts of our country for nearly a century." We noted evidence in the record reflecting the subsisting and pervasive discriminatory—and therefore unconstitutional—use of literacy tests. The Act's new remedies, includ[ing] the suspension of [literacy tests,] were deemed necessary given the ineffectiveness of the existing voting rights laws and the slow costly character of case-by-case litigation. After South Carolina v. Katzenbach, the Court continued to acknowledge the necessity of using strong remedial and preventive measures to respond to the widespread and persisting deprivation of constitutional rights resulting from this country's history of racial discrimination. See Oregon v. Mitchell; City of Rome; Katzenbach v. Morgan.

Any suggestion that Congress has a substantive, non-remedial power under the Fourteenth Amendment is not supported by our case law. In Oregon v. Mitchell, a majority of the Court concluded Congress had exceeded its enforcement powers by enacting legislation lowering the minimum age of voters from 21 to 18 in state and local elections. The five Members of the Court who reached this conclusion explained that the legislation intruded into an area reserved by the Constitution to the States. Four of these five [all but Justice Black] were explicit in rejecting the position that § 5 endowed Congress with the power to establish the meaning of constitutional provisions.

There is language in our opinion in Katzenbach v. Morgan which could be interpreted as acknowledging a power in Congress to enact legislation that expands the rights contained in § 1 of the Fourteenth Amendment. This is not a necessary interpretation, however, or even the best one. In Morgan, the Court considered the constitutionality of § 4(e) of the Voting Rights Act of 1965, which provided that no person who had successfully completed the sixth primary grade in a public school in, or a private school accredited by, the Commonwealth of Puerto Rico in which the language of instruction was other than English could be denied the right to vote because of an inability to read or write English. New York's Constitution, on the other hand, required voters to be able to read and write English. The Court provided two related rationales for its conclusion that § 4(e) could "be viewed as a measure to secure for the Puerto Rican community residing in New York nondiscriminatory treatment by government." Under the first rationale, Congress could prohibit New York from denying the right to vote to large segments of its Puerto Rican community, in order to give Puerto Ricans "enhanced political power" that would be "helpful in gaining nondiscriminatory treatment in public services for the entire Puerto Rican community." Section 4(e) thus could be justified as a remedial measure to deal with "discrimination in governmental services." The second rationale, an alternative holding, did not address discrimination in the provision of public services but "discrimination in establishing voter qualifications." The Court perceived a factual basis on which Congress could have concluded that New York's literacy requirement "constituted an invidious discrimination in violation of the Equal Protection Clause." Both rationales for upholding § 4(e) rested on unconstitutional discrimination by New York and Congress' reasonable attempt to combat it.

[If] Congress could define its own powers by altering the Fourteenth Amendment's meaning, no longer would the Constitution be "superior paramount law, unchangeable by ordinary means." It would be "on a level with ordinary legislative acts, and, like other acts, . . . alterable when the legislature shall please to alter it." Marbury v. Madison. Under this approach, it is difficult to conceive of a principle that would limit congressional power. Shifting legislative majorities could change the Constitution and effectively circumvent the difficult and detailed amendment process contained in Article V.

We now turn to consider whether RFRA can be considered enforcement legislation under § 5 of the Fourteenth Amendment. Respondent contends that RFRA is a proper exercise of Congress' remedial or preventive power [because] it prevents and remedies laws which are enacted with the unconstitutional object of targeting religious beliefs and practices. To avoid the difficulty of proving such violations, it is said, Congress can simply invalidate any law which imposes a substantial burden on a religious practice unless it is justified by a compelling interest and is the least restrictive means of accomplishing that interest. If Congress can prohibit laws with discriminatory effects in order to prevent racial discrimination in violation of the Equal Protection Clause, then it can do the same, respondent argues, to promote religious liberty.

While preventive rules are sometimes appropriate remedial measures, there must be a congruence between the means used and the ends to be achieved. The appropriateness of remedial measures must be considered in light of the evil presented. [In] contrast to the record which confronted Congress and the judiciary in the voting rights cases, RFRA's legislative record lacks examples of modern instances of generally applicable laws passed because of religious bigotry. The history of persecution in this country detailed in the hearings mentions no episodes occurring in the past 40 years. Rather, the emphasis of the hearings was on laws of general applicability which place incidental burdens on religion.

[This] lack of support in the legislative record, however, is not RFRA's most serious shortcoming. [As] a general matter, it is for Congress to determine the method by which it will reach a decision. Regardless of the state of the legislative record, RFRA cannot be considered remedial, preventive legislation, if those terms are to have any meaning. RFRA is so out of proportion to a supposed remedial or preventive object that it cannot be understood as responsive to, or designed to prevent, unconstitutional behavior. It appears, instead, to attempt a substantive change in constitutional protections. Preventive measures prohibiting certain types of laws may be appropriate when there is reason to believe that many of the laws affected by the congressional enactment have a significant likelihood of being unconstitutional. Remedial legislation under § 5 "should be adapted to the mischief and wrong which the [Fourteenth] Amendment was intended to provide against." Civil Rights Cases.

RFRA is not so confined. Sweeping coverage ensures its intrusion at every level of government, displacing laws and prohibiting official actions of almost every description and regardless of subject matter. [The] reach and scope of RFRA distinguish it from other measures passed under Congress' enforcement power, even in the area of voting rights. In South Carolina v. Katzenbach, the challenged provisions were confined to those regions of the country where voting discrimination had been most flagrant, and affected a discrete class of state laws, i.e., state voting laws. [The] provisions restricting and banning literacy tests, upheld in Katzenbach v. Morgan and Oregon v. Mitchell attacked a particular type of voting qualification. [In] City of Rome, the Court rejected a challenge to the constitutionality of a Voting Rights Act provision [imposed] only on jurisdictions with a history of intentional racial discrimination in voting. [This] is not to say, of course, that § 5 legislation requires termination dates, geographic restrictions or egregious predicates. Where, however, a congressional enactment pervasively prohibits constitutional state action in an effort to remedy or to prevent unconstitutional state action, limitations of this kind tend to ensure Congress' means are proportionate to ends legitimate under § 5.

The stringent test RFRA demands of state laws reflects a lack of proportionality or congruence between the means adopted and the legitimate end to be achieved. If an objector can show a substantial burden on his free exercise, the State must demonstrate a compelling governmental interest and show that the law is the least restrictive means of furthering its interest. Claims that a law substantially burdens someone's exercise of religion will often be difficult to contest. Requiring a State to demonstrate a compelling interest and show that it has adopted the least restrictive means of achieving that interest is the most demanding test known to constitutional law. [Laws] valid under Smith would fall under RFRA without regard to whether they had the object of stifling or punishing free exercise. We make these observations not to reargue the position of the majority in Smith but to illustrate the substantive alteration of its holding attempted by RFRA. Even assuming RFRA would be interpreted in effect to mandate some lesser test, say one equivalent to intermediate scrutiny, the statute nevertheless would require searching judicial scrutiny of state law with the attendant likelihood of invalidation. This is a considerable congressional intrusion into the States' traditional prerogatives and general authority to regulate for the health and welfare of their citizens.

The substantial costs RFRA exacts, both in practical terms of imposing a heavy litigation burden on the States and in terms of curtailing their traditional general regulatory power, far exceed any pattern or practice of unconstitutional conduct under the Free Exercise Clause as interpreted in Smith. Simply put, RFRA is not designed to identify and counteract state laws likely to be unconstitutional because of their treatment of religion. [In] addition, the Act imposes in every case a least restrictive means requirement [which] also indicates that the legislation is broader than is appropriate if the goal is to prevent and remedy constitutional violations.

[Our] national experience teaches that the Constitution is preserved best when each part of the government respects both the Constitution and the proper actions and determinations of the other branches. When the Court has interpreted the Constitution, it has acted within the province of the Judicial Branch, which embraces the duty to say what the law is. Marbury v. Madison. When the political branches of the Government act against the background of a judicial interpretation of the Constitution already issued, it must be understood that in later cases and controversies the Court will treat its precedents with the respect due them under settled principles, including stare decisis, and contrary expectations must be disappointed. RFRA was designed to control cases and controversies, such as the one before us; but as the provisions of the federal statute here invoked are beyond congressional authority, it is this Court's precedent, not RFRA, which must control.

It is for Congress in the first instance to "determine whether and what legislation is needed to secure the guarantees of the Fourteenth Amendment," and its conclusions are entitled to much deference. Katzenbach v. Morgan. Congress' discretion is not unlimited, however, and the courts retain the power, as they have since Marbury v. Madison, to determine if Congress has exceeded its authority under the Constitution. Broad as the power of Congress is under the Enforcement Clause of the Fourteenth Amendment, RFRA contradicts vital principles necessary to maintain separation of powers and the federal balance.

[Reversed.][2]

Page 1015. Add new note 3e, "The Implications of Boerne":

Did Boerne simply repudiate an unusually flagrant attempt by Congress to overturn the substance of one of the Court's own decisions by means of statute rather than constitutional amendment? Or did it announce a new stricter standard of scrutiny for all statutes claimed to enforce the civil rights guaranteed by the Fourteenth Amendment? Two decisions that sharply divided the Court at the end of the 1998–99 Term suggested that Congress must demonstrate a clear justification for the exercise of its civil rights enforcement power against the states, even where it offers no challenge to the Court's substantive interpretation of those rights. The cases arose from two statutes enacted by Congress in order to expressly abrogate state sovereign immunity against patent and trademark suits. Under the Court's holding in Seminole Tribe v. Florida (1996; 13th ed., p. 226), Congress could not enact such legislation under its Article I powers. But Seminole Tribe did not disturb the Court's earlier holdings that Congress may subject nonconsenting states to lawsuits in federal court pursuant to its powers under § 5 of the Fourteenth Amendment. Thus, the constitutionality of the patent and trademark statutes in question turned on whether they were validly enacted pursuant to Congress' powers under § 5 of the Fourteenth Amendment. In both cases, the Court concluded that they were not.

In FLORIDA PREPAID POSTSECONDARY EDUCATION EXPENSE BOARD v. COLLEGE SAVINGS BANK, 119 S.Ct. 2199 (1999), the Court, by a 5–4 vote, invalidated the Patent and Plant Variety Protection Remedy Clarification Act, which had expressly abrogated the states' sovereign immunity from claims of patent infringement. The case arose from a patent infringement claim brought under the Act by a New Jersey bank against a Florida agency that had allegedly copied the bank's patented college tuition savings program. The bank and the United States defended the statute as an exercise of Congress's power to prevent state deprivations of property, here in the form of patent rights, without due process of law. Chief Justice REHNQUIST, writing for the Court, reiterated that " 'appropriate' legislation pursuant to the Enforcement Clause of the Fourteenth Amendment could abrogate state sovereignty," and that "the 'provisions of this article,' to which § 5 refers, include the Due Process Clause of the Fourteenth Amendment." "But," he continued, "the legislation must

2. Justice Stevens joined Justice Kennedy's opinion for the Court and also filed a separate concurrence stating that RFRA was unconstitutional under the Establishment Clause. Justice O'Connor dissented, stating that, "if I agreed with the Court's standard in Smith, I would join the opinion" of the Court, but arguing at length that Smith had misinterpreted the Free Exercise Clause and should be reexamined by directing the parties to brief that question and setting the case for reargument. Justice Breyer joined Justice O'Connor's dissent except insofar as it suggested that, "assuming Smith is correct, § 5 of the Fourteenth Amendment would [not] authorize Congress to enact [RFRA]." Justice Souter filed a dissent stating that in the absence of reconsideration of Smith, about which he had "serious doubts," the congressional authority questions "cannot now be soundly decided"; thus he would dismiss the writ of certiorari as improvidently granted. Justice Scalia, joined by Justice Stevens, filed a concurrence disputing Justice O'Connor's historical evidence for the claim that that Smith misinterpreted the Free Exercise Clause. For excerpts of the debate between the concurrence and the dissent over the interpretation of free exercise, see p. 149 below.

nonetheless be 'appropriate' under § 5 as that term was construed in City of Boerne. [There we] held that for Congress to invoke § 5, it must identify conduct transgressing the Fourteenth Amendment's substantive provisions, and must tailor its legislative scheme to remedying or preventing such conduct."

Turning to the question whether the Patent Remedy Act could be viewed as permissibly remedial or preventive legislation within the meaning of Boerne, the Chief Justice continued: "The underlying conduct at issue here is state infringement of patents and the use of sovereign immunity to deny patent owners compensation for the invasion of their patent rights. [In] enacting the Patent Remedy Act, however, Congress identified no pattern of patent infringement by the States, let alone a pattern of constitutional violations. Unlike the undisputed record of racial discrimination confronting Congress in the voting rights cases, Congress came up with little evidence of infringing conduct on the part of the States. [Moreover, Congress] barely considered the availability of state remedies for patent infringement and hence whether the States' conduct might have amounted to a constitutional violation under the Fourteenth Amendment. [The] legislative record thus suggests that the Patent Remedy Act does not respond to a history of 'widespread and persisting deprivation of constitutional rights' of the sort Congress has faced in enacting proper prophylactic § 5 legislation. Boerne. Instead, Congress appears to have enacted this legislation in response to a handful of instances of state patent infringement that do not necessarily violate the Constitution. Though the lack of support in the legislative record is not determinative, identifying the targeted constitutional wrong or evil is still a critical part of our § 5 calculus. [Here], the record at best offers scant support for Congress' conclusion that States were depriving patent owners of property without due process of law by pleading sovereign immunity in federal-court patent actions.

"Because of this lack, the provisions of the Patent Remedy Act are 'so out of proportion to a supposed remedial or preventive object that [they] cannot be understood as responsive to, or designed to prevent, unconstitutional behavior.' [Despite] subjecting States to this expansive liability, Congress did nothing to limit the coverage of the Act to cases involving arguable constitutional violations, such as where a State refuses to offer any state-court remedy for patent owners whose patents it had infringed. Nor did it make any attempt to confine the reach of the Act by limiting the remedy to certain types of infringement, such as nonnegligent infringement or infringement authorized pursuant to state policy; or providing for suits only against States with questionable remedies or a high incidence of infringement. Instead, Congress made all States immediately amenable to suit in federal court for all kinds of possible patent infringement and for an indefinite duration. [The] Patent Remedy Act's indiscriminate scope offends [the] principle [of proportionality set forth in Boerne], and is particularly incongruous in light of the scant support for the predicate unconstitutional conduct that Congress intended to remedy. In sum, it simply cannot be said that 'many of [the acts of infringement] affected by the congressional enactment have a significant likelihood of being unconstitutional.' The historical record and the scope of coverage therefore make it clear that the Patent Remedy Act cannot be sustained under § 5 of the Fourteenth Amendment."

Justice STEVENS dissented, joined by Justices Souter, Ginsburg and Breyer. Emphasizing the need for federal uniformity in patent law, he argued that it was "appropriate" under Boerne for Congress to conclude that state remedies would be inadequate to "guarantee patentees due process in infringement actions against state defendants," and thus appropriate to pass the Patent Remedy Act as a preventive measure. Asserting that the Court had gone beyond the limits set forth in Boerne, he warned that "[t]he Court's opinion today threatens to read Congress' power to pass prophylactic legislation out of § 5 altogether."

In COLLEGE SAVINGS BANK v. FLORIDA PREPAID POSTSECONDARY EDUCATION EXPENSE BOARD, 119 S. Ct. 2219 (1999), the Court, reviewing a case arising between the same parties over the same conduct, and dividing along identical lines, invalidated the Trademark Remedy Clarification Act, which had subjected states to federal lawsuits by their business competitors for false and misleading advertising. Justice SCALIA's opinion for the Court held that the rights protected by the federal statute were not the kind of rights that qualify as property rights protected by the due process clause. Accordingly, he found that Congress lacked authority to enact the statute under § 5 of the Fourteenth Amendment. Justices STEVENS and BREYER filed dissents criticizing the Court's extension of Seminole Tribe.

United States v. Morrison

120 S.Ct. 1740 (2000).

Chief Justice REHNQUIST delivered the opinion of the Court.

[This case arose from a rape claim brought by a student at Virginia Polytechnic Institute, Christy Brzonkala, against two football players also enrolled at the university. She filed a complaint under the Virginia Tech disciplinary system, but one of the accused was not punished and the other's punishment was eventually suspended. She dropped out of school and sued both men and Virginia Tech in federal district court under the challenged statute.]

In these cases we consider the constitutionality of 42 U.S.C. § 13981, which provides a federal civil remedy for the victims of gender-motivated violence. [Section] 13981 was part of the Violence Against Women Act of 1994, [which] states that "[a]ll persons within the United States shall have the right to be free from crimes of violence motivated by gender." To enforce that right, [the law] declares: "A person (including a person who acts under color of any statute, ordinance, regulation, custom, or usage of any State) who commits a crime of violence motivated by gender and thus deprives another of the right [to be free of such crimes] shall be liable to the party injured, in an action for the recovery of compensatory and punitive damages, injunctive and declaratory relief, and such other relief as a court may deem appropriate."

[Every] law enacted by Congress must be based on one or more of its powers enumerated in the Constitution. [Congress] explicitly identified the sources of federal authority on which it relied in enacting § 13981 [as including] "section 5 of the Fourteenth Amendment to the Constitution [and] section 8 of Article I of the Constitution."

[In section II of the opinion, the Chief Justice found no authority for the provision in the Commerce Clause of Article I, section 8, clause 3. This part of the opinion is reported above at p. 10.]

III. Because we conclude that the Commerce Clause does not provide Congress with authority to enact § 13981, we address petitioners' alternative argument that the section's civil remedy should be upheld as an exercise of Congress' remedial power under § 5 of the Fourteenth Amendment. [Petitioners'] § 5 argument is founded on an assertion that there is pervasive bias in various state justice systems against victims of gender-motivated violence. This assertion is supported by a voluminous congressional record. Specifically, Congress received evidence that many participants in state justice systems are perpetuating an array of erroneous stereotypes and assumptions. Congress concluded that these discriminatory stereotypes often result in insufficient investigation and prosecution of gender-motivated crime, inappropriate focus on the behavior and credibility of the victims of that crime, and unacceptably lenient punishments for those who are actually convicted of gender-motivated violence. Petitioners contend that this bias denies victims of gender-motivated violence the equal protection of the laws and that Congress therefore acted appropriately in enacting a private civil remedy against the perpetrators of gender-motivated violence to both remedy the States' bias and deter future instances of discrimination in the state courts.

As our cases have established, state-sponsored gender discrimination violates equal protection unless it " 'serves "important governmental objectives and ... the discriminatory means employed" are "substantially related to the achievement of those objectives." ' " United States v. Virginia [1996; 13th ed., p. 704]. However, the language and purpose of the Fourteenth Amendment place certain limitations on the manner in which Congress may attack discriminatory conduct. These limitations are necessary to prevent the Fourteenth Amendment from obliterating the Framers' carefully crafted balance of power between the States and the National Government. Foremost among these limitations is the time-honored principle that the Fourteenth Amendment, by its very terms, prohibits only state action.

Shortly after the Fourteenth Amendment was adopted, we decided two cases interpreting the Amendment's provisions, United States v. Harris, 106 U.S. 629 (1883), and the Civil Rights Cases [1883; 13th ed., p. 921]. In Harris, the Court considered a challenge to § 2 of the Civil Rights Act of 1871. That section sought to punish "private persons" for "conspiring to deprive any one of the equal protection of the laws enacted by the State." We concluded that this law exceeded Congress' § 5 power because the law was "directed exclusively against the action of private persons, without reference to the laws of the State, or their administration by her officers." [We] reached a similar conclusion in the Civil Rights Cases. In those consolidated cases, we held that the public accommodation provisions of the Civil Rights Act of 1875, which applied to purely private conduct, were beyond the scope of the § 5 enforcement power.

[Petitioners] argue that, unlike the situation in the Civil Rights Cases, here there has been gender-based disparate treatment by state authorities, whereas in those cases there was no indication of such state action. There is abundant evidence, however, to show that the Congresses that enacted the Civil Rights Acts of 1871 and 1875 had a purpose similar to that of Congress in enacting

§ 13981: There were state laws on the books bespeaking equality of treatment, but in the administration of these laws there was discrimination against newly freed slaves. [But] even if that distinction were valid, we do not believe it would save § 13981's civil remedy. For the remedy is simply not "corrective in its character, adapted to counteract and redress the operation of such prohibited [s]tate laws or proceedings of [s]tate officers." Civil Rights Cases. Or, as we have phrased it in more recent cases, prophylactic legislation under § 5 must have a "congruence and proportionality between the injury to be prevented or remedied and the means adopted to that end." Florida Prepaid; Boerne v. Flores. [Section] 13981 is not aimed at proscribing discrimination by officials which the Fourteenth Amendment might not itself proscribe; it is directed not at any State or state actor, but at individuals who have committed criminal acts motivated by gender bias.

In the present cases, for example, § 13981 visits no consequence whatever on any Virginia public official involved in investigating or prosecuting Brzonkala's assault. The section is, therefore, unlike any of the § 5 remedies that we have previously upheld. [Section] 13981 is also different from these previously upheld remedies in that it applies uniformly throughout the Nation. Congress' findings indicate that the problem of discrimination against the victims of gender-motivated crimes does not exist in all States, or even most States. [For] these reasons, we conclude that Congress' power under § 5 does not extend to the enactment of § 13981. [Affirmed.]

Justice BREYER, with whom Justice STEVENS joins, dissenting.[1]

[Justice Breyer first expressed the view that Congress had authority under the Commerce Clause to enact the violence against women law.] Given my conclusion on the Commerce Clause question, I need not consider Congress' authority under § 5 of the Fourteenth Amendment. Nonetheless, I doubt the Court's reasoning rejecting that source of authority. [Petitioners claim] that Congress used § 5 to remedy the actions of state actors, namely, those States which, through discriminatory design or the discriminatory conduct of their officials, failed to provide adequate (or any) state remedies for women injured by gender-motivated violence—a failure that the States, and Congress, documented in depth. [This] Court has held that Congress at least sometimes can enact remedial "[l]egislation ... [that] prohibits conduct which is not itself unconstitutional." Flores. The statutory remedy does not in any sense purport to "determine what constitutes a constitutional violation." Id. It intrudes little upon either States or private parties. It may lead state actors to improve their own remedial systems, primarily through example. It restricts private actors only by imposing liability for private conduct that is, in the main, already forbidden by state law. Why is the remedy "disproportionate"? And given the relation between remedy and violation—the creation of a federal remedy to substitute for constitutionally inadequate state remedies—where is the lack of "congruence"?

The majority adds that Congress found that the problem of inadequacy of state remedies "does not exist in all States, or even most States." But Congress

1. Justice Souter wrote a lengthy dissent, joined by Justices Stevens, Ginsburg and Breyer, from the majority's Commerce Clause holding. Justices Souter and Ginsburg joined portions of Justice Breyer's dissent with respect to the Commerce Clause holding. See p. 10 above.

had before it the task force reports of at least 21 States documenting constitutional violations. And it made its own findings about pervasive gender-based stereotypes hampering many state legal systems, sometimes unconstitutionally so. The record nowhere reveals a congressional finding that the problem "does not exist" elsewhere. Why can Congress not take the evidence before it as evidence of a national problem? This Court has not previously held that Congress must document the existence of a problem in every State prior to proposing a national solution. And the deference this Court gives to Congress' chosen remedy under § 5, suggests that any such requirement would be inappropriate.

Page 1017 n.2. Add to footnote 2:

In DICKERSON v. UNITED STATES, 120 S. Ct. 2326 (2000), the Court invalidated Congress's attempt to overturn the Miranda safeguards by statute. Chief Justice REHNQUIST, writing for the 7–2 majority, stated: "In Miranda v. Arizona, 384 U.S. 436 (1966), we held that certain warnings must be given before a suspect's statement made during custodial interrogation could be admitted in evidence. In the wake of that decision, Congress enacted 18 U.S.C. § 3501, which in essence laid down a rule that the admissibility of such statements should turn only on whether or not they were voluntarily made [under the totality of the circumstances]. We hold that Miranda, being a constitutional decision of this Court, may not be in effect overruled by an Act of Congress, and we decline to overrule Miranda ourselves. [Congress] retains the ultimate authority to modify or set aside any judicially created rules of evidence and procedure that are not required by the Constitution. But Congress may not legislatively supersede our decisions interpreting and applying the Constitution. See, e.g., City of Boerne v. Flores. This case therefore turns on whether the Miranda Court announced a constitutional rule or merely exercised its supervisory authority to regulate evidence in the absence of congressional direction."

The Chief Justice concluded that Miranda had set forth a constitutional rule that Congress may not supersede legislatively. He noted that it and its companion cases applied to proceedings in state courts, over which the Supreme Court has constitutional but not supervisory authority, and that the Miranda opinion "is replete with statements indicating that the majority thought it was announcing a constitutional rule." He rejected the argument that § 3501 was a constitutionally sufficient substitute for Miranda, as it "explicitly eschews a requirement of pre-interrogation warnings in favor of an approach that looks to the administration of such warnings as only one factor in determining the voluntariness of a suspect's confession." Finally he noted that, "[w]hether or not we would agree with Miranda's reasoning and its resulting rule, were we addressing the issue in the first instance, the principles of stare decisis weigh heavily against overruling it now."

Justice SCALIA dissented, joined by Justice Thomas. He insisted that the Miranda warnings did not amount to a constitutional requirement, but "rather only 'prophylactic' rules that go beyond the right against compelled self-incrimination. [By] disregarding congressional action that [does] not violate the Constitution, the Court flagrantly offends fundamental principles of separation of powers, and arrogates to itself prerogatives reserved to the representatives of the people. [Today's] judgment converts Miranda from a milestone of judicial overreaching into the very Cheops' Pyramid (or perhaps the Sphinx would be a better analogue) of judicial arrogance."

Page 1020. Replace note 5.c on EEOC v. Wyoming with:

In KIMEL v. FLORIDA BOARD OF REGENTS, 120 S.Ct. 631 (2000), the Court ruled by a vote of 5–4 that Congress had exceeded its Fourteenth Amendment remedial authority in allowing state employees to sue the states for damages for violations of the Age Discrimination in Employment Act (ADEA). After noting that the Fourteenth Amendment was the sole source of congressional authority to abrogate sovereign immunity, see page 33 above, the Court examined the ADEA under the test announced in City of Boerne v. Flores. Because the ADEA failed the "congruence and proportionality test," the majority held, Congress's attempt to abrogate the states' sovereign immunity was unconstitutional.

Justice O'CONNOR, joined by Chief Justice Rehnquist and Justices Scalia, Kennedy, and Thomas, noted that the antidiscrimination protections of the ADEA for state employees far exceeded the requirements of Equal Protection. "Applying the 'congruence and proportionality' test, [we] conclude that the ADEA is not 'appropriate legislation' under § 5 of the Fourteenth Amendment. [The] substantive requirements the ADEA imposes on state and local governments are disproportionate to any unconstitutional conduct that conceivably could be targeted by the Act. We have considered claims of unconstitutional age discrimination under the Equal Protection Clause three times. See, e.g., Massachusetts Bd. of Retirement v. Murgia, [1976; 13th ed., p. 734]. In all three cases, we held that the age classifications at issue did not violate the Equal Protection Clause. [These] decisions thus demonstrate that the constitutionality of state classifications on the basis of age cannot be determined on a person-by-person basis. Our Constitution permits States to draw lines on the basis of age when they have a rational basis for doing so at a class-based level, even if it 'is probably not true' that those reasons are valid in the majority of cases.

"[The ADEA], through its broad restriction on the use of age as a discriminating factor, prohibits substantially more state employment decisions and practices than would likely be held unconstitutional under the applicable equal protection [standard]. [Congress], through the ADEA, has effectively elevated the standard for analyzing age discrimination to heightened scrutiny. [Congress] never identified any pattern of age discrimination by the States, much less any discrimination whatsoever that rose to the level of constitutional violation. [Congress] had virtually no reason to believe that state and local governments were unconstitutionally discriminating against their employees on the basis of age. [In] light of the indiscriminate scope of the Act's substantive requirements, and the lack of evidence of widespread and unconstitutional age discrimination by the States, we hold that the ADEA is not a valid exercise of Congress' power under § 5 of the Fourteenth Amendment. The ADEA's purported abrogation of the States' sovereign immunity is accordingly invalid."

Justice THOMAS, joined by Justice Kennedy, concurred with the Court's Fourteenth Amendment analysis, but thought the constitutional question unnecessary because the ADEA did not evince an unmistakable intention to abrogate the states' sovereign immunity.

In dissent, Justice STEVENS, joined by Justices Souter, Ginsburg, and Breyer, did not reach the Fourteenth Amendment issue, since he thought the ADEA's abrogation of sovereign immunity justified under the Commerce Power. [See page 33 above for dissenting and concurring opinions].

CHAPTER 11

Freedom of Speech—Why Government Restricts Speech—Unprotected and Less Protected Expression

Section 5. Sexually Explicit Expression

Page 1174. Add to end of Note 3 on indecent programming on cable television:

In UNITED STATES v. PLAYBOY ENTERTAINMENT GROUP, 120 S.Ct. 1878 (2000), the Court, by a vote of 5–4, invalidated provisions of a federal telecommunications law that required cable operators either to fully scramble sexually explicit programming or, if they were unable to do so because of "signal bleed," to confine such programming to late-night hours when children were unlikely to view it. Writing for the Court, Justice KENNEDY, joined by Justices Stevens, Souter, Thomas and Ginsburg, held the law subject to strict scrutiny on the grounds that it was content-based, and that its time channeling requirement significantly restricted cable operators' speech even though it did not impose a complete prohibition: "The distinction between laws burdening and laws banning speech is but a matter of degree. The Government's content-based burdens must satisfy the same rigorous scrutiny as its content-based bans." He distinguished erogenous zoning cases as "irrelevant," writing that "the lesser scrutiny afforded regulations targeting the secondary effects of crime or declining property values has no application to content-based regulations targeting the primary effects of protected speech." He likewise distinguished broadcasting cases, reasoning that cable systems, unlike broadcasters, "have the capacity to block unwanted channels on a household-by-household basis," and that "targeted blocking is less restrictive than banning."

Applying strict scrutiny, Justice Kennedy wrote: "When a plausible, less restrictive alternative is offered to a content-based speech restriction, it is the Government's obligation to prove that the alternative will be ineffective to achieve its goals. The Government has not met that burden here." He found such an alternative in a different provision of the law requiring cable operators to block undesired channels at individual households upon request, and rejected, at least without a better record, a variety of government arguments as to why such voluntary blocking might be ineffective.

Justice SCALIA dissented on the ground that lesser scrutiny should apply to regulation of commercial trafficking in sexual speech, a proposition that Justice STEVENS disputed in a separate concurrence. Justice THOMAS concurred separately to express the view that the government might regulate much sexual cable programming as obscene under the Miller test, but that its attempt to regulate merely indecent sexual speech on cable was not defensible.

Justice BREYER dissented, joined by Chief Justice Rehnquist and Justices O'Connor and Scalia. He concluded that the voluntary opt-out provision was not a "*similarly* practical and *effective* way to accomplish [the time-channeling provision's] child-protecting objective," and argued for applying a First Amendment narrow tailoring standard that would afford "a degree of leeway [for] the legislature when it chooses among possible alternatives in light of predicted comparative effects."

Page 1174. Replace Note 4, "Indecency on the Internet," with:

Reno v. American Civil Liberties Union

521 U.S. 844, 117 S.Ct. 2329, 138 L.Ed.2d 874 (1997).

Justice STEVENS delivered the opinion of the Court.

At issue is the constitutionality of two statutory provisions enacted to protect minors from "indecent" and "patently offensive" communications on the Internet. Notwithstanding the legitimacy and importance of the congressional goal of protecting children from harmful materials, we agree with the three-judge District Court that the statute abridges "the freedom of speech" protected by the First Amendment.

The District Court made extensive findings of fact: [The] Internet is an international network of interconnected computers [that now] enable tens of millions of people to communicate with one another and to access vast amounts of information from around the world. The Internet is "a unique and wholly new medium of worldwide human communication." The Internet has experienced "extraordinary growth." [About] 40 million people used the Internet at the time of trial, a number that is expected to mushroom to 200 million by 1999. Individuals can obtain access to the Internet from many different sources. [Most] colleges and universities provide access for their students and faculty; many corporations provide their employees with access through an office network; many communities and local libraries provide free access; and an increasing number of storefront "computer coffee shops" provide access for a small hourly fee. Several major national "online services" [offer] access to their own extensive proprietary networks as well as a link to the much larger resources of the Internet.

Anyone with access to the Internet may take advantage of a wide variety of communication and information retrieval methods. [E-mail] enables an individual to send an electronic message—generally akin to a note or letter—to another individual or to a group of addressees. [A] mail exploder is a sort of e-mail group. [Newsgroups] also serve groups of regular participants, but these postings may be read by others as well. [In] addition to posting a message that can be read later, two or more individuals wishing to communicate more immediately can enter a chat room [by] typing messages to one another that appear almost immediately on the others' computer screens.

The best known category of communication over the Internet is the World Wide Web, which allows users to search for and retrieve information stored in remote computers, as well as, in some cases, to communicate back to designated sites. [The] Web is [comparable,] from the readers' viewpoint, to both a vast library including millions of readily available and indexed publications and a sprawling mall offering goods and services. From the publishers' point of view, it constitutes a vast platform from which to address and hear from a world-wide audience of millions of readers, viewers, researchers, and buyers. Any person or organization with a computer connected to the Internet can "publish" information. Publishers include government agencies, educational institutions, commercial entities, advocacy groups, and individuals. Publishers may either make their material available to the entire pool of Internet users, or confine access to a selected group, such as those willing to pay for the privilege. "No single organization controls any membership in the Web, nor is there any centralized point from which individual Web sites or services can be blocked from the Web."

Sexually explicit material on the Internet includes text, pictures, and chat and "extends from the modestly titillating to the hardest-core." These files are created, named, and posted in the same manner as material that is not sexually explicit, and may be accessed either deliberately or unintentionally during the course of an imprecise search. "Once a provider posts its content on the Internet, it cannot prevent that content from entering any community." [Some] of the communications over the Internet that originate in foreign countries are also sexually explicit. [The] "odds are slim" that a user would enter a sexually explicit site by accident. Unlike communications received by radio or television, "the receipt of information on the Internet requires a series of affirmative steps more deliberate and directed than merely turning a dial. A child requires some sophistication and some ability to read to retrieve material and thereby to use the Internet unattended."

Systems have been developed to help parents control the material that may be available on a home computer with Internet access. A system may either limit a computer's access to an approved list of sources that have been identified as containing no adult material, it may block designated inappropriate sites, or it may attempt to block messages containing identifiable objectionable features. "Although parental control software currently can screen for certain suggestive words or for known sexually explicit sites, it cannot now screen for sexually explicit images." Nevertheless, the evidence indicates that "a reasonably effective method by which parents can prevent their children from accessing sexually explicit and other material which parents may believe is inappropriate for their children will soon be available."

The problem of age verification differs for different uses of the Internet. The District Court categorically determined that there "is no effective way to determine the identity or the age of a user who is accessing material through e-mail, mail exploders, newsgroups or chat rooms." The Government offered no evidence that there was a reliable way to screen recipients and participants in such fora for age. [Technology] exists by which an operator of a Web site may condition access on the verification of requested information such as a credit card number or an adult password. Credit card verification is only feasible, however, either in connection with a commercial transaction in which the card is used, or by payment to a verification agency. Using credit card possession as a surrogate for proof of age would impose costs on non-commercial Web sites that would require many of them to shut down. [Commercial] pornographic sites that charge their users for access have assigned them passwords as a method of age verification. The record does not contain any evidence concerning the reliability of these technologies. Even if passwords are effective for commercial purveyors of indecent material, the District Court found that an adult password requirement would impose significant burdens on noncommercial sites, both because they would discourage users from accessing their sites and because the cost of creating and maintaining such screening systems would be "beyond their reach."

[Two provisions of] the "Communications Decency Act of 1996" (CDA) [are] challenged in this case. [The "indecent transmission" provision, 47 U.S.C. § 223 (a),] prohibits the knowing transmission of obscene or indecent messages to any recipient under 18 years of age. It provides in pertinent part: "(a) Whoever—(1) in interstate or foreign communications— . . . (B) by means of a telecommunications device knowingly—(i) makes, creates, or solicits, and (ii) initiates the transmission of, any comment, request, suggestion, proposal, image, or other communication which is obscene or indecent, knowing that the recipient of the communication is under 18 years of age, regardless of whether the maker of such communication placed the call or initiated the communication; . . . [or] (2) knowingly permits any telecommunications facility under his control to be used for any activity prohibited by paragraph (1) with the intent that it be used for such activity, shall be fined [or] imprisoned not more than two years, or both."

The ["patently offensive display" provision, 47 U.S.C. § 223 (d),] prohibits the knowing sending or displaying of patently offensive messages in a manner that is available to a person under 18 years of age. It provides: "(d) Whoever—(1) in interstate or foreign communications knowingly—(A) uses an interactive computer service to send to a specific person or persons under 18 years of age, or (B) uses any interactive computer service to display in a manner available to a person under 18 years of age, any comment, request, suggestion, proposal, image, or other communication that, in context, depicts or describes, in terms patently offensive as measured by contemporary community standards, sexual or excretory activities or organs, regardless of whether the user of such service placed the call or initiated the communication; or (2) knowingly permits any telecommunications facility under such person's control to be used for an activity prohibited by paragraph (1) with the intent that it be used for such activity, shall be fined [or] imprisoned not more than two years, or both." The breadth of these prohibitions is qualified by two affirmative defenses.[1]

The judgment of the District Court enjoins the Government from enforcing the prohibitions in § 223(a)(1)(B) insofar as they relate to "indecent" commu-

1. [47 U.S.C.] § 223(e)(5) provides: (5) It is a defense to a prosecution under subsection (a)(1)(B) or (d) of this section, or under subsection (a)(2) of this section with respect to the use of a facility for an activity under subsection (a)(1)(B) of this section that a person—(A) has taken, in good faith, reasonable, effective, and appropriate actions under the circumstances to restrict or prevent access by minors to a communication specified in such subsections, which may involve any appropriate measures to restrict minors from such communications, including any method which is feasible under available technology; or (B) has restricted access to such communication by requiring use of a verified credit card, debit account, adult access code, or adult personal identification number. [Footnote by Justice Stevens.]

nications, but expressly preserves the Government's right to investigate and prosecute the obscenity or child pornography activities prohibited therein. The injunction against enforcement of §§ 223(d)(1) and (2) is unqualified because those provisions contain no separate reference to obscenity or child pornography. [We] conclude that the judgment should be affirmed.

In arguing for reversal, the Government [relies upon] Ginsberg v. New York, 390 U.S. 629 (1968); FCC v. Pacifica Foundation [1978; 13th ed., p. 1164]; and Renton v. Playtime Theatres, Inc. [1986; 13th ed., p. 1162]. A close look at these cases, however, raises—rather than relieves—doubts concerning the constitutionality of the CDA. In Ginsberg, we upheld the constitutionality of a New York statute that prohibited selling to minors under 17 years of age material that was considered obscene as to them even if not obscene as to adults. [But] the statute upheld in Ginsberg was narrower than the CDA. First, we noted in Ginsberg that "the prohibition against sales to minors does not bar parents who so desire from purchasing the magazines for their children." Under the CDA, by contrast, neither the parents' consent—nor even their participation—in the communication would avoid the application of the statute. Second, the New York statute applied only to commercial transactions, whereas the CDA contains no such limitation. Third, the New York statute cabined its definition of material that is harmful to minors with the requirement that it be "utterly without redeeming social importance for minors." The CDA fails to provide us with any definition of the term "indecent" [and] omits any requirement that the "patently offensive" material covered by § 223(d) lack serious literary, artistic, political, or scientific value. Fourth, the New York statute defined a minor as a person under the age of 17, whereas the CDA, in applying to all those under 18 years, includes an additional year of those nearest majority.

In Pacifica, we upheld a declaratory order of the FCC, holding that the broadcast of a recording of a 12-minute monologue entitled "Filthy Words" ["could] have been the subject of administrative sanctions." [There] are significant differences between the order upheld in Pacifica and the CDA. First, the order in Pacifica, issued by an agency that had been regulating radio stations for decades, targeted a specific broadcast that represented a rather dramatic departure from traditional program content in order to designate when—rather than whether—it would be permissible to air such a program in that particular medium. The CDA's broad categorical prohibitions are not limited to particular times and are not dependent on any evaluation by an agency familiar with the unique characteristics of the Internet. Second, unlike the CDA, the Commission's declaratory order was not punitive; we expressly refused to decide whether the indecent broadcast "would justify a criminal prosecution." Finally, the Commission's order applied to a medium which as a matter of history had "received the most limited First Amendment protection," in large part because warnings could not adequately protect the listener from unexpected program content. The Internet, however, has no comparable history. Moreover, the District Court found that the risk of encountering indecent material by accident is remote because a series of affirmative steps is required to access specific material.

In Renton, we upheld a zoning ordinance that kept adult movie theatres out of residential neighborhoods. The ordinance was aimed, not at the content of the films shown in the theaters, but rather at the "secondary effects"—such as crime and deteriorating property values—that these theaters fostered. [According] to the Government, the CDA is constitutional because it constitutes a sort of "cyberzoning" on the Internet. But the CDA applies broadly to the entire universe of cyberspace. And the purpose of the CDA is to protect children from the primary effects of "indecent" and "patently offensive" speech, rather than any "secondary" effect of such speech. Thus, the CDA is a content-based blanket restriction on speech, and, as such, cannot be "properly analyzed as a form of time, place, and manner regulation." These precedents, then, surely do not require us to uphold the CDA and are fully consistent with the application of the most stringent review of its provisions.

[Some] of our cases have recognized special justifications for regulation of the broadcast media that are not applicable to other speakers, see Red Lion Broadcasting Co. v. FCC [1969; 13th ed., p. 1450]; FCC v. Pacifica. In these cases, the Court relied on the history of extensive government regulation of the broadcast medium; the scarcity of available frequencies at its inception; and its "invasive" nature, see Sable Communications v. FCC [1989; 13th ed., p. 1171]. Those factors are not present in cyberspace. Neither before nor after the enactment of the CDA have the vast democratic fora of the Internet been subject to the type of government supervision and regulation that has attended the broadcast industry. Moreover, the Internet is not as "invasive" as radio or television. The District Court specifically found that "communications over the Internet do not 'invade' an individual's home or appear on one's computer screen unbidden. Users seldom encounter content 'by accident.' " It also found that "almost all sexually explicit images are preceded by warnings as to the content." We distinguished Pacifica in Sable on just this basis, [explaining that the "dial-a-porn medium] requires the listener to take affirmative steps to receive the communication."

[Finally,] unlike the conditions that prevailed when Congress first authorized regulation of the broadcast spectrum, the Internet can hardly be considered a "scarce" expressive commodity. It provides relatively unlimited, low-cost capacity for communication of all kinds, [including] not only traditional print and news services, but also audio, video, and still images, as well as interactive, real-time dialogue. Through the use of chat rooms, any person with a phone line can become a town crier with a voice that resonates farther than it could from any soapbox. Through the use of Web pages, mail exploders, and newsgroups, the same individual can become a pamphleteer. As the District Court found, "the content on the Internet is as diverse as human thought." We agree with its conclusion that our cases provide no basis for qualifying the level of First Amendment scrutiny that should be applied to this medium.

Regardless of whether the CDA is so vague that it violates the Fifth Amendment, the many ambiguities concerning the scope of its coverage render it problematic for purposes of the First Amendment. [The] Government argues that the statute is no more vague than the obscenity standard this Court established in Miller v. California [1973; 13th ed., p. 1132]. But that is not so. [The purportedly analogous] second prong of the Miller test [contains] a critical requirement that is omitted from the CDA: that the proscribed ["patently offensive"] material be "specifically defined by the applicable state law." [Moreover,] the Miller definition is limited to "sexual conduct," whereas the

CDA extends also to include "excretory activities" as well as "organs" of both a sexual and excretory nature. [Just] because a definition including three limitations is not vague, it does not follow that one of those limitations, standing by itself, is not vague. Each of Miller's additional two prongs—that, taken as a whole, the material appeal to the "prurient" interest, and that it "lack serious literary, artistic, political, or scientific value"—critically limits the uncertain sweep of the obscenity definition. The [latter] requirement is particularly important because, unlike the "patently offensive" and "prurient interest" criteria, it is not judged by contemporary community standards. This "societal value" requirement, absent in the CDA, allows appellate courts to impose some limitations and regularity on the definition by setting, as a matter of law, a national floor for socially redeeming value. The Government's contention that courts will be able to give such legal limitations to the CDA's standards is belied by Miller's own rationale for having juries determine whether material is "patently offensive" according to community standards: that such questions are essentially ones of fact. In contrast to Miller and our other previous cases, the CDA thus presents a greater threat of censoring speech that, in fact, falls outside the statute's scope. [That] danger provides further reason for insisting that the statute not be overly broad.

We are persuaded that the CDA lacks the precision that the First Amendment requires when a statute regulates the content of speech. In order to deny minors access to potentially harmful speech, the CDA effectively suppresses a large amount of speech that adults have a constitutional right to receive and to address to one another. That burden on adult speech is unacceptable if less restrictive alternatives would be at least as effective in achieving the legitimate purpose that the statute was enacted to serve.

[It] is true that we have repeatedly recognized the governmental interest in protecting children from harmful materials. But that interest does not justify an unnecessarily broad suppression of speech addressed to adults. [In] arguing that the CDA does not so diminish adult communication, the Government relies on the incorrect factual premise that prohibiting a transmission whenever it is known that one of its recipients is a minor would not interfere with adult-to-adult communication. The findings of the District Court make clear that this premise is untenable. Given the size of the potential audience for most messages, in the absence of a viable age verification process, the sender must be charged with knowing that one or more minors will likely view it. Knowledge that, for instance, one or more members of a 100–person chat group will be minor—and therefore that it would be a crime to send the group an indecent message—would surely burden communication among adults.

The District Court found that at the time of trial existing technology did not include any effective method for a sender to prevent minors from obtaining access to its communications on the Internet without also denying access to adults. The Court found no effective way to determine the age of a user who is accessing material through e-mail, mail exploders, newsgroups, or chat rooms. As a practical matter, the Court also found that it would be prohibitively expensive for noncommercial—as well as some commercial—speakers who have Web sites to verify that their users are adults. These limitations must inevitably curtail a significant amount of adult communication on the Internet. By contrast, the District Court found that "despite its limitations, currently available user-based software suggests that a reasonably effective method by which parents can prevent their children from accessing sexually explicit and other material which parents may believe is inappropriate for their children will soon be widely available."

The breadth of the CDA's coverage is wholly unprecedented. [It] is not limited to commercial speech or commercial entities. Its open-ended prohibitions embrace all nonprofit entities and individuals posting indecent messages or displaying them on their own computers in the presence of minors. The general, undefined terms "indecent" and "patently offensive" cover large amounts of nonpornographic material with serious educational or other value. Moreover, the "community standards" criterion as applied to the Internet means that any communication available to a nation-wide audience will be judged by the standards of the community most likely to be offended by the message. [The] strength of the Government's interest in protecting minors is not equally strong throughout the coverage of this broad statute. Under the CDA, a parent allowing her 17-year-old to use the family computer to obtain information on the Internet that she, in her parental judgment, deems appropriate could face a lengthy prison term. Similarly, a parent who sent his 17-year-old college freshman information on birth control via e-mail could be incarcerated even though neither he, his child, nor anyone in their home community, found the material "indecent" or "patently offensive," if the college town's community thought otherwise.

The breadth of this content-based restriction of speech imposes an especially heavy burden on the Government to explain why a less restrictive provision would not be as effective as the CDA. It has not done so. The arguments in this Court have referred to possible alternatives such as requiring that indecent material be "tagged" in a way that facilitates parental control of material coming into their homes, making exceptions for messages with artistic or educational value, providing some tolerance for parental choice, and regulating some portions of the Internet—such as commercial web sites—differently than others, such as chat rooms. Particularly in the light of the absence of any detailed findings by the Congress, or even hearings addressing the special problems of the CDA, we are persuaded that the CDA is not narrowly tailored if that requirement has any meaning at all.

In an attempt to curtail the CDA's facial overbreadth, the Government [contends] that the CDA is constitutional because it leaves open ample "alternative channels" of communication. [This] argument is unpersuasive because the CDA regulates speech on the basis of its content. A "time, place, and manner" analysis is therefore inapplicable. [The] Government's position is equivalent to arguing that a statute could ban leaflets on certain subjects as long as individuals are free to publish books. [The] Government also asserts that the "knowledge" requirement of both §§ 223(a) and (d), especially when coupled with the "specific child" element found in § 223(d), saves the CDA from overbreadth. Because both sections prohibit the dissemination of indecent messages only to persons known to be under 18, the Government argues, it does not require transmitters to "refrain from communicating indecent material to adults." [This] argument ignores the fact that most Internet fora—including chat rooms, newsgroups, mail exploders, and the Web—are open to all comers. [Even] the strongest reading of the "specific person" requirement of

§ 223(d) cannot save the statute. It would confer broad powers of censorship, in the form of a "heckler's veto," upon any opponent of indecent speech who might simply log on and inform the would-be discoursers that his 17–year-old child would be present.

The Government's [remaining] arguments focus on the defenses provided in § 223(e)(5). First, relying on the "good faith, reasonable, effective, and appropriate actions" provision, the Government suggests that "tagging" provides a defense that saves the constitutionality of the Act. The suggestion assumes that transmitters may encode their indecent communications in a way that would indicate their contents, thus permitting recipients to block their reception with appropriate software. It is the requirement that the good faith action must be "effective" that makes this defense illusory. The Government recognizes that its proposed screening software does not currently exist. Even if it did, there is no way to know whether a potential recipient will actually block the encoded material. Without the impossible knowledge that every guardian in America is screening for the "tag," the transmitter could not reasonably rely on its action to be "effective."

[The] Government [also] relies on the [defense that] applies when the transmitter has restricted access by requiring use of a verified credit card or adult identification. Such verification is not only technologically available but actually is used by commercial providers of sexually explicit material. [Under] the findings of the District Court, however, it is not economically feasible for most noncommercial speakers to employ such verification. Accordingly, this defense would not significantly narrow the statute's burden on noncommercial speech. Even with respect to the commercial pornographers that would be protected by the defense, the Government failed to adduce any evidence that these verification techniques actually preclude minors from posing as adults.

[We] agree with the District Court's conclusion that the CDA places an unacceptably heavy burden on protected speech, and that the defenses do not constitute the sort of "narrow tailoring" that will save an otherwise patently invalid unconstitutional provision. In Sable, we remarked that the speech restriction at issue there amounted to " 'burning the house to roast the pig.' " The CDA, casting a far darker shadow over free speech, threatens to torch a large segment of the Internet community.

[Finally,] the Government [argues that an] interest in fostering the growth of the Internet provides an independent basis for upholding the constitutionality of the CDA. The Government apparently assumes that the unregulated availability of "indecent" and "patently offensive" material on the Internet is driving countless citizens away from the medium because of the risk of exposing themselves or their children to harmful material. We find this argument singularly unpersuasive. [The] record demonstrates that the growth of the Internet has been and continues to be phenomenal. As a matter of constitutional tradition, in the absence of evidence to the contrary, we presume that governmental regulation of the content of speech is more likely to interfere with the free exchange of ideas than to encourage it. The interest in encouraging freedom of expression in a democratic society outweighs any theoretical but unproven benefit of censorship.

[Affirmed.]

Justice O'CONNOR, with whom Chief Justice REHNQUIST joins, concurring in the judgment in part and dissenting in part.

I write separately to explain why I view the CDA as little more than an attempt by Congress to create "adult zones" on the Internet. [The] creation of "adult zones" is by no means a novel concept. States have long denied minors access to certain establishments frequented by adults. States have also denied minors access to speech deemed to be "harmful to minors." The Court has previously sustained such zoning laws, but only if they respect the First Amendment rights of adults and minors. That is to say, a zoning law is valid if (i) it does not unduly restrict adult access to the material; and (ii) minors have no First Amendment right to read or view the banned material. As applied to the Internet as it exists in 1997, the "display" provision and some applications of the "indecency transmission" and "specific person" provisions fail to adhere to the first of these limiting principles by restricting adults' access to protected materials in certain circumstances. Unlike the Court, however, I would invalidate the provisions only in those circumstances.

[The] Court in Ginsberg concluded that the New York law created a constitutionally adequate adult zone simply because, on its face, it denied access only to minors. The Court did not question—and therefore necessarily assumed—that an adult zone, once created, would succeed in preserving adults' access while denying minors' access to the regulated speech. Before today, there was no reason to question this assumption, for the Court has previously only considered laws that operated in the physical world, a world that with two characteristics that make it possible to create "adult zones": geography and identity. See Lessig, Reading the Constitution in Cyberspace, 45 Emory L. J. 869, 886 (1996). A minor can see an adult dance show only if he enters an establishment that provides such entertainment. And should he attempt to do so, the minor will not be able to conceal completely his identity (or, consequently, his age). Thus, the twin characteristics of geography and identity enable the establishment's proprietor to prevent children from entering the establishment, but to let adults inside.

The electronic world is fundamentally different. Because it is no more than the interconnection of electronic pathways, cyberspace allows speakers and listeners to mask their identities. Cyberspace undeniably reflects some form of geography; chat rooms and Web sites, for example, exist at fixed "locations" on the Internet. Since users can transmit and receive messages on the Internet without revealing anything about their identities or ages, however, it is not currently possible to exclude persons from accessing certain messages on the basis of their identity. Cyberspace differs from the physical world in another basic way: Cyberspace is malleable. Thus, it is possible to construct barriers in cyberspace and use them to screen for identity, making cyberspace more like the physical world and, consequently, more amenable to zoning laws. This transformation of cyberspace is already underway. Internet speakers (users who post material on the Internet) have begun to zone cyberspace itself through the use of "gateway" technology. Such technology requires Internet users to enter information about themselves—perhaps an adult identification number or a credit card number—before they can access certain areas of cyberspace, much like a bouncer checks a person's driver's license before admitting him to a nightclub. Internet users who access information have not attempted to zone cyberspace itself, but have tried to limit their own power to access information in cyberspace, much as a parent controls what her children watch on television by installing a lock box. This user-based zoning is accomplished through the use of screening software [or] browsers with screening capabilities, both of which search addresses and text for keywords that are associated with "adult" sites and, if the user wishes, blocks access to such sites. The Platform for Internet Content Selection (PICS) project is designed to facilitate user-based zoning by encouraging Internet speakers to rate the content of their speech using codes recognized by all screening programs.

Despite this progress, the transformation of cyberspace is not complete. [Gateway] technology is not ubiquitous in cyberspace, and because without it "there is no means of age verification," cyberspace still remains largely unzoned—and unzoneable. User-based zoning is also in its infancy. For it to be effective, (i) an agreed-upon code (or "tag") would have to exist; (ii) screening software or browsers with screening capabilities would have to be able to recognize the "tag"; and (iii) those programs would have to be widely available—and widely used—by Internet users. At present, none of these conditions is true.

Although the prospects for the eventual zoning of the Internet appear promising, I agree with the Court that we must evaluate the constitutionality of the CDA as it applies to the Internet as it exists today. Given the present state of cyberspace, I agree with the Court that the "display" provision cannot pass muster. Until gateway technology is available throughout cyberspace, and it is not in 1997, a speaker cannot be reasonably assured that the speech he displays will reach only adults because it is impossible to confine speech to an "adult zone." Thus, the only way for a speaker to avoid liability under the CDA is to refrain completely from using indecent speech. But this forced silence impinges on the First Amendment right of adults to make and obtain this speech and, for all intents and purposes, "reduces the adult population [on the Internet] to reading only what is fit for children."

The "indecency transmission" and "specific person" provisions present a closer issue, for they are not unconstitutional in all of their applications. [The] "indecency transmission" provision makes it a crime to transmit knowingly an indecent message to a person the sender knows is under 18 years of age. The "specific person" provision proscribes the same conduct, although it does not as explicitly require the sender to know that the intended recipient of his indecent message is a minor. Appellant urges the Court to construe the provision to impose such a knowledge requirement, and I would do so. So construed, both provisions are constitutional as applied to a conversation involving only [one] adult and one or more minors—e.g., when an adult speaker sends an e-mail knowing the addressee is a minor, or when an adult and minor converse by themselves or with other minors in a chat room. In this context, these provisions are no different from the law we sustained in Ginsberg. Restricting what the adult may say to the minors in no way restricts the adult's ability to communicate with other adults.

[The] analogy to Ginsberg breaks down, however, when more than one adult is a party to the conversation. If a minor enters a chat room otherwise occupied by adults, the CDA effectively requires the adults in the room to stop using indecent speech. [The] CDA is therefore akin to a law that makes it a crime for a bookstore owner to sell pornographic magazines to anyone once a minor enters his store. Even assuming such a law might be constitutional in the physical world as a reasonable alternative to excluding minors completely from the store, the absence of any means of excluding minors from chat rooms in cyberspace restricts the rights of adults to engage in indecent speech in those rooms. The "indecency transmission" and "specific person" provisions share this defect.

[I] agree with the Court that the provisions are overbroad in that they cover any and all communications between adults and minors, regardless of how many adults might be part of the audience to the communication. [But] I would therefore sustain the "indecency transmission" and "specific person" provisions to the extent they apply to the transmission of Internet communications where the party initiating the communication knows that all of the recipients are minors.

The Court neither "accepts nor rejects" the argument that the CDA is facially overbroad because it substantially interferes with the First Amendment rights of minors. I would reject it. Ginsberg established that minors may constitutionally be denied access to material that is obscene as to minors. [Because] the CDA denies minors the right to obtain material that is "patently offensive"—even if it has some redeeming value for minors and even if it does not appeal to their prurient interests—the CDA could ban some speech that is "indecent" [but not] obscene as to minors. I do not deny this possibility, but to prevail in a facial challenge, it is not enough for a plaintiff to show "some" overbreadth. Our cases require a proof of "real" and "substantial" overbreadth. [The] universe of material that is "patently offensive," but which nonetheless has some redeeming value for minors or does not appeal to their prurient interest—is a very small one. [Accordingly,] in my view, the CDA does not burden a substantial amount of minors' constitutionally protected speech.

Thus, the constitutionality of the CDA as a zoning law hinges on the extent to which it substantially interferes with the First Amendment rights of adults. Because the rights of adults are infringed only by the "display" provision and by the "indecency transmission" and "specific person" provisions as applied to communications involving more than one adult, I would invalidate the CDA only to that extent. Insofar as the "indecency transmission" and "specific person" provisions prohibit the use of indecent speech in communications between an adult and one or more minors, however, they can and should be sustained.

SECTION 6. COMMERCIAL SPEECH

Page 1195. Add to Note 2 on differential treatment of commercial speech:

In LOS ANGELES POLICE DEPARTMENT v. UNITED REPORTING, 120 S.Ct. 483 (1999), the Court rejected a facial attack on a state law that permitted arrest records to be disclosed for "scholarly, journalistic, political, or governmental" purposes, but not in order "to sell a product or service." The opinion of the Court by Chief Justice REHNQUIST found that "the section in question is not an abridgment of anyone's right to engage in speech, be it commercial or otherwise, but simply a law regulating access to information in the hands of the police department." In separate concurrences, Justice SCALIA, joined by Justice Thomas, insisted that the discriminatory denial of such access to a commercial vendor might be found unconstitutional as applied; Justice GINSBURG, joined by Justices O'Connor, Souter and Breyer, suggested that such discrimination would be legitimate because viewpoint-neutral. Justice STEVENS, joined by Justice Kennedy, dissented, reasoning that protection of privacy was an insufficient justification for "making [information] available to scholars, news media, politicians, and others, while denying access to a narrow category of persons solely because they intend to use the information for [a] commercial speech purpose that the State finds objectionable."

Page 1201. Add after Liquormart:

In GREATER NEW ORLEANS BROADCASTING ASSOCIATION v. UNITED STATES, 119 S. Ct. 1923 (1999), the Court unanimously invalidated a 65–year-old federal law banning broadcast advertising of lotteries and casino gambling as an impermissible restriction of commercial speech under the Central Hudson test. The statute, now codified at 18 U.S.C. § 1304, prohibited radio and television broadcasting of "any advertisement of or information concerning any lottery, gift enterprise, or similar scheme," but contained various exemptions, including exemptions for advertisements of state-conducted lotteries and gaming advertisements by Native American tribes. The statute was challenged on First Amendment grounds by Louisiana broadcasters who sought to broadcast promotional advertisements for lawful gaming at private, for-profit casinos in Louisiana and neighboring Mississippi. Writing for the Court, Justice STEVENS noted that "petitioners as well as certain judges, scholars, and amici curiae have advocated repudiation of the Central Hudson standard and implementation of a more straightforward and stringent test for assessing the validity of governmental restrictions on commercial speech," but held that, "[i]n this case, there is no need to break new ground," for Central Hudson, as interpreted in more recent cases, provided an adequate basis for decision.

Applying that test, Justice Stevens continued: "All parties to this case agree that the messages petitioners wish to broadcast [would] satisfy the first part of the Central Hudson test [as they are] not misleading and concern[] lawful activities. The second part of the Central Hudson test asks whether the asserted governmental interest served by the speech restriction is substantial. The Solicitor General identifies two such interests: (1) reducing the social costs associated with 'gambling' or 'casino gambling,' and (2) assisting States that 'restrict gambling' or 'prohibit casino gambling' within their own borders. [We] can accept the characterization of these two interests as 'substantial,' but that conclusion is by no means self-evident. [Despite] its awareness of the potential social costs, Congress has not only sanctioned casino gambling for Indian tribes through tribal-state compacts, but [has] generally exempted state-run lotteries and casinos from federal gambling legislation. [The] federal policy of discouraging gambling in general, and casino gambling in particular, is now decidedly equivocal. The third part of the Central Hudson test asks whether the speech restriction directly and materially advances the asserted governmental interest. [The] fourth part of the test complements the direct-advancement inquiry of the third, asking whether the speech restriction is not more extensive than necessary to serve the interests that support it.

"[As] applied to petitioners' case, § 1304 cannot satisfy these standards. With regard to the first asserted interest—alleviating the social costs of casino gambling by limiting demand—the Government contends that its broadcasting restrictions directly advance that interest because 'promotional' broadcast advertising concerning casino gambling increases demand for such gambling, which in turn increases the amount of casino gambling that produces those social costs. [While] it is no doubt fair to assume that more advertising would have some impact on overall demand for gambling, it is also reasonable to assume that much of that advertising would merely channel gamblers to one casino rather than another. More important, any measure of the effectiveness of the Government's attempt to minimize the social costs of gambling cannot ignore Congress' simultaneous encouragement of tribal casino gambling, which may well be growing at a rate exceeding any increase in gambling [that] private casino advertising could produce.

"[In any case, the] operation of § 1304 and its attendant regulatory regime is so pierced by exemptions and inconsistencies that the Government cannot hope to exonerate it. See Rubin [v. Coors (1995); 13th ed., p. 1197]. Under current law, a broadcaster may not carry advertising about privately operated commercial casino gambling, regardless of the location of the station or the casino. On the other hand, advertisements for tribal casino gambling authorized by state compacts [are] subject to no such broadcast ban, even if the broadcaster is located in or broadcasts to a jurisdiction with the strictest of antigambling policies. Government-operated, nonprofit, and 'occasional and ancillary' commercial casinos are likewise exempt. [The] Government presents no convincing reason for pegging its speech ban to the identity of the owners or operators of the advertised casinos. [And while Congress'] failure to institute [direct] regulation of private casino gambling does not necessarily compromise the constitutionality of § 1304, it does undermine the asserted justifications for the restriction before us. There surely are practical and nonspeech-related forms of regulation—including a prohibition or supervision of gambling on credit; limitations on the use of cash machines on casino premises; controls on admissions; pot or betting limits; location restrictions; and licensing requirements—that could more directly and effectively alleviate some of the social costs of casino gambling.

"The second interest asserted by the Government—['assisting'] States with policies that disfavor private casinos—adds little to its case. We cannot see how this broadcast restraint, ambivalent as it is, might directly and adequately further any state interest in dampening consumer demand for casino gambling if it cannot achieve the same goal with respect to the similar federal interest. [Even] assuming that the state policies on which the Federal Government seeks to embellish are more coherent and pressing than their federal counterpart, [Congress'] choice here was [not] a reasonable accommodation of competing State and private interests. Rather, the regulation distinguishes among the indistinct, permitting a variety of speech that poses the same risks the Government purports to fear, while banning messages unlikely to cause any harm at all." Justice Stevens distinguished the statute upheld in Edge Broadcasting (1993; 13th ed. p. 1196) as more closely serving an actual government interest in " 'accommodating the policies of both lottery and nonlottery States.' " He concluded: "Accordingly, respondents cannot overcome the presumption that the speaker and the audience, not the Government, should be left to assess the value of accurate and nonmisleading information about lawful conduct. Had the Federal Government adopted a more coherent policy, or accommodated the rights of speakers in States that have legalized the underlying conduct, this might be a different case. But under current federal law, as applied to petitioners and the messages that they wish to convey, the broadcast prohibition in [§ 1304] violates the First Amendment." Chief Justice Rehnquist and Justice Thomas wrote brief separate concurrences.

Page 1202. Add to end of Note 1, "What standard of scrutiny?":

In GLICKMAN v. WILEMAN BROS., 521 U.S. 457 (1997), the Court did not reach the question of how to interpret Central Hudson, because it found that the challenged regulations did not implicate speech at all. By a vote of 5–4, the Court rejected a challenge by fruit producers to mandatory fees for generic fruit advertising, finding that the fees did not amount to compelled speech or association within the Court's precedents. (For the compelled speech and association aspects of the case, see p. 73 below.) In dissent, Justice SOUTER, joined by Chief Justice Rehnquist and Justice Scalia, would have applied Central Hudson, reasoning that the fees did amount to compelled speech and that "laws requiring an individual to engage in or pay for expressive activities are reviewed under the same standard that applies to laws prohibiting one from engaging in or paying for such activities." He would have proceeded to apply a relatively stringent version of that test, finding the government's justification inadequate with respect both to ends and means.

First, in Justice Souter's view, the forced advertising requirements, which applied only to selected agricultural commodities and geographic locations, were "so random and so randomly implemented [as] to unsettle any inference that the Government's asserted interest [in stabilizing markets and maintaining prices] is either substantial or even real. [The] list includes onions but not garlic, tomatoes but not cucumbers, [and] so on. The selection is puzzling. [A] correlation with nothing more than the priorities of particular interest groups gives no reassuring answer." Second, although the Court usually presumes that advertising increases demand, the government had not established that its particular advertising program would likely be more effective than private substitutes; a mere assertion of the possibility of " 'free riders' if promotion were to become wholly voluntary" was insufficient. Third, the "mandatory advertising schemes for California peaches, plums, and nectarines fail [the] narrow tailoring requirement because they deny handlers any credit toward their assessments for some or all of their individual advertising expenditures." Such credits were given for private advertising of "almonds, filberts, raisins, walnuts, olives and Florida Indian River grapefruit," and the government had not explained why branded advertising might not likewise contribute to the collective goal in the stone-fruit context: "A consumer galvanized by respondents' depiction of 'Mr. Plum' might turn down a plum by any other name, but I doubt it." Justice Souter concluded: "Although the government's obligation is not a heavy one in Central Hudson, [we] have understood it to call for some showing beyond plausibility, and there has been none here."

Justice THOMAS dissented separately, reiterating the view he expressed in Liquormart that "a higher standard" than Central Hudson's "should be applied to all speech, whether commercial or not," but adding that the regulations here failed even Central Hudson.

CHAPTER 12

FREEDOM OF SPEECH—HOW GOVERNMENT RESTRICTS SPEECH—MODES OF ABRIDGMENT AND STANDARDS OF REVIEW

SECTION 1. THE DISTINCTION BETWEEN CONTENT-BASED AND CONTENT-NEUTRAL REGULATIONS

B. CONTENT-NEUTRAL LAWS AND SYMBOLIC CONDUCT

Page 1234. Insert after Barnes v. Glen Theatre:

The Court revisited the constitutionality of public nudity bans as applied to nude dancing in CITY OF ERIE v. PAP'S A.M., 120 S.Ct. 1382 (2000). The Pennsylvania Supreme Court, employing strict scrutiny, had upheld the free speech right of an establishment called Kandyland to feature totally nude erotic dancing by women, reasoning that the law was not content-neutral but sought to "impact negatively on the erotic message of the dance," and finding no clear precedent in the fragmented Barnes opinions. Reversing, the Court again fragmented in its reasoning. Justice O'CONNOR, writing for the Court in a plurality opinion joined by Chief Justice Rehnquist and Justices Kennedy and Breyer, found that government restrictions on public nudity should be evaluated under the O'Brien test as content-neutral restrictions on symbolic conduct. She rejected any reading of the Erie ordinance as content-based, finding it instead aimed at "combat[ing] the negative secondary effects associated with nude dancing establishments," such as the promotion of " 'violence, public intoxication, prostitution, and other serious criminal activity.' " Justice O'Connor found this justification sufficient to satisfy O'Brien, even in the absence of a specific evidentiary record of such secondary effects.

Justice SCALIA, joined by Justice Thomas, concurred in the judgment, reiterating his view in Barnes that a public nudity law such as Erie's is a "general law regulating conduct and not specifically directed at expression," and thus subject to no First Amendment scrutiny at all. He continued: "[E]ven if one hypothesizes that the city's object was to suppress only nude dancing, that would not establish an intent to suppress what (if anything) nude dancing communicates. I do not feel the need, as the Court does, to identify some 'secondary effects' associated with nude dancing that the city could properly seek to eliminate. (I am highly skeptical, to tell the truth, that the addition of pasties and g-strings will at all reduce the tendency of establishments such as Kandyland to attract crime and prostitution, and hence to foster sexually transmitted disease.) The traditional power of government to foster good morals (bonos mores), and the acceptability of the traditional judgment (if Erie wishes to endorse it) that nude public dancing itself is immoral, have not been repealed by the First Amendment."

Justice SOUTER filed a separate opinion concurring in part and dissenting in part. He agreed that O'Brien was the right test, but insisted that "intermediate scrutiny requires a regulating government to make some demonstration of an evidentiary basis for the harm it claims to flow from the expressive activity, and for the alleviation expected from the restriction imposed." He found the evidentiary record in the case "deficient" under this standard, finding not facts but "emotionalism" in the statements made by city council members. In requiring a better empirical justification for the law in order to satisfy the O'Brien standard, Justice Souter took the unusual step of confessing error about his own prior opinion in Barnes: "Careful readers, and not just those on the Erie City Council, will of course realize that my partial dissent rests on a demand for an evidentiary basis that I failed to make when I concurred in Barnes. I should have demanded the evidence then, too, and my mistake calls to mind Justice Jackson's foolproof explanation of a lapse of his own, when he quoted Samuel Johnson, 'Ignorance, sir, ignorance.' "

Justice STEVENS, joined by Justice Ginsburg, dissented, opposing the plurality's extension of the "secondary effects" test from zoning cases to what he characterized as a "total ban" on a medium of expression. He also criticized the plurality's lenient application of that test: "To believe that the mandatory addition of pasties and a G-string will have any kind of noticeable impact on secondary effects requires nothing short of a titanic surrender to the implausible." He would have found that the Erie ordinance was impermissibly aimed at nude dancing rather than nudity in general, and invalidated it.

SECTION 2. GOVERNMENT'S POWER TO LIMIT SPEECH IN ITS CAPACITY AS PROPRIETOR, EDUCATOR, EMPLOYER AND PATRON

A. SPEECH IN PUBLIC FORUMS AND OTHER GOVERNMENT PROPERTY

Page 1266. Add to Note 2.b, after Madsen v. Women's Health Center:

In SCHENCK v. PRO–CHOICE NETWORK OF WESTERN NEW YORK, 519 U.S. 357 (1997), the Court again reviewed a First Amendment challenge to an injunction against protestors outside an abortion clinic. The injunction, issued by a federal district after a serious of large-scale protests and blockades, banned "demonstrating within fifteen feet from either side or edge of, or in front of, doorways or doorway entrances, parking lot entrances, driveways and driveway entrances of" clinic facilities, or "within fifteen feet of any person or vehicle seeking access to or leaving such facilities." Anti-abortion counselors could approach persons entering or exiting clinics in order to make "non-threatening" conversation with them, but if requested to "cease and desist," they had to retreat 15 feet from the people they had been counseling. As construed by the Court, the injunction thus created two kinds of buffer zones: "fixed buffer zones" and "floating buffer zones." Applying the standard set forth in Madsen, Chief Justice REHNQUIST, writing for the Court, struck down the floating buffer zones but upheld the fixed buffer zones:

"We strike down the floating buffer zones around people entering and leaving the clinics because they burden more speech than is necessary to serve the relevant governmental interests. The floating buffer zones prevent defendants—except for two sidewalk counselors, while they are tolerated by the targeted individual—from communicating a message from a normal conversational distance or handing leaflets to people entering or leaving the clinics who are walking on the public sidewalks. [Since] the buffer zone floats, protesters on the public sidewalks who wish (i) to communicate their message to an incoming or outgoing patient or clinic employee and (ii) to remain as close as possible (while maintaining an acceptable conversational distance) to this individual, must move as the individual moves, maintaining 15 feet of separation. But this would be difficult to accomplish [without stepping into the street or into other persons' floating buffer zones.] With clinic escorts leaving the clinic to pick up incoming patients and entering the clinic to drop them off, it would be quite difficult for a protester who wishes to engage in peaceful expressive activities to know how to remain in compliance with the injunction."

In contrast, the Court upheld the fixed buffer zones around clinic doorways, driveways, and driveway entrances, reasoning that such buffer zones were necessary to ensure that people and vehicles trying to enter or exit the clinic property or clinic parking lots could do so. Chief Justice Rehnquist wrote: "As in Madsen, the record shows that protesters purposefully or effectively blocked or hindered people from entering and exiting the clinic doorways, from driving up to and away from clinic entrances, and from driving in and out of clinic parking lots. Based on this conduct [the] District Court was entitled to conclude that the only way to ensure access was to move back the demonstrations away from the driveways and parking lot entrances. [Although] one might quibble about whether 15 feet is too great or too small a distance if the goal is to ensure access, we defer to the District Court's reasonable assessment of the number of feet necessary to keep the entrances clear."

Justice SCALIA, joined by Justices Kennedy and Thomas, dissented from the decision insofar as it upheld fixed buffer zones. He argued that the majority opinion had mischaracterized the zones as intended to preserve unimpeded clinic access, when they were in fact grounded at least in part on the impermissible purpose of protecting listeners from having to hear "unwanted" speech. Justice BREYER dissented from the decision insofar as it struck down the floating buffer zones, arguing that "the preliminary injunction's language does not necessarily create the kind of 'floating bubble' that leads the Court to find the injunction unconstitutionally broad."

In HILL v. COLORADO, 120 S.Ct. 2480 (2000), the Court reviewed a statute, as opposed to an injunction, challenged for limiting the speech of abortion protestors outside abortion clinics, and upheld it by a vote of 6–3. The statute makes it unlawful within the vicinity of a health care facility for anyone to "knowingly approach" within eight feet of another person, without that person's consent, "for the purpose of passing a leaflet or handbill to, displaying a sign to, or engaging in oral protest, education, or counseling with such other person...." Justice STEVENS delivered the opinion of the Court, joined by Chief Justice Rehnquist and Justices O'Connor, Souter, Ginsburg and Breyer.

He found the statute a valid, content-neutral time, place and manner regulation under the Ward test. It was content-neutral, he wrote, because it regulated not speech but "the places where some speech may occur," it was not adopted because of disagreement with a message, and it was justified by interests in access and privacy that were unrelated to ideas. He declined to find a content basis in the distinction between approaches for "protest, education or counseling" and for other purposes, such as "pure social or random conversation." He concluded that the statute "applies to all 'protest,' to all 'counseling,' and to all demonstrators whether or not the demonstration concerns abortion, and whether they oppose or support the woman who has made an abortion decision. That is the level of neutrality that the Constitution demands." He went on to hold that the statute was narrowly tailored to important interests in privacy and access and left protestors adequate alternative means of getting their message across. Justice SOUTER filed a concurrence, joined by Justices O'Connor, Ginsburg and Breyer, emphasizing that the statute addressed "not the content of speech but the circumstances of its delivery," and thus was properly evaluated as content-neutral.

Vigorous dissents were filed by Justice SCALIA, joined by Justice Thomas, and by Justice KENNEDY. Justice Scalia argued that the floating buffer zone around oral communication was "obviously and undeniably content-based," because "[w]hether a speaker must obtain permission before approaching within eight feet—and whether he will be sent to prison for failing to do so—depends entirely on what he intends to say when he gets there." He would have applied strict scrutiny, which the statute could not survive: "Suffice it to say that if protecting people from unwelcome communications (the governmental interest the Court posits) is a compelling state interest, the First Amendment is a dead letter. And if forbidding peaceful, nonthreatening, but uninvited speech from a distance closer than eight feet is a 'narrowly tailored' means of preventing the obstruction of entrance to medical facilities (the governmental interest the State asserts) narrow tailoring must refer not to the standards of Versace, but to those of Omar the tentmaker." He bitterly accused the Court of distorting First Amendment law in order to "sustain this restriction upon the free speech of abortion opponents": "Does the deck seem stacked? You bet." Justice Kennedy likewise would have found the law content-based as restrictive of particular topics, and denied that "citizens have a right to avoid unpopular speech in a public forum." He added that the statute interfered with an important First Amendment interest in "immediacy": "Here the citizens who claim First Amendment protection seek it for speech which, if it is to be effective, must take place at the very time and place a grievous moral wrong, in their view, is about to occur. The Court tears away from the protesters the guarantees of the First Amendment when they most need it."

Page 1288. Add after Note 7:

8. *Candidate debate on public television.* In ARKANSAS EDUCATIONAL TELEVISION COMM'N (AETC) v. FORBES, 523 U.S. 666 (1998), the Court rejected a free speech challenge to the exclusion of a candidate from a candidate debate televised by a public broadcasting station. The challenge was brought by Ralph Forbes, who had gained enough signatures to run on the ballot as an independent for Arkansas's third congressional district seat, but was regarded by the debate producers as lacking enough popular support to warrant inclu-

sion in the debate along with the Democratic and Republican candidates. Justice KENNEDY, writing the 6–3 decision of the Court, upheld the exclusion, finding that "the candidate debate was subject to constitutional constraints applicable to nonpublic fora under our forum precedents," but that "the broadcaster's decision to exclude the candidate was a reasonable, viewpoint-neutral exercise of journalistic discretion" that satisfied the First Amendment.

Justice Kennedy cautioned that, "having first arisen in the context of streets and parks, the public forum doctrine should not be extended in a mechanical way to the very different context of public television broadcasting," where "broad rights of access for outside speakers would be antithetical, as a general rule, to the discretion that stations and their editorial staff must exercise to fulfill their journalistic purpose and statutory obligations." Thus First Amendment obligations might not apply at all to most public television programming. But the First Amendment does apply in the limited context of publicly televised candidate debates, he wrote, because they are "by design a forum for political speech by the candidates" and have "exceptional significance in the electoral process."

The issue then was whether Forbes' exclusion from the debate was subject to the stricter standards applicable to a designated public forum or the more deferential standards applicable to a nonpublic forum, and Justice Kennedy concluded that nonpublic forum rules applied here: "Under our precedents, the AETC debate was not a designated public forum. To create a forum of this type, the government must intend to make the property 'generally available' to a class of speakers. [Widmar.] [The] government does not create a designated public forum when it does no more than reserve eligibility for access to the forum to a particular class of speakers, whose members must then, as individuals, 'obtain permission,' to use it. [Perry, Cornelius.]" Under this test, he reasoned, "the debate was a nonpublic forum": "Here, the debate did not have an open-microphone format. [AETC] did not make its debate generally available to candidates for Arkansas' Third Congressional District seat. Instead, [AETC] reserved eligibility for participation in the debate to candidates for the Third Congressional District seat (as opposed to some other seat). At that point, [AETC] made candidate-by-candidate determinations as to which of the eligible candidates would participate in the debate." Justice Kennedy suggested that this "distinction between general and selective access furthers First Amendment interests. By recognizing the distinction, we encourage the government to open its property to some expressive activity in cases where, if faced with an all-or-nothing choice, it might not open the property at all." Under the standards applicable to nonpublic forums, the majority opinion found Forbes's exclusion reasonable and viewpoint-neutral: "There is no substance to Forbes' suggestion that he was excluded because his views were unpopular or out of the mainstream. His own objective lack of support, not his platform, was the criterion."

Justice STEVENS dissented, joined by Justices Souter and Ginsburg: "[T]he First Amendment will not tolerate arbitrary definitions of the scope of the forum. [The] dispositive issue in this case [is] not whether AETC created a designated public forum or a nonpublic forum, as the Court concludes, but whether AETC defined the contours of the debate forum with sufficient specificity to justify the exclusion of a ballot-qualified candidate." Justice

Stevens analogized AETC's decision to exclude Forbes to the exercise of impermissibly standardless discretion to exclude speakers from the public forum: "No written criteria cabined the discretion of the AETC staff. Their subjective judgment about a candidate's 'viability' or 'newsworthiness' allowed them wide latitude either to permit or to exclude a third participant in any debate. [The] importance of avoiding arbitrary or viewpoint-based exclusions from political debates militates strongly in favor of requiring the controlling state agency to use (and adhere to) pre-established, objective criteria to determine who among qualified candidates may participate."

D. SPEECH SUBSIDIZED BY PUBLIC FUNDS

Page 1325. Add after Rosenberger v. Rector:

After a long and heated political debate that began in 1989 with public controversy over the exhibition of photographs by Robert Mapplethorpe and Andres Serrano with funding from the National Endowment for the Arts (NEA), the question whether government may limit the content of art produced by artists receiving public arts grants finally reached the Court in NATIONAL ENDOWMENT FOR THE ARTS v. FINLEY, 524 U.S. 569 (1998). The case arose from a facial challenge by four individual performance artists and an artists' organization to a 1990 congressional amendment, codified at 20 U.S.C. § 954(d)(1), requiring the Chairperson of the NEA to ensure that "artistic excellence and artistic merit are the criteria by which [grant] applications are judged, taking into consideration general standards of decency and respect for the diverse beliefs and values of the American public." By a vote of 8–1, the Court held the law constitutional on its face. Justice O'CONNOR wrote the opinion of the Court: "Respondents argue that the provision is a paradigmatic example of viewpoint discrimination because it rejects any artistic speech that either fails to respect mainstream values or offends standards of decency. The premise of respondents' claim is that § 954(d)(1) constrains the agency's ability to fund certain categories of artistic expression. The NEA, however, reads the provision as merely hortatory, and contends that it stops well short of an absolute restriction. [It] is clear [that] the text of § 954(d)(1) imposes no categorical requirement. [The] criteria in § 954(d)(1) inform the assessment of artistic merit, but Congress declined to disallow any particular viewpoints. [That] § 954(d)(1) admonishes the NEA merely to take 'decency and respect' into consideration [undercuts] respondents' argument that the provision inevitably will be utilized as a tool for invidious viewpoint discrimination. In cases where we have struck down legislation as facially unconstitutional, the dangers were both more evident and more substantial. [See, e.g., R.A.V. v. City of St. Paul.] [Given] the varied interpretations of the criteria [of decency and respect] and the vague exhortation to 'take them into consideration,' it seems unlikely that this provision will introduce any greater element of selectivity than the determination of 'artistic excellence' itself.

"[Any] content-based considerations that may be taken into account in the grant-making process are a consequence of the nature of arts funding. The NEA has limited resources and it must deny the majority of the grant applications that it receives, including many that propose 'artistically excellent' projects. The agency may decide to fund particular projects for a wide variety of reasons, 'such as the technical proficiency of the artist, the creativity of the work, the anticipated public interest in or appreciation of the work, the work's contemporary relevance, its educational value, its suitability for or appeal to special audiences (such as children or the disabled), its service to a rural or isolated community, or even simply that the work could increase public knowledge of an art form.' [It] would be 'impossible to have a highly selective grant program without denying money to a large amount of constitutionally protected expression.' The 'very assumption' of the NEA is that grants will be awarded according to the 'artistic worth of competing applications,' and absolute neutrality is simply 'inconceivable.'

"Respondent's reliance on our decision in Rosenberger v. Rector and Visitors of Univ. of Va. [1995; 13th ed., p.1324] is therefore misplaced. In Rosenberger, a public university declined to authorize disbursements from its Student Activities Fund to finance the printing of a Christian student newspaper. We held that by subsidizing the Student Activities Fund, the University had created a limited public forum, from which it impermissibly excluded all publications with religious editorial viewpoints. Although the scarcity of NEA funding does not distinguish this case from Rosenberger, the competitive process according to which the grants are allocated does. In the context of arts funding, in contrast to many other subsidies, the Government does not indiscriminately 'encourage a diversity of views from private speakers.' The NEA's mandate is to make aesthetic judgments, and the inherently content-based 'excellence' threshold for NEA support sets it apart from the subsidy at issue in Rosenberger—which was available to all student organizations that were 'related to the educational purpose of the University,'—and from comparably objective decisions on allocating public benefits, such as access to a school auditorium or a municipal theater [see Lamb's Chapel; Conrad]."

While rejecting the facial challenge to the decency and respect provision, Justice O'Connor held out the possibility that particular applications of such criteria might violate the Free Speech Clause: "Respondents do not allege discrimination in any particular funding decision. [Thus,] we have no occasion here to address an as-applied challenge in a situation where the denial of a grant may be shown to be the product of invidious viewpoint discrimination. If the NEA were to leverage its power to award subsidies on the basis of subjective criteria into a penalty on disfavored viewpoints, then we would confront a different case. We have stated that, even in the provision of subsidies, the Government may not 'aim at the suppression of dangerous ideas,' and if a subsidy were 'manipulated' to have a 'coercive effect,' then relief could be appropriate. [Likewise,] a more pressing constitutional question would arise if government funding resulted in the imposition of a disproportionate burden calculated to drive 'certain ideas or viewpoints from the marketplace.' Unless and until § 954(d)(1) is applied in a manner that raises concern about the suppression of disfavored viewpoints, however, we uphold the constitutionality of the provision."

Justice SCALIA, joined by Justice Thomas, concurred only in the judgment, arguing that there was no need to read § 954(d)(1) as merely hortatory because it was constitutional even if mandatory and clearly viewpoint-based: " 'The operation was a success, but the patient died.' What such a procedure is to medicine, the Court's opinion in this case is to law. It sustains the constitutionality of § 954(d)(1) by gutting it. The most avid congressional opponents of the provision could not have asked for more. I write separately because, unlike the Court, I think that § 954(d)(1) must be evaluated as written. [By] its terms, it establishes content-and viewpoint-based criteria upon which grant applications are to be evaluated. And that is perfectly constitutional.

"[It] is entirely, 100% clear that decency and respect are to be taken into account in evaluating applications. This is so apparent that I am at a loss to understand what the Court has in mind [when] it speculates that the statute is merely 'advisory.' [This] does not mean that those factors must always be dispositive, but it does mean that they must always be considered. [Such] factors need not be conclusive to be discriminatory. To the extent a particular applicant exhibits disrespect for the diverse beliefs and values of the American public or fails to comport with general standards of decency, the likelihood that he will receive a grant diminishes. [The] decisionmaker, all else being equal, will favor applications that display decency and respect, and disfavor applications that do not. This unquestionably constitutes viewpoint discrimination. [If] viewpoint discrimination in this context is unconstitutional, the law is invalid unless there are some situations in which the decency and respect factors do not constitute viewpoint discrimination. And there is none. The applicant who displays 'decency,' that is, 'conformity to prevailing standards of propriety or modesty,' and the applicant who displays 'respect,' that is, 'deferential regard,' for the diverse beliefs and values of the American people, will always have an edge over an applicant who displays the opposite.

"The Court devotes so much of its opinion to explaining why this statute means something other than what it says that it neglects to cite the constitutional text governing our analysis. The First Amendment reads: 'Congress shall make no law . . . abridging the freedom of speech.' To abridge is 'to contract, to diminish; to deprive of.' With the enactment of § 954(d)(1), Congress did not abridge the speech of those who disdain the beliefs and values of the American public, nor did it abridge indecent speech. Those who wish to create indecent and disrespectful art are as unconstrained now as they were before the enactment of this statute. Avant-garde artistes such as respondents remain entirely free to epater les bourgeois;[2] they are merely deprived of the additional satisfaction of having the bourgeoisie taxed to pay for it. It is preposterous to equate the denial of taxpayer subsidy with measures 'aimed at the suppression of dangerous ideas.' One might contend, I suppose, that a threat of rejection by the only available source of free money would constitute coercion and hence

2. "Which they do quite well. The oeuvres d'art for which the four individual plaintiffs in this case sought funding have been described as follows: Finley's controversial show, 'We Keep Our Victims Ready,' contains three segments. In the second segment, Finley visually recounts a sexual assault by stripping to the waist and smearing chocolate on her breasts and by using profanity to describe the assault. Holly Hughes' monologue 'World Without End' is a somewhat graphic recollection of the artist's realization of her lesbianism and reminiscence of her mother's sexuality. John Fleck, in his stage performance 'Blessed Are All the Little Fishes,' confronts alcoholism and Catholicism. During the course of the performance, Fleck appears dressed as a mermaid, urinates on the stage and creates an altar out of a toilet bowl by putting a photograph of Jesus Christ on the lid. Tim Miller derives his performance 'Some Golden States' from childhood experiences, from his life as a homosexual, and from the constant threat of AIDS. Miller uses vegetables in his performances to represent sexual symbols." [Footnote by Justice Scalia.]

'abridgment' within the meaning of the First Amendment. I would not agree with such a contention, which would make the NEA the mandatory patron of all art too indecent, too disrespectful, or even too kitsch to attract private support. But even if one accepts the contention, it would have no application here. The NEA is far from the sole source of funding for art—even indecent, disrespectful, or just plain bad art. Accordingly, the Government may earmark NEA funds for projects it deems to be in the public interest without thereby abridging speech.

"Respondents, relying on Rosenberger, argue that viewpoint-based discrimination is impermissible unless the government is the speaker or the government is 'disbursing public funds to private entities to convey a governmental message.' It is impossible to imagine why that should be so; one would think that directly involving the government itself in the viewpoint discrimination (if it is unconstitutional) would make the situation even worse. Respondents are mistaken. It is the very business of government to favor and disfavor points of view on (in modern times, at least) innumerable subjects—which is the main reason we have decided to elect those who run the government, rather than save money by making their posts hereditary. And it makes not a bit of difference, insofar as either common sense or the Constitution is concerned, whether these officials further their (and, in a democracy, our) favored point of view by achieving it directly (having government-employed artists paint pictures, for example, or government-employed doctors perform abortions); or by advocating it officially (establishing an Office of Art Appreciation, for example, or an Office of Voluntary Population Control); or by giving money to others who achieve or advocate it (funding private art classes, for example, or Planned Parenthood). None of this has anything to do with abridging anyone's speech. Rosenberger found the viewpoint discrimination unconstitutional, not because funding of 'private' speech was involved, but because the government had established a limited public forum—to which the NEA's granting of highly selective (if not highly discriminating) awards bears no resemblance. The nub of the difference between me and the Court is that I regard the distinction between 'abridging' speech and funding it as a fundamental divide, on this side of which the First Amendment is inapplicable."

Justice SOUTER alone dissented: "The decency and respect proviso mandates viewpoint-based decisions in the disbursement of government subsidies, and the Government has wholly failed to explain why the statute should be afforded an exemption from the fundamental rule of the First Amendment that viewpoint discrimination in the exercise of public authority over expressive activity is unconstitutional. [Because] 'the normal definition of "indecent" ... refers to nonconformance with accepted standards of morality' [Pacifica], restrictions turning on decency, especially those couched in terms of 'general standards of decency,' are quintessentially viewpoint based: they require discrimination on the basis of conformity with mainstream mores. [Just] as self-evidently, a statute disfavoring speech that fails to respect America's 'diverse beliefs and values' is the very model of viewpoint discrimination; it penalizes any view disrespectful to [the] ideology, opinions, or convictions of a significant segment of the American public. [It does not matter that § 954(d)(1)] admonishes the NEA merely to take 'decency and respect' into consideration, not to make funding decisions specifically on those grounds. [What] if the statute required a panel to apply criteria 'taking into consideration the centrality of

Christianity to the American cultural experience,' or 'taking into consideration whether the artist is a communist,' or 'taking into consideration the political message conveyed by the art,' or even 'taking into consideration the superiority of the white race'? Would the Court hold these considerations facially constitutional, merely because the statute had no requirement to give them any particular, much less controlling, weight? I assume not.

"[The] Government calls attention to the roles of government-as-speaker and government-as-buyer, in which the government is of course entitled to engage in viewpoint discrimination: if the Food and Drug Administration launches an advertising campaign on the subject of smoking, it may condemn the habit without also having to show a cowboy taking a puff on the opposite page; and if the Secretary of Defense wishes to buy a portrait to decorate the Pentagon, he is free to prefer George Washington over George the Third. The Government freely admits, however, that it neither speaks through the expression subsidized by the NEA, nor buys anything for itself with its NEA grants. [When] the Government acts as a patron, financially underwriting the production of art by private artists and impresarios for independent consumption, [this] patronage falls embarrassingly on the wrong side of the line between government-as-buyer or -speaker and government-as-regulator-of-private-speech. [Thus,] Rosenberger [controls] here. The NEA, like the student activities fund in Rosenberger, is a subsidy scheme created to encourage expression of a diversity of views from private speakers. [Given] this congressional choice to sustain freedom of expression, Rosenberger teaches that the First Amendment forbids decisions based on viewpoint popularity. So long as Congress chooses to subsidize expressive endeavors at large, it has no business requiring the NEA to turn down funding applications of artists and exhibitors who [defy] our tastes, our beliefs, or our values."

SECTION 3. IMPERMISSIBLE FORMS OF SPEECH-RESTRICTIVE LAW: OVERBREADTH, VAGUENESS AND PRIOR RESTRAINT

B. VAGUENESS

Page 1339. Insert at end of subsection B:

Does the First Amendment prohibition on vagueness extend to vague conditions on public subsidies for speech? In NATIONAL ENDOWMENT FOR THE ARTS v. FINLEY, 524 U.S. 569 (1998), the Court unanimously answered that question no. The decision upheld against facial challenge a 1990 amendment to the statutes authorizing arts grants by the National Endowment for the Arts (NEA) that required the Chairperson of the NEA to ensure that "artistic excellence and artistic merit are the criteria by which [grant] applications are judged, taking into consideration general standards of decency and respect for the diverse beliefs and values of the American public." Writing for the Court, Justice O'CONNOR stated: "Under the First and Fifth Amendments, speakers are protected from arbitrary and discriminatory enforcement of vague standards. The terms of the [NEA] provision are undeniably opaque, and if they appeared in a criminal statute or regulatory scheme, they could raise substantial vagueness concerns. It is unlikely, however, that speakers will be compelled to steer too far clear of any 'forbidden area' in the context of grants of this nature. We recognize, as a practical matter, that artists may conform their speech to what they believe to be the decision-making criteria in order to acquire funding. But when the Government is acting as patron rather than as sovereign, the consequences of imprecision are not constitutionally severe." While filing a lone dissent arguing that the provision amounted to unconstitutional viewpoint discrimination, Justice SOUTER agreed that the provision was not unconstitutionally vague: "The necessary imprecision of artistic-merit-based criteria justifies tolerating a degree of vagueness that might be intolerable when applying the First Amendment to attempts to regulate political discussion."

Can Finley be reconciled with earlier decisions invalidating the denial of government jobs to those who failed to swear loyalty oaths that the Court found impermissibly vague? See, e.g., Cramp, Baggett v. Bullitt, 13th ed. p. 1392.

CHAPTER 13

Rights Ancillary to Freedom of Speech

Section 2. Freedom of Association

D. The Right *Not* to Associate

Page 1399. Add to Note 1, after Abood v. Detroit Board of Educ.:

May the government compel producers to contribute fees to finance generic advertising of their products, even if they object to the advertising? This issue reached the Court in GLICKMAN v. WILEMAN BROS., 521 U.S. 457 (1997). By a vote of 5–4, the Court upheld against First Amendment challenge certain agricultural marketing orders assessing California fruit growers the costs of generic advertising of California nectarines, plums, and peaches. The court of appeals had invalidated the assessments as compelling commercial speech without satisfying intermediate scrutiny under Central Hudson (see 13th ed., p. 1189; see also p. 70 above) because the government had not shown that collective generic advertising was more effective than individual advertising and thus "directly advanced" its purposes. The Supreme Court reversed. Justice STEVENS, writing for the Court, found that the assessments did not raise a First Amendment issue at all, but rather "simply a question of economic policy for Congress and the Executive to resolve." He reasoned:

"Three characteristics of the regulatory scheme at issue distinguish it from laws that we have found to abridge the freedom of speech protected by the First Amendment. First, the marketing orders impose no restraint on the freedom of any producer to communicate any message to any audience. Second, they do not compel any person to engage in any actual or symbolic speech. Third, they do not compel the producers to endorse or to finance any political or ideological views. Indeed, since all of the respondents are engaged in the business of marketing California nectarines, plums, and peaches, it is fair to presume that they agree with the central message of the speech that is generated by the generic program."

Justice Stevens found that these features distinguished the regulations from those held to have unconstitutionally compelled speech in earlier cases: "The use of assessments to pay for advertising does not require respondents to repeat an objectional message out of their own mouths, cf. West Virginia Bd. of Ed. v. Barnette [1943; 13th ed., p. 1362], require them to use their own property to convey an antagonistic ideological message, cf. Wooley v. Maynard [1977; 13th ed., p. 1363], Pacific Gas & Elec. Co. v. Public Util. Comm'n of Cal. [1986 (plurality opinion); 13th ed., p. 1367] force them to respond to a hostile message when they 'would prefer to remain silent,' or require them to be publicly identified or associated with another's message, cf. PruneYard Shopping Center v. Robins [1980; 13th ed. p. 1366]. Respondents are not required themselves to speak, but are merely required to make contributions for advertising. With trivial exceptions [none] of the generic advertising conveys any message with which respondents disagree. Furthermore, the advertising is attributed not to them, but to the California Tree Fruit Agreement."

He also found the compelled funding here distinct from that involved in the Abood line of cases (see 13th ed., p. 1397): "Abood, and the cases that follow it, did not announce a broad First Amendment right not to be compelled to provide financial support for any organization that conducts expressive activities. Rather, Abood merely recognized a First Amendment interest in not being compelled to contribute to an organization whose expressive activities conflict with one's 'freedom of belief.' [In Abood we] found that compelled contributions for political purposes unrelated to collective bargaining implicated First Amendment interests because they interfere with the values lying at the 'heart of the First Amendment.' Here, however, requiring respondents to pay the assessments cannot be said to engender any crisis of conscience. None of the advertising in this record promotes any particular message other than encouraging consumers to buy California tree fruit. Neither the fact that respondents may prefer to foster that message independently in order to promote and distinguish their own products, nor the fact that they think more or less money should be spent fostering it, makes this case comparable to those in which an objection rested on political or ideological disagreement with the content of the message." Moreover, he noted that nothing in the Abood line of cases barred the assessment of fees for non-ideological purposes " 'germane' to the purpose for which compelled association was justified." Here, he noted, "the generic advertising of California peaches and nectarines is unquestionably germane to the purposes of the marketing orders [and] the assessments are not used to fund ideological activities."

Justice Stevens concluded that under appropriately deferential scrutiny the assessments were clearly constitutional: "Generic advertising is intended to stimulate consumer demand for an agricultural product in a regulated market. That purpose is legitimate and consistent with the regulatory goals of the overall statutory scheme. [Whether] the benefits from the advertising justify its cost is a question that [involves] the exercise of policy judgments that are better made by producers and administrators than by judges."

Justice SOUTER dissented, joined by Chief Justice Rehnquist and Justice Scalia and in part by Justice Thomas. He would have affirmed the court of appeals, finding that the marketing assessments implicated commercial speech, not mere economic conduct; that they were thus subject to the Central Hudson test generally applicable to commercial speech; and that, under that test, the government's justifications were inadequate. He disagreed centrally with the majority's application of Abood: "The Court's first mistaken conclusion lies in treating Abood as permitting any enforced subsidy for speech that is germane to permissible economic regulation, in the sense that it relates to the subject matter of the regulation and tends to further its objectives. But Abood and its subsequent line of cases is not nearly so permissive as the Court makes out. [Rather,] to survive scrutiny under Abood, a mandatory fee must not only be germane to some otherwise legitimate regulatory scheme; it must also be justified by vital policy interests of the government and not add significantly to the burdening of free speech inherent in achieving those interests. [Here,] produce markets can be directly regulated in the interest of stability and growth without espousing the virtues of fruit. They were, indeed, for a quarter century, and still are under the many agricultural marketing orders that authorize no advertising schemes. [The] challenged burden on dissenters' First Amendment rights is substantially greater than anything inherent in regulation of the [relevant] commercial transactions. Thus, the Abood line does not permit this program merely because it is germane to the marketing orders.

"The Court's second misemployment of Abood and its successors is its reliance on them for the proposition that when government neither forbids speech nor attributes it to an objector, it may compel subsidization for any objectionable message that is not political or ideological. [While] it is perfectly true that cases like [Abood] did involve political or ideological speech, [nothing] in those cases suggests that government has free rein to compel funding of nonpolitical speech (which might include art, for example, as well as commercial advertising).

"[An] apparent third ground for the Court's conclusion that the First Amendment is not implicated here is its assumption that respondents do not disagree with the advertisements they object to subsidizing. But this assumption is doubtful and would be beside the point even if true. [Respondents] do claim to disagree with the messages of some promotions they are being forced to fund: some of the ads promote specific varieties of plums, peaches, and nectarines marketed by respondents' competitors but not by respondents; other ads characterize California tree fruits as a generic and thus fungible commodity, whereas respondents believe that their produce is superior to most grown in California. [In] any event, the requirement of disagreement finds no legal warrant in our compelled-speech cases. [The] Abood cases themselves protect objecting employees from being forced to subsidize ideological union activities unrelated to collective bargaining, without any requirement that the objectors declare that they disagree with the positions espoused by the union. Requiring a profession of disagreement is likewise at odds with our holding [in Hurley] that no articulable message is necessary for expression to be protected. [What] counts here [is] not whether respondents fail to disagree with the generalized message of the generic ads that California fruit is good, but that they do indeed deny that the general message is as valuable and worthy of their support as more particular claims about the merits of their own brands."

Justice THOMAS also filed a dissent. He agreed with Justice Souter that the compelled assessments plainly implicated speech, not mere economic conduct. He would have applied strict scrutiny (hence his partial concurrence in Justice Souter's dissent), but would have found that the government's justifications failed even the "more lenient Central Hudson test."

In the latest First Amendment challenge to a mandatory fee requirement, the Court upheld a public university's requirement that students contribute to a student activity fund used in part to support student organizations engaging in political or ideological speech. In BOARD OF REGENTS OF THE UNIVERSITY OF WISCONSIN v. SOUTHWORTH, 120 S.Ct. 1346 (2000), the Court rejected students' attempt to analogize their fee requirement to the one invalidated in Abood v. Detroit Board [1977; 13th ed., p. 1397] and Keller v.

State Bar [1990; 13th ed., p. 1398]. Justice KENNEDY wrote for a unanimous Court: "In Abood and Keller the constitutional rule took the form of limiting the required subsidy to speech germane to the purposes of the union or bar association. [But] the standard of germane speech as applied to student speech at a university is unworkable. [The] speech the University seeks to encourage in the program before us is distinguished not by discernable limits but by its vast, unexplored bounds. To insist upon asking what speech is germane would be contrary to the very goal the University seeks to pursue. It is not for the Court to say what is or is not germane to the ideas to be pursued in an institution of higher learning." He cautioned, though, that "the University must provide some protection to its students' First Amendment interests. [The] proper measure, and the principal standard of protection for objecting students, we conclude, is the requirement of viewpoint neutrality in the allocation of funding support." While upholding the fee program in most respects, he remanded the portion of the University's program that allowed activity funding by student referendum for further review for viewpoint neutrality. Justice SOUTER, joined by Justices Stevens and Breyer, concurred only in the judgment, cautioning that too rigid an approach to viewpoint neutrality in the university setting might ultimately conflict with principles of academic freedom.

Page 1400. Insert at end of Note 2, Compulsory membership:

In BOY SCOUTS OF AMERICA v. DALE, 120 S.Ct. 2446 (2000), a closely divided Court upheld the First Amendment expressive association right of the Boy Scouts to exclude an otherwise qualified scoutmaster, James Dale, on the ground that he had avowed his homosexuality. Writing for the 5–4 majority, Chief Justice REHNQUIST held that New Jersey may not constitutionally apply its public accommodations law, which bars discrimination on the basis of sexual orientation, to require the Boy Scouts to admit Dale: "The forced inclusion of an unwanted person in a group infringes the group's freedom of expressive association if the presence of that person affects in a significant way the group's ability to advocate public or private viewpoints. [To] determine whether a group is protected by the First Amendment's expressive associational right, we must determine whether the group engages in 'expressive association.'

"[The] Boy Scouts is a private, nonprofit organization. According to its mission statement: 'It is the mission of the Boy Scouts of America to serve others by helping to instill values in young people and, in other ways, to prepare them to make ethical choices over their lifetime in achieving their full potential. The values we strive to instill are based on those found in the Scout Oath—On my honor I will do my best to do my duty to God and my country and to obey the Scout Law; To help other people at all times; To keep myself physically strong, mentally awake, and morally straight'—and Scout Law—'A Scout is: Trustworthy Obedient Loyal Cheerful Helpful Thrifty Friendly Brave Courteous Clean Kind Reverent.' Thus, the general mission of the Boy Scouts is clear: '[T]o instill values in young people.' The Boy Scouts seeks to instill these values by having its adult leaders spend time with the youth members, instructing and engaging them in activities like camping, archery, and fishing. During the time spent with the youth members, the scoutmasters and assistant scoutmasters inculcate them with the Boy Scouts' values—both expressly and by example. It seems indisputable that an association that seeks to transmit such a system of values engages in expressive activity.

"Given that the Boy Scouts engages in expressive activity, we must determine whether the forced inclusion of Dale as an assistant scoutmaster would significantly affect the Boy Scouts' ability to advocate public or private viewpoints. This inquiry necessarily requires us first to explore, to a limited extent, the nature of the Boy Scouts' view of homosexuality. The values the Boy Scouts seeks to instill are 'based on' those listed in the Scout Oath and Law. Boy Scouts explains that the Scout Oath and Law provide 'a positive moral code for living; they are a list of do's rather than don'ts.' The Boy Scouts asserts that homosexual conduct is inconsistent with the values embodied in the Scout Oath and Law, particularly with the values represented by the terms 'morally straight' and 'clean.' Obviously, the Scout Oath and Law do not expressly mention sexuality or sexual orientation. And the terms 'morally straight' and 'clean' are by no means self-defining. Different people would attribute to those terms very different meanings. For example, some people may believe that engaging in homosexual conduct is not at odds with being 'morally straight' and 'clean.' And others may believe that engaging in homosexual conduct is contrary to being 'morally straight' and 'clean.' The Boy Scouts says it falls within the latter category.

"The New Jersey Supreme Court analyzed the Boy Scouts' beliefs and found that the 'exclusion of members solely on the basis of their sexual orientation is inconsistent with Boy Scouts' commitment to a diverse and 'representative' membership ... [and] contradicts Boy Scouts' overarching objective to reach 'all eligible youth.' But our cases reject this sort of inquiry; it is not the role of the courts to reject a group's expressed values because they disagree with those values or find them internally inconsistent. The Boy Scouts asserts that it 'teach[es] that homosexual conduct is not morally straight,' and that it does 'not want to promote homosexual conduct as a legitimate form of behavior.' We accept the Boy Scouts' assertion.

"We must then determine whether Dale's presence as an assistant scoutmaster would significantly burden the Boy Scouts' desire to not 'promote homosexual conduct as a legitimate form of behavior.' As we give deference to an association's assertions regarding the nature of its expression, we must also give deference to an association's view of what would impair its expression. That is not to say that an expressive association can erect a shield against antidiscrimination laws simply by asserting that mere acceptance of a member from a particular group would impair its message. But here Dale, by his own admission, is one of a group of gay Scouts who have 'become leaders in their community and are open and honest about their sexual orientation.' Dale was the copresident of a gay and lesbian organization at college and remains a gay rights activist. Dale's presence in the Boy Scouts would, at the very least, force the organization to send a message, both to the youth members and the world, that the Boy Scouts accepts homosexual conduct as a legitimate form of behavior.

"Hurley [1995; 13th ed., p. 1371] is illustrative on this point. There we considered whether the application of Massachusetts' public accommodations law to require the organizers of a private St. Patrick's Day parade to include among the marchers an Irish–American gay, lesbian, and bisexual group, GLIB, violated the parade organizers' First Amendment rights. We noted that the parade organizers did not wish to exclude the GLIB members because of their sexual orientations, but because they wanted to march behind a GLIB banner. [Here], we have found that the Boy Scouts believes that homosexual conduct is inconsistent with the values it seeks to instill in its youth members. [As] the presence of GLIB in Boston's St. Patrick's Day parade would have interfered with the parade organizers' choice not to propound a particular point of view, the presence of Dale as an assistant scoutmaster would just as surely interfere with the Boy Scout's choice not to propound a point of view contrary to its beliefs.

"[Having] determined that the Boy Scouts is an expressive association and that the forced inclusion of Dale would significantly affect its expression, we inquire whether the application of New Jersey's public accommodations law to require that the Boy Scouts accept Dale as an assistant scoutmaster runs afoul of the Scouts' freedom of expressive association. We conclude that it does. [We] recognized in cases such as Roberts [v. Jaycees (1984); 13th ed., p. 1399] that States have a compelling interest in eliminating discrimination against women in public accommodations. But [we] went on to conclude that the enforcement of these statutes would not materially interfere with the ideas that the organization sought to express. [We] have already concluded that a state requirement that the Boy Scouts retain Dale as an assistant scoutmaster would significantly burden the organization's right to oppose or disfavor homosexual conduct. The state interests embodied in New Jersey's public accommodations law do not justify such a severe intrusion on the Boy Scouts' rights to freedom of expressive association. That being the case, we hold that the First Amendment prohibits the State from imposing such a requirement through the application of its public accommodations law.

"[That] homosexuality has gained greater societal acceptance [is] scarcely an argument for denying First Amendment protection to those who refuse to accept these views. We are not, as we must not be, guided by our views of whether the Boy Scouts' teachings with respect to homosexual conduct are right or wrong; public or judicial disapproval of a tenet of an organization's expression does not justify the State's effort to compel the organization to accept members where such acceptance would derogate from the organization's expressive message. The judgment of the New Jersey Supreme Court is reversed."

In dissent, Justice STEVENS, joined by Justices Souter, Ginsburg and Breyer, denied that the Boy Scouts had proclaimed any anti-gay philosophy: "It is plain as the light of day that neither [of the] principles—'morally straight' and 'clean'—says the slightest thing about homosexuality." Nor did he find any other clear statement of such a principle by the Boy Scouts prior to Dale's dismissal. "A State's antidiscrimination law does not impose a 'serious burden' or a 'substantial restraint' upon the group's 'shared goals' if the group itself is unable to identify its own stance with any clarity." Justice Stevens wrote further that "Dale's inclusion in the Boy Scouts is nothing like the case in Hurley. His participation sends no cognizable message to the Scouts or to the world. Unlike GLIB, Dale did not carry a banner or a sign; he did not distribute any fact sheet; and he expressed no intent to send any message. If there is any kind of message being sent, then, it is by the mere act of joining the Boy

Scouts. Such an act does not constitute an instance of symbolic speech under the First Amendment.'' He concluded: ''The only apparent explanation for the majority's holding, then, is that homosexuals are simply so different from the rest of society that their presence alone—unlike any other individual's—should be singled out for special First Amendment treatment.'' He suggested that the harm done by ''atavistic'' antigay opinions should not ''be aggravated by the creation of a constitutional shield for a policy that is itself the product of a habitual way of thinking about strangers.'' Justice SOUTER filed a separate dissent joined by Justices Ginsburg and Breyer.

SECTION 3. MONEY AND POLITICAL CAMPAIGNS

Page 1410. Add to Note 1, The Court's methodology in Buckley:

The Court indicated strong adherence to its Buckley methodology, over the dissent of three justices who would largely abandon it, in NIXON v. SHRINK MISSOURI GOVERNMENT PAC, 120 S.Ct. 897 (2000). This case involved a challenge to Missouri's limits on contributions to candidates for state office. A candidate for state auditor challenged the $1075 limit on any individual contribution for that office, arguing that even if the $1000 federal contribution limits upheld in Buckley were constitutional, inflation had eroded the value of such a sum in the quarter century that had elapsed, and that such a limit was too restrictive to be constitutional today. The Court rejected his argument.

Writing for the 6–3 majority, Justice SOUTER, joined by Chief Justice Rehnquist and Justices Stevens, O'Connor, Ginsburg and Breyer, reiterated that contribution limits are subject to considerably greater deference than expenditure limits when challenged under the First Amendment, and will survive if ''closely drawn'' to a ''sufficiently important interest'' such as prevention of corruption and the appearance of corruption. He went on to reject the challengers' argument that the state must adduce strong empirical evidence of such corruption or its appearance: ''The state statute is not void [for] want of evidence. The quantum of empirical evidence needed to satisfy heightened judicial scrutiny of legislative judgments will vary up or down with the novelty and plausibility of the justification raised. Buckley demonstrates that the dangers of large, corrupt contributions and the suspicion that large contributions are corrupt are neither novel nor implausible. [While] the record does not show that the Missouri Legislature relied on the evidence and findings accepted in Buckley, the evidence introduced into the record [here] is enough to show that the substantiation of the congressional concerns reflected in Buckley has its counterpart supporting the Missouri law.'' Justice Souter also rejected the argument that the $1075 was too low in terms of real purchasing power to be constitutional under Buckley: ''In Buckley, we specifically rejected the contention that $1,000, or any other amount, was a constitutional minimum below which legislatures could not regulate. [We] asked [instead] whether the contribution limitation was so radical in effect as to render political association ineffective. [Thus,] the issue in later cases cannot be truncated to a narrow question about the power of the dollar.'' Justices Stevens and Breyer filed separate concurrences.

Justice KENNEDY dissented, emphasizing that Buckley's "wooden" contribution/expenditure distinction had had "adverse, unintended consequences"—specifically, it "has forced a forced a substantial amount of political speech underground, as contributors and candidates devise ever more elaborate methods of avoiding contribution limits, limits which take no account of rising campaign costs. [Soft] money may be contributed to political parties in unlimited amounts, and is used often to fund so-called issue advocacy, advertisements that promote or attack a candidate's positions without specifically urging his or her election or defeat. [Thus] has the Court's decision given us covert speech. This mocks the First Amendment. The current system would be unfortunate, and suspect under the First Amendment, had it evolved from a deliberate legislative choice; but its unhappy origins are in our earlier decree in Buckley, which by accepting half of what Congress did (limiting contributions) but rejecting the other (limiting expenditures) created a misshapen system, one which distorts the meaning of speech." He concluded: "I would overrule Buckley and then free Congress or state legislatures to attempt some new reform, if, based upon their own considered view of the First Amendment, it is possible to do so. Until any reexamination takes place, however, the existing distortion of speech caused by the half-way house we created in Buckley ought to be eliminated. The First Amendment ought to be allowed to take its own course without further obstruction from the artificial system we have imposed. It suffices here to say that the law in question does not come even close to passing any serious scrutiny."

Justice THOMAS likewise dissented, joined by Justice Scalia. He described as a "curious anomaly" the majority's willingness to give less protection to campaign contributions than to other forms of speech less central to the political process. He questioned Buckley's contribution/expenditure distinction, stating that "the Constitution leaves it entirely up to citizens and candidates to determine who shall speak, the means they will use, and the amount of speech sufficient to inform and persuade." Finally, he criticized the majority for in effect lowering the standard of scrutiny applied to contribution regulations, suggesting that it had "permit[ted] vague and unenumerated harms to suffice as a compelling reason for the government to smother political speech," and argued that the Missouri law should have been subject to strict scrutiny, which it could not survive.

Page 1419. Add after Meyer v. Grant:

In BUCKLEY v. AMERICAN CONSTITUTIONAL LAW FOUNDATION, 119 S. Ct. 636 (1999), the Court invalidated three conditions Colorado had placed on the ballot-initiative process in the aftermath of its defeat in Meyer v. Grant: a requirement that initiative-petition circulators be registered voters, a requirement that they each wear an identification badge bearing the circulator's name, and a requirement that proponents of an initiative report the names and addresses of all paid circulators and the amount paid to each circulator. Justice GINSBURG, writing for the Court, stated: "[W]e are satisfied that, as in Meyer, the restrictions in question significantly inhibit communication with voters about proposed political change, and are not warranted by the state interests (administrative efficiency, fraud detection, informing voters) alleged to justify those restrictions." The registration requirement, she concluded, "produces a speech diminution of the very kind produced by the ban on paid circulators at issue in Meyer," by "decreas[ing] the pool of potential circulators." She found the state's "strong interest in policing lawbreakers among petition circulators" insufficient to justify the requirement, because that interest was adequately served by an extant requirement that each circulator file with the state an affidavit attesting to name and address. Justice Ginsburg similarly found the state interest in policing misconduct inadequate to justify the name-badge requirement, as the affidavit requirement sufficed to serve this interest without inhibiting petitioning activities by exposing circulators to " 'heat of the moment' harassment" by listeners. Indeed, she found the forced-speech requirement here "more severe" than the signed-leaflet requirement struck down in McIntyre v. Ohio Elections Commission (1995; 13th ed. p. 1364), because "[p]etition circulation is the less fleeting encounter," and "the badge requirement compels personal name identification at the precise moment when the circulator's interest in anonymity is greatest." Finally, Justice Ginsburg found the reporting requirement invalid under the "exacting scrutiny" required by Buckley v. Valeo (1976; 13th ed. p. 1381), as other disclosure requirements that informed voters of the source and amount of money spent by proponents to get a measure on the ballot made the "added benefit of revealing the names of paid circulators and amounts paid to each circulator [hardly] apparent."

Justice THOMAS concurred in the judgment, noting that he would have applied strict scrutiny to each provision struck down by the majority. Justice O'CONNOR, joined by Justice Breyer, concurred in the judgment in part and dissented in part. She agreed that the name-badge requirement should be subject to and invalidated under strict scrutiny, because it burdened the "one-on-one, communicative aspect of petition circulation." But she would have upheld the registration and disclosure requirements as "permissible regulation[s] of the electoral process," subject merely to "review for reasonableness," as they "only indirectly and incidentally burden[ed] the communicative aspects of petition circulation." Preventing fraud and increasing information to the electorate were, in her view, more than adequate to satisfy this standard. Chief Justice REHNQUIST, dissenting, would have upheld both the registration requirement and the reporting requirement as serving "substantial interests" in fraud prevention that "are sufficiently narrowly tailored to satisfy the First Amendment."

SECTION 4. FREEDOM OF THE PRESS

D. DIFFERENTIAL REGULATION OF THE BROADCAST MEDIA

Page 1454. Add after Note 6:

7. *Speaker access to public television.* ARKANSAS EDUCATIONAL TELEVISION COMM'N (AETC) v. FORBES, 523 U.S. 666 (1998), which rejected a free speech challenge to the exclusion of a candidate from a candidate debate televised by a public broadcasting station, see p. 130 above, raised the question of what First Amendment constraints apply to the exercise of journalistic judgment by public broadcasters. Justice KENNEDY, writing for the majority, suggested that First Amendment obligations of neutrality might not apply at all to most decisions by public broadcasters to exclude speakers: "In

the case of television broadcasting, [broad] rights of access for outside speakers would be antithetical, as a general rule, to the discretion that stations and their editorial staff must exercise to fulfill their journalistic purpose and statutory obligations. [Television] broadcasters enjoy the 'widest journalistic freedom' consistent with their public responsibilities. Among the broadcaster's responsibilities is the duty to schedule programming that serves the 'public interest, convenience, and necessity.' Public and private broadcasters alike are not only permitted, but indeed required, to exercise substantial editorial discretion in the selection and presentation of their programming. As a general rule, the nature of editorial discretion counsels against subjecting broadcasters to claims of viewpoint discrimination. Programming decisions would be particularly vulnerable to claims of this type because even principled exclusions rooted in sound journalistic judgment can often be characterized as viewpoint-based. Much like a university selecting a commencement speaker, a public institution selecting speakers for a lecture series, or a public school prescribing its curriculum, a broadcaster by its nature will facilitate the expression of some viewpoints instead of others. Were the judiciary to require, and so to define and approve, pre-established criteria for access, it would risk implicating the courts in judgments that should be left to the exercise of journalistic discretion. [This] is not to say the First Amendment would bar the legislative imposition of neutral rules for access to public broadcasting. Instead, we say that, in most cases, the First Amendment of its own force does not compel public broadcasters to allow third parties access to their programming." The majority in AETC nonetheless applied a First Amendment requirement of viewpoint neutrality in the particular context of a televised candidate debate, finding it satisfied as Forbes was excluded on the basis of popularity, not platform.

In dissent, Justice STEVENS wrote that a public broadcaster ought to be subject to greater obligations of neutrality than the majority had enforced. Echoing his dissent in FCC v. League of Women Voters [1984; 13th ed., p. 1320], he wrote: "Because AETC is owned by the State, deference to its interest in making ad hoc decisions about the political content of its programs necessarily increases the risk of government censorship and propaganda in a way that protection of privately owned broadcasters does not."

Page 1460. Add at the end of Note 2, "The Internet and the First Amendment":

The Court's first answer to these questions came in RENO v. ACLU, 521 U.S. 844 (1997), which is reported above at p. 78. Writing for the Court, Justice STEVENS exhaustively recounted the three-judge district court's findings about the characteristics of the Internet, and expressly rejected any analogy between the Internet and the broadcasting medium: "[Decisions such as Red Lion v. FCC and FCC v. Pacifica] relied on the history of extensive government regulation of the broadcast medium; the scarcity of available frequencies at its inception; and its 'invasive' nature. Those factors are not present in cyberspace. [The] vast democratic fora of the Internet [have never] been subject to the type of government supervision and regulation that has attended the broadcast industry. Moreover, the Internet is not as 'invasive' as radio or television. The District Court specifically found that 'communications over the Internet do not "invade" an individual's home or appear on one's computer screen unbidden. Users seldom encounter content "by accident." ' [Finally,] unlike the conditions that prevailed when Congress first authorized regulation of the broadcast spectrum, the Internet can hardly be considered a 'scarce' expressive commodity. It provides relatively unlimited, low-cost capacity for communication of all kinds, [including] not only traditional print and news services, but also audio, video, and still images, as well as interactive, real-time dialogue. Through the use of chat rooms, any person with a phone line can become a town crier with a voice that resonates farther than it could from any soapbox. Through the use of Web pages, mail exploders, and newsgroups, the same individual can become a pamphleteer. As the District Court found, 'the content on the Internet is as diverse as human thought.' We agree with its conclusion that our cases provide no basis for qualifying the level of First Amendment scrutiny that should be applied to this medium."

CHAPTER 14

The Religion Clauses: Free Exercise and Establishment

Section 2. The Free Exercise of Religion

B. Neutral Laws Adversely Affecting Religion: Are Religious Exemptions Constitutionally Compelled?

Page 1497. Add to Note 1, "The history of religious exemptions":

In CITY OF BOERNE v. FLORES, 521 U.S. 507 (1997), which held that Congress lacked authority to enact a statute applying the Sherbert rather than the Smith standard to claims of religious exemption from generally applicable state laws (see p. 98 above), Justices O'Connor and Scalia engaged in a lively colloquy on whether or not historical evidence supported the Smith standard.

Justice O'CONNOR's dissent argued that "the historical evidence casts doubt on the Court's current interpretation of the Free Exercise Clause." She noted that various colonial charters and acts had stated that religious practice should not be interfered with unless it caused some specified public harm: for example, because it was "unfaithfull to the Lord Proprietary, or molest[ed] or conspire[d] against the civill Government" (Maryland Act Concerning Religion, 1649); or was "us[ed] to licentiousness and profaneness [or] to the civil injury, or outward disturbance of others" (Charter of Rhode Island, 1663). "In other words," she argued, "when religious beliefs conflicted with civil law, religion prevailed unless important state interests militated otherwise." Likewise, she noted, early state constitutions quite commonly "guaranteed free exercise of religion or liberty of conscience, limited by particular defined state interests." For example, the New York Constitution of 1777 guaranteed free exercise but provided that it "shall not be so construed as to excuse acts of licentiousness, or justify practices inconsistent with the peace or safety of this State." Other states similarly provided for free exercise subject to the constraints of "the public peace" (New Hampshire) or the "peace or safety of the State" (Maryland, Georgia). Justice O'Connor also cited the Northwest Ordinance of 1787, which established a bill of rights for the northwest territory providing that: "No person, demeaning himself in a peaceable and orderly manner, shall ever be molested on account of his mode of worship or religious sentiments."

From this evidence, Justice O'Connor concluded that, "around the time of the drafting of the Bill of Rights, it was generally accepted that the right to 'free exercise' required, where possible, accommodation of religious practice." She suggested that otherwise, "there would have been no need to specify" licentiousness or other justifications for interference. Rather, she argued, "these documents make sense only if the right to free exercise was viewed as generally superior to ordinary legislation, to be overridden only when necessary to secure important government purposes." A particularly protective example, she noted, could be found in James Madison's draft free exercise clause for the Virginia Declaration of Rights, which, though not ultimately adopted, would have provided that "no man [ought] on account of religion to be [subjected] to any penalties or disabilities, unless under color of religion the preservation of equal liberty, and the existence of the State be manifestly endangered."

Justice O'Connor next cited early examples of religious accommodation in the colonies and states. For example, some colonial governments created alternatives to oath requirements to accommodate Quakers and other Protestant sects that did not permit the swearing of allegiance to civil government; some colonies and the Continental Congress exempted Quakers and Mennonites from military service; some states with established churches exempted religious objectors from tithes. From these examples she concluded that state legislatures favored religious accommodations when possible, and that "it is reasonable to presume that the drafters and ratifiers of the First Amendment—many of whom served in state legislatures—assumed courts would apply the Free Exercise Clause similarly."

Finally, Justice O'Connor interpreted the writings of various framers as supporting this interpretation. For example, she read Madison's Memorial and Remonstrance as suggesting that religious duty might prevail over civil law whether that law was directed at religion or was more generally applicable. She concluded: "As the historical sources [show,] the Free Exercise Clause is properly understood as an affirmative guarantee of the right to participate in religious activities without impermissible governmental interference, even where a believer's conduct is in tension with a law of general application."

Justice SCALIA, the author of Smith, wrote a separate concurrence in Boerne disputing Justice O'Connor's historical claims. He argued that "[t]he material that the dissent claims is at odds with Smith either has little to say about the issue or is in fact more consistent with Smith than with the dissent's interpretation of the Free Exercise Clause." As he read the early colonial and state free exercise clauses, they were "a virtual restatement of Smith: Religious exercise shall be permitted so long as it does not violate general laws governing conduct." On his reading, avoiding "licentiousness" or disturbance of public "peace" or "order" simply meant "obeying the laws" or avoiding "'the occurrence of illegal actions.'" He argued that it was impossible to derive Sherbert's compelling interest test from caveats about mere "peace and order."

Justice Scalia also discounted evidence of early legislative accommodations: "that legislatures sometimes (though not always) found it 'appropriate' to accommodate religious practices does not establish that accommodation was understood to be constitutionally mandated by the Free Exercise Clause." Likewise, as to writings such as Madison's Remonstrance, there was "no reason to think they were meant to describe what was constitutionally required (and judicially enforceable), as opposed to what was thought to be legislatively or even morally desirable."

He concluded that "the most telling point made by the dissent is to be found, not in what it says, but in what it fails to say. Had the understanding in the period surrounding the ratification of the Bill of Rights been that the various forms of accommodation discussed by the dissent were constitutionally required (either by State Constitutions or by the Federal Constitution), it would be surprising not to find a single state or federal case refusing to enforce a generally applicable statute because of its failure to make accommodation. Yet the dissent cites none—and to my knowledge, [none] exists." Accordingly, he found, the "historical evidence does nothing to undermine the conclusion" in Smith that "the people" rather than the Court should decide questions of religious exemption.

SECTION 3. THE ESTABLISHMENT CLAUSE

A. ENSHRINING OFFICIAL BELIEFS

Page 1513. Insert after Lee v. Weisman:

Relying on Lee, the Court struck down another attempt at school prayer in SANTA FE INDEPENDENT SCH. DIST. v. DOE, 120 S.Ct. 2266 (2000). Under the school program at issue in the case, the student body was empowered to vote each year on whether to have a student speaker preceding football games, and who the speaker would be. Justice STEVENS, joined by Justices O'Connor, Kennedy, Souter, Ginsburg, and Breyer, explained that the mere fact that the speech was student-initiated did not make the program constitutional: "[T]he majoritarian process implemented by the District guarantees, by definition, that minority candidates will never prevail and that their views will be effectively silenced. [While] Santa Fe's majoritarian election might ensure that most of the students are represented, it does nothing to protect the minority; indeed, it likely serves to intensify their offense." Although the chosen speaker was not obligated to deliver a prayer, "the expressed purposes of the policy encourage the selection of a religious message, and that is precisely how the students understand the policy."

He explained: "[T]he invocation is [delivered] to a large audience assembled as part of a regularly scheduled, school-sponsored function conducted on school property. The message is broadcast over the school's public address system, [subject] to the control of school officials. [In] this context the members of the listening audience must perceive the pregame message as a public expression of the views of the majority of the student body delivered with the approval of the school administration. [Regardless] of the listener's support for, or objection to, the message, an objective Santa Fe High School student will unquestionably perceive the inevitable pregame prayer as stamped with her school's seal of approval."

Justice Stevens rejected the school district's attempt to distinguish the case from Lee on the coercion issue: "The District [argues] that attendance at the commencement ceremonies at issue in Lee 'differs dramatically' from attendance at high school football games. [Attendance] at a high school football game, unlike showing up for class, is certainly not required in order to receive a diploma. [There] are some students, however, such as cheerleaders, members of the band, and, of course, the team members themselves, for whom seasonal commitments mandate their attendance, sometimes for class credit. The District also minimizes the importance to many students of attending and participating in extracurricular activities as part of a complete educational experience.

[To] assert that high school students do not feel immense social pressure, or have a truly genuine desire, to be involved in the extracurricular event that is American high school football is 'formalistic in the extreme.' [For] many [students], the choice between whether to attend these games or to risk facing a personally offensive religious ritual is in no practical sense an easy one. The Constitution [demands] that the school may not force this difficult choice upon these students for '[i]t is a tenet of the First Amendment that the State cannot require one of its citizens to forfeit his or her rights and benefits as the price of resisting conformance to state-sponsored religious practice.' Even if we regard every high school student's decision to attend a home football game as purely voluntary, we are nevertheless persuaded that the delivery of a pregame prayer has the improper effect of coercing those present to participate in an act of religious worship. For 'the government may no more use social pressure to enforce orthodoxy than it may use more direct means.' As in Lee, '[w]hat to most believers may seem nothing more than a reasonable request that the nonbeliever respect their religious practices, in a school context may appear to the nonbeliever or dissenter to be an attempt to employ the machinery of the State to enforce a religious orthodoxy.' The constitutional command will not permit the District 'to exact religious conformity from a student as the price' of joining her classmates at a varsity football game."

Chief Justice REHNQUIST, dissenting along with Justices Scalia and Thomas, objected that the majority's decision "bristles with hostility to all things religious in public life. [Respondents] in this case challenged the [program] before it had been put into practice. [The] fact that a policy might 'operate unconstitutionally under some conceivable set of circumstances is insufficient to render it wholly invalid.' [Therefore], the question is not whether the district's policy may be applied in violation of the Establishment Clause, but whether it inevitably will be." Because it was possible for the school district's policy to be applied in nonreligious ways, the Chief Justice saw no reason to sustain the facial challenge.

B. FINANCIAL AID TO RELIGIOUS INSTITUTIONS

Page 1541. Replace Grand Rapids School Dist. v. Ball and Aguilar v. Felton with:

Agostini v. Felton

521 U.S. 203, 117 S.Ct. 1997, 138 L.Ed.2d 391 (1997).

Justice O'CONNOR delivered the opinion of the Court.

In Aguilar v. Felton, 473 U.S. 402 (1985), this Court held that the Establishment Clause of the First Amendment barred the city of New York from sending public school teachers into parochial schools to provide remedial education to disadvantaged children pursuant to a congressionally mandated program. On remand, the [district court] entered a permanent injunction reflecting our ruling. Twelve years later, petitioners—the parties bound by that injunction—seek relief from its operation. Petitioners maintain that Aguilar cannot be squared with our intervening Establishment Clause jurisprudence and ask that we explicitly recognize what our more recent cases already dictate: Aguilar is no longer good law. We agree with petitioners that Aguilar is not consistent with our subsequent Establishment Clause decisions and further conclude that, on the facts presented here, petitioners are entitled under

Federal Rule of Civil Procedure 60(b)(5) to relief from the operation of the District Court's prospective injunction.

[Title] I of the Elementary and Secondary Education Act of 1965 [channels] federal funds, through the States, to "local educational agencies" (LEA's) [to] provide remedial education, guidance, and job counseling to [students who are] failing, or [at] risk of failing, the State's student performance standards. Title I funds must be made available to all eligible children, regardless of whether they attend public schools, and the services provided to children attending private schools must be "equitable in comparison to services and other benefits for public school children." An LEA providing services to children enrolled in private schools is subject to a number of constraints that are not imposed when it provides aid to public schools. Title I services may be provided only to those private school students eligible for aid, and cannot be used to provide services on a "school-wide" basis. In addition, the LEA must retain complete control over Title I funds; retain title to all materials used to provide Title I services; and provide those services through public employees or other persons independent of the private school and any religious institution. The Title I services themselves must be "secular, neutral, and nonideological," and must "supplement, and in no case supplant, the level of services" already provided by the private school.

Petitioner Board of Education of the City of New York (Board), an LEA, first applied for Title I funds in 1966 and has grappled ever since with how to provide Title I services to the private school students within its jurisdiction. Approximately 10% of the total number of students eligible for Title I services are private school students. Recognizing that more than 90% of the private schools within the Board's jurisdiction are sectarian, the Board initially arranged to transport children to public schools for after-school Title I instruction. But this enterprise was largely unsuccessful. Attendance was poor, teachers and children were tired, and parents were concerned for the safety of their children.

The Board [later] implemented the plan we evaluated in Aguilar v. Felton. That plan called for the provision of Title I services [by public employees] on private school premises during school hours. Before any public employee could provide Title I instruction at a private school, she would be given a detailed set of written and oral instructions emphasizing the secular purpose of Title I and setting out the rules to be followed to ensure that this purpose was not compromised. Specifically, employees would be told that (i) they were employees of the Board and accountable only to their public school supervisors; (ii) they had exclusive responsibility for selecting students for the Title I program and could teach only those children who met the eligibility criteria for Title I; (iii) their materials and equipment would be used only in the Title I program; (iv) they could not engage in team-teaching or other cooperative instructional activities with private school teachers; and (v) they could not introduce any religious matter into their teaching or become involved in any way with the religious activities of the private schools. All religious symbols were to be removed from classrooms used for Title I services. The rules acknowledged that it might be necessary for Title I teachers to consult with a student's regular classroom teacher to assess the student's particular needs and progress, but admonished instructors to limit those consultations to mutual professional concerns regarding the student's education. To ensure compliance with these rules, a publicly employed field supervisor was to attempt to make at least one unannounced visit to each teacher's classroom every month.

In 1978, six federal taxpayers—respondents here—sued the Board in the District Court. [The] District Court granted summary judgment for the Board, but the Court of Appeals for the Second Circuit reversed. [In] a 5–4 decision, this Court affirmed on the ground that the Board's Title I program necessitated an "excessive entanglement of church and state in the administration of [Title I] benefits." On remand, the District Court permanently enjoined the Board "from using public funds for any plan or program under [Title I] to the extent that it requires, authorizes or permits public school teachers and guidance counselors to provide teaching and counseling services on the premises of sectarian schools within New York City."

The Board [reverted] to its prior practice of providing instruction at public school sites, at leased sites, and in mobile instructional units (essentially vans converted into classrooms) parked near the sectarian school. The Board also offered computer-aided instruction, which could be provided "on premises" because it did not require public employees to be physically present on the premises of a religious school. It is not disputed that the additional costs of complying with Aguilar's mandate are significant. Since the 1986–1987 school year, the Board has spent over $100 million providing computer-aided instruction, leasing sites and mobile instructional units, and transporting students to those sites. [These] "Aguilar costs" [reduce] the amount of Title I money an LEA has available for remedial education, and LEA's have had to cut back on the number of students who receive Title I benefits.

[The] question we must answer is a simple one: Are petitioners entitled to relief from the District Court's permanent injunction under Rule 60(b)? Rule 60(b)(5), [states]: "On motion and upon such terms as are just, the court may relieve a party . . . from a final judgment [or] order . . . [when] it is no longer equitable that the judgment should have prospective application." [We have] held that it is appropriate to grant a Rule 60(b)(5) motion when the party seeking relief from an injunction or consent decree can show "a significant change either in factual conditions or in law." [Petitioners argue] that there have been two significant legal developments since Aguilar was decided: [in Bd. of Educ. of Kiryas Joel v. Grumet (1994); 13th ed., p. 1551,] a majority of Justices [Justices O'Connor and Kennedy in their concurrences and Justice Scalia joined by Chief Justice Rehnquist and Justice Thomas in dissent] have expressed their views that Aguilar should be reconsidered or overruled [and] Aguilar has in any event been undermined by subsequent Establishment Clause decisions, including Witters v. Washington Dept. of Servs. for Blind [1986; 13th ed., p. 1544], Zobrest v. Catalina Foothills School Dist. [1993; 13th ed., p. 1545], and Rosenberger v. Rector and Visitors of Univ. of Va. [1995; 13th ed., p. 1546]. [The] statements made by five Justices in Kiryas Joel do not, in themselves, furnish a basis for concluding that our Establishment Clause jurisprudence has changed. [The] question of Aguilar's propriety was not before us [there]. [Thus,] petitioners' ability to satisfy the prerequisites of Rule 60(b)(5) hinges on whether our later Establishment Clause cases have so undermined Aguilar that it is no longer good law.

In order to evaluate whether Aguilar has been eroded by our subsequent Establishment Clause cases, it is necessary to understand the rationale upon which Aguilar, as well as its companion case, School Dist. of Grand Rapids v. Ball, 473 U.S. 373 (1985), rested. In Ball, the Court evaluated two programs implemented by the School District of Grand Rapids, Michigan. The district's Shared Time program, the one most analogous to Title I, provided remedial and "enrichment" classes, at public expense, to students attending nonpublic schools. The classes were taught during regular school hours by publicly employed teachers, using materials purchased with public funds, on the premises of nonpublic schools. [Distilled] to essentials, the Court's conclusion that the Shared Time program in Ball had the impermissible effect of advancing religion rested on three assumptions: (i) any public employee who works on the premises of a religious school is presumed to inculcate religion in her work; (ii) the presence of public employees on private school premises creates a symbolic union between church and state; and (iii) any and all public aid that directly aids the educational function of religious schools impermissibly finances religious indoctrination, even if the aid reaches such schools as a consequence of private decisionmaking. Additionally, in Aguilar there was a fourth assumption: that New York City's Title I program necessitated an excessive government entanglement with religion because public employees who teach on the premises of religious schools must be closely monitored to ensure that they do not inculcate religion.

Our more recent cases have undermined the assumptions upon which Ball and Aguilar relied. To be sure, the general principles we use to evaluate whether government aid violates the Establishment Clause have not changed since Aguilar was decided. For example, we continue to ask whether the government acted with the purpose of advancing or inhibiting religion [and] to explore whether the aid has the "effect" of advancing or inhibiting religion. What has changed since we decided Ball and Aguilar is our understanding of the criteria used to assess whether aid to religion has an impermissible effect.

As we have repeatedly recognized, government inculcation of religious beliefs has the impermissible effect of advancing religion. Our cases subsequent to Aguilar have, however, modified in two significant respects the approach we use to assess indoctrination. First, we have abandoned the presumption [that] the placement of public employees on parochial school grounds inevitably results in the impermissible effect of state-sponsored indoctrination or constitutes a symbolic union between government and religion. [Zobrest] expressly rejected the notion—relied on in Ball and Aguilar—that, solely because of her presence on private school property, a public employee will be presumed to inculcate religion in the students. Zobrest also implicitly repudiated [the] assumption [that] the presence of a public employee on private school property creates an impermissible "symbolic link" between government and religion. Justice Souter contends that [the] sign-language interpreter in Zobrest is unlike the remedial instructors in Ball and Aguilar because signing, "[cannot] be understood as an opportunity to inject religious content in what [is] supposed to be secular instruction." [In] Zobrest, however, we did not expressly or implicitly rely upon [that] basis. The signer in Zobrest had the same opportunity to inculcate religion in the performance of her duties as do Title I employees, and there is no genuine basis upon which to confine Zobrest's underlying rationale—that public employees will not be presumed to inculcate religion—to sign-language interpreters.

Second, we have departed from the rule relied on in Ball that all government aid that directly aids the educational function of religious schools is invalid. In Witters, we held that the Establishment Clause did not bar a State from issuing a vocational tuition grant to a blind person who wished to use the grant to attend a Christian college and become a pastor, missionary, or youth director. [We] observed that the tuition grants were " 'made available generally without regard to the sectarian-nonsectarian [nature] of the institution benefited' " [and that the] grants were disbursed directly to students [and thus that] any money that ultimately went to religious institutions did so "only as a result of the genuinely independent and private choices of" individuals. The same logic applied in Zobrest.

Zobrest and Witters make clear that, under current law, the Shared Time program in Ball and New York City's Title I program in Aguilar will not, as a matter of law, be deemed to have the effect of advancing religion through indoctrination. [First,] there is no reason to presume that, simply because she enters a parochial school classroom, a full-time public employee such as a Title I teacher will depart from her assigned duties and instructions and embark on religious indoctrination, any more than there was a reason in Zobrest to think an interpreter would inculcate religion by altering her translation of classroom lectures. [Zobrest] also repudiates Ball's assumption that the presence of Title I teachers in parochial school classrooms will, without more, create the impression of a "symbolic union" between church and State. Justice Souter maintains that [Title] I continues to foster a "symbolic union" between the Board and sectarian schools because it mandates "the involvement of public teachers in the instruction provided within sectarian schools," and "fuses public and private faculties." Justice Souter does not disavow the notion [that] Title I services may be provided to sectarian school students in off-campus locations. [We] do not see any perceptible (let alone dispositive) difference in the degree of symbolic union between a student receiving remedial instruction in a classroom on his sectarian school's campus and one receiving instruction in a van parked just at the school's curbside.

Nor under current law can we conclude that a program placing full-time public employees on parochial campuses to provide Title I instruction would impermissibly finance religious indoctrination. In all relevant respects, the provision of instructional services under Title I is indistinguishable from the provision of sign-language interpreters [in Zobrest]. Both programs make aid available only to eligible recipients. That aid is provided to students at whatever school they choose to attend. [And,] as in Zobrest, Title I services are by law supplemental to the regular curricula. [They] do not, therefore, "relieve sectarian schools of costs they otherwise would have borne in educating their students." [Contrary to Justice Souter's suggestion, no] Title I funds ever reach the coffers of religious schools. [Title] I funds are instead distributed to a public agency (an LEA) that dispenses services directly to the eligible students within its boundaries, no matter where they choose to attend school. [Nor is Justice Souter correct that] Title I services supplant the remedial instruction and guidance counseling already provided in New York City's sectarian schools. [We] are unwilling to speculate that all sectarian schools provide remedial instruction and guidance counseling to their students, and are unwilling to presume that the Board would violate Title I regulations by continuing to provide Title I services to students who attend a sectarian school that has curtailed its remedial instruction program in response to Title I. What is most fatal to the argument that New York City's Title I program directly subsidizes religion is that it applies with equal force when those services are provided off-campus, and Aguilar implied that providing the services off-campus is entirely consistent with the Establishment Clause. [Because] the incentive is the same either way, we find no logical basis upon which to conclude that Title I services are an impermissible subsidy of religion when offered on-campus, but not when offered off-campus.

[Where] aid is allocated on the basis of neutral, secular criteria that neither favor nor disfavor religion, and is made available to both religious and secular beneficiaries on a nondiscriminatory basis, [the] aid is less likely to have the effect of advancing religion. In Ball and Aguilar, the Court gave this consideration no weight. Before and since those decisions, we have sustained programs that provided aid to all eligible children regardless of where they attended school. See, e.g., Everson; Mueller v. Allen; Witters; Zobrest. Applying this reasoning to New York City's Title I program, it is clear that Title I services are allocated on the basis of criteria that neither favor nor disfavor religion. The services are available to all children who meet the Act's eligibility requirements, no matter what their religious beliefs or where they go to school. The Board's program does not, therefore, give aid recipients any incentive to modify their religious beliefs or practices in order to obtain those services.

We turn now to Aguilar's conclusion that New York City's Title I program resulted in an excessive entanglement between church and state. [The] factors we use to assess whether an entanglement is "excessive" are similar to the factors we use to examine "effect." That is, to assess entanglement, we have looked to "the character and purposes of the institutions that are benefited, the nature of the aid that the State provides, and the resulting relationship between the government and religious authority." [Thus,] it is simplest to treat [entanglement] as an aspect of the inquiry into a statute's effect. Not all entanglements, of course, have the effect of advancing or inhibiting religion. [Entanglement] must be "excessive" before it runs afoul of the Establishment Clause.

The pre-Aguilar Title I program does not result in an "excessive" entanglement that advances or inhibits religion. [The] Court's finding of "excessive" entanglement in Aguilar rested on three grounds: (i) the program would require "pervasive monitoring by public authorities" to ensure that Title I employees did not inculcate religion; (ii) the program required "administrative cooperation" between the Board and parochial schools; and (iii) the program might increase the dangers of "political divisiveness." Under our current understanding of the Establishment Clause, the last two considerations are insufficient by themselves to create an "excessive" entanglement. They are present no matter where Title I services are offered, and no court has held that Title I services cannot be offered off-campus. Further, the assumption underlying the first consideration has been undermined. [After] Zobrest we no longer presume that public employees will inculcate religion simply because they happen to be in a sectarian environment. Since we have abandoned the assumption that properly instructed public employees will fail to discharge their duties faithfully, we must also discard the assumption that pervasive monitoring of Title I teachers is required.

To summarize, New York City's Title I program does not run afoul of any of three primary criteria we currently use to evaluate whether government aid has the effect of advancing religion: it does not result in governmental indoctrination; define its recipients by reference to religion; or create an excessive entanglement. We therefore hold that a federally funded program providing supplemental, remedial instruction to disadvantaged children on a neutral basis is not invalid under the Establishment Clause when such instruction is given on the premises of sectarian schools by government employees pursuant to a program containing safeguards such as those present here. The same considerations that justify this holding require us to conclude that this carefully constrained program also cannot reasonably be viewed as an endorsement of religion. Accordingly, we must acknowledge that Aguilar, as well as the portion of Ball addressing Grand Rapids' Shared Time program, are no longer good law.

[Stare decisis] does not prevent us from overruling a previous decision where there has been a significant change in or subsequent development of our constitutional law. [Our] Establishment Clause jurisprudence has changed significantly since we decided Ball and Aguilar, so our decision to overturn those cases rests on far more than "a present doctrinal disposition to come out differently from the Court of [1985]." Casey. We therefore overrule Ball and Aguilar to the extent those decisions are inconsistent with our current understanding of the Establishment Clause. [We] are only left to decide whether this change in law entitles petitioners to relief under Rule 60(b)(5). We conclude that it does. [We] reverse the judgment of the Court of Appeals and remand to the District Court with instructions to vacate its [1985] order.

Justice SOUTER, with whom Justices STEVENS and GINSBURG join, and with whom Justice BREYER joins as to Part II, dissenting.

I. [I] believe Aguilar was a correct and sensible decision, and my only reservation about its opinion is that the emphasis on the excessive entanglement produced by monitoring religious instructional content obscured those facts that independently called for the application of two central tenets of Establishment Clause jurisprudence. The State is forbidden to subsidize religion directly and is just as surely forbidden to act in any way that could reasonably be viewed as religious endorsement. [The] flat ban on subsidization antedates the Bill of Rights and has been an unwavering rule in Establishment Clause cases, qualified only by the conclusion [that] state exactions from college students are not the sort of public revenues subject to the ban. See Rosenberger v. Rector. The rule expresses the hard lesson learned over and over again in the American past and in the experiences of the countries from which we have come, that religions supported by governments are compromised just as surely as the religious freedom of dissenters is burdened when the government supports religion. [The] ban against state endorsement of religion addresses the same historical lessons. Governmental approval of religion tends to reinforce the religious message (at least in the short run) and, by the same token, to carry a message of exclusion to those of less favored views. The human tendency, of course, is to forget the hard lessons, and to overlook the history of governmental partnership with religion when a cause is worthy, and bureaucrats have programs. That tendency to forget is the reason for having the Establishment Clause (along with the Constitution's other structural and libertarian guarantees), in the hope of stopping the corrosion before it starts.

These principles were violated by the programs at issue in Aguilar and Ball, as a consequence of several significant features common to both: [each] provided classes on the premises of the religious schools, covering a wide range of subjects including some at the core of primary and secondary education, like reading and mathematics; while their services were termed "supplemental," the programs and their instructors necessarily assumed responsibility for teaching subjects that the religious schools would otherwise have been obligated to provide; the public employees carrying out the programs had broad responsibilities involving the exercise of considerable discretion; while the programs offered aid to nonpublic school students generally (and Title I went to public school students as well), participation by religious school students in each program was extensive; and, finally, aid [flowed] directly to the schools in the form of classes and programs, as distinct from indirect aid that reaches schools only as a result of independent private choice.

What, therefore, was significant in Aguilar and Ball about the placement of state-paid teachers into the physical and social settings of the religious schools was not only the consequent temptation of some of those teachers to reflect the schools' religious missions in the rhetoric of their instruction, with a resulting need for monitoring and the certainty of entanglement. What was so remarkable was that the schemes in issue assumed a teaching responsibility indistinguishable from the responsibility of the schools themselves. The obligation of primary and secondary schools to teach reading necessarily extends to teaching those who are having a hard time at it, and the same is true of math. Calling some classes remedial does not distinguish their subjects from the schools' basic subjects, however inadequately the schools may have been addressing them. [If] a State may constitutionally enter the schools to teach [remedial education,] it must in constitutional principle be free to assume, or assume payment for, the entire cost of instruction provided in any ostensibly secular subject in any religious school.

It may be objected that there is some subsidy in remedial education even when it takes place off the religious premises. [In] these circumstances, too, what the State does, the religious school need not do; the schools save money and the program makes it easier for them to survive and concentrate their resources on their religious objectives. This argument [does] nothing to undermine the sense of drawing a line between remedial teaching on and off-premises. [If] the aid is delivered outside of the schools, it is less likely to supplant some of what would otherwise go on inside them and to subsidize what remains. On top of that, the difference in the degree of reasonably perceptible endorsement is substantial. Sharing the teaching responsibilities within a school having religious objectives is far more likely to telegraph approval of the school's mission than keeping the State's distance would do. [When,] moreover, the aid goes overwhelmingly to one religious denomination, minimal contact between state and church is the less likely to feed the resentment of other religions that would like access to public money for their own worthy projects. In sum, if a line is to be drawn short of barring all state aid to religious schools for teaching standard subjects, the Aguilar–Ball line was a sensible one capable of principled adherence. It is no less sound, and no less necessary, today.

II. The [Court's] holding that Aguilar and the portion of Ball addressing the Shared Time program are "no longer good law" rests on mistaken reading. [Zobrest] is no [sanction] for overruling Aguilar or any portion of Ball. In Zobrest the Court did indeed recognize that the Establishment Clause lays down no absolute bar to placing public employees in a sectarian school, but the rejection of such a per se rule was hinged expressly on the nature of the employee's job, sign-language interpretation (or signing) and the circumscribed role of the signer. [The Court explained:] "The task of a sign-language interpreter seems to us quite different from that of a teacher or guidance counselor.... Nothing in this record suggests that a sign-language interpreter would do more than accurately interpret whatever material is presented to the class as a whole. In fact, ethical guidelines require interpreters to 'transmit everything that is said in exactly the same way it was intended.'" The signer could thus be seen as more like a hearing aid than a teacher, and the signing could not be understood as an opportunity to inject religious content in what was supposed to be secular instruction. Zobrest accordingly holds only that in these limited circumstances where a public employee simply translates for one student the material presented to the class for the benefit of all students, the employee's presence in the sectarian school does not violate the Establishment Clause. [Nor did] Zobrest, implicitly or otherwise, repudiate the view that the involvement of public teachers in the instruction provided within sectarian schools looks like a partnership or union and implies approval of the sectarian aim. On the subject of symbolic unions and the strength of their implications, the lesson of Zobrest is merely that less is less.

The Court next claims that Ball rested on the assumption that "any and all public aid that directly aids the educational function of religious schools impermissibly finances religious indoctrination, even if the aid reaches such schools as a consequence of private decision-making." [This] mischaracterizes Ball. [Ball] did not establish that "any and all" such aid to religious schools necessarily violates the Establishment Clause. It held that the Shared Time program subsidized the religious functions of the parochial schools by taking over a significant portion of their responsibility for teaching secular subjects. The Court noted that it had "never accepted the mere possibility of subsidization ... as sufficient to invalidate an aid program," and instead enquired whether the effect of the proffered aid was "direct and substantial" (and, so, unconstitutional) or merely "indirect and incidental" (and, so, permissible) emphasizing that the question "is one of degree." Witters and Zobrest did nothing to repudiate the principle, emphasizing rather the limited nature of the aid at issue in each case as well as the fact that religious institutions did not receive it directly from the State.

It is [puzzling] to find the Court insisting that the aid scheme administered under Title I and considered in Aguilar was comparable to the programs in Witters and Zobrest. Instead of aiding isolated individuals within a school system, New York City's Title I program before Aguilar served about 22,000 private school students, all but 52 of whom attended religious schools. Instead of serving individual blind or deaf students, as such, Title I funded instruction in core subjects (remedial reading, reading skills, remedial mathematics, English as a second language) and provided guidance services. Instead of providing a service the school would not otherwise furnish, the Title I services necessarily relieved a religious school of "an expense that it otherwise would have assumed," and freed its funds for other, and sectarian uses.

Finally, instead of aid that comes to the religious school indirectly in the sense that its distribution results from private decisionmaking, a public educational agency distributes Title I aid in the form of programs and services directly to the religious schools. In Zobrest and Witters, it was fair to say that individual students were themselves applicants for individual benefits. [But] under Title I, a local educational agency [may] receive federal funding by proposing programs approved to serve individual students who meet the criteria of need, which it then uses to provide such programs at the religious schools; students eligible for such programs may not apply directly for Title I funds. In sum, nothing since Ball and Aguilar and before this case has eroded the distinction between "direct and substantial" and "indirect and incidental." That principled line is being breached only here and now. [And if] a scheme of government aid results in support for religion in some substantial degree, or in endorsement of its value, the formal neutrality of the scheme does not render the Establishment Clause helpless or the holdings in Aguilar and Ball inapposite.

III. Finally, there is the issue of precedent. [Since] Aguilar came down, no case has held that there need be no concern about a risk that publicly paid school teachers may further religious doctrine; no case has repudiated the distinction between direct and substantial aid and aid that is indirect and incidental; no case has held that fusing public and private faculties in one religious school does not create an impermissible union or carry an impermissible endorsement; and no case has held that direct subsidization of religious education is constitutional or that the assumption of a portion of a religious school's teaching responsibility is not direct subsidization.

[The] object of Title I is worthy without doubt, and the cost of compliance is high. [But] constitutional lines have to be drawn, and on one side of every one of them is an otherwise sympathetic case that provokes impatience with the Constitution and with the line. But constitutional lines are the price of constitutional government.

Justice GINSBURG, with whom Justices STEVENS, SOUTER, and BREYER join, dissenting.

The Court today finds a way to rehear a legal question decided in respondents' favor in this very case some 12 years ago. Subsequent decisions, the majority says, have undermined Aguilar and justify our immediate reconsideration. This Court's Rules do not countenance the rehearing here granted. For good reason, a proper application of those rules and the Federal Rules of Civil Procedure would lead us to defer reconsideration of Aguilar until we are presented with the issue in another case.

[Under] settled practice, the sole question [under Rule 60(b)] would be: Did the District Court abuse its discretion when it concluded that neither the facts nor the law had so changed as to warrant alteration of the injunction? The majority [recognizes] that Aguilar had not been overruled, but remained the governing Establishment Clause law, until this very day. Because Aguilar had not been overruled at the time the District Court acted, the law the District Court was bound to respect had not changed. The District Court therefore did not abuse its discretion in denying petitioners' Rule 60(b) motion.

[In] an effort to make today's use of Rule 60(b) appear palatable, the Court describes its decision not as a determination of whether Aguilar should be overruled, but as an exploration whether Aguilar already has been "so undermined ... that it is no longer good law." But nothing can disguise the reality that, until today, Aguilar had not been overruled. Good or bad, it was in fact the law. Despite the problematic use of Rule 60(b), the Court "sees no reason to wait for a 'better vehicle.'" There are such vehicles in motion. [Unlike] the majority, I find just cause to await the arrival of [another] case in which our review appropriately may be sought, before deciding whether Aguilar should remain the law of the land. That cause lies in the maintenance of integrity in the interpretation of procedural rules, preservation of the responsive, non-agenda-setting character of this Court, and avoidance of invitations to reconsider old cases based on "speculations on chances from changes in [the Court's membership]."

In MITCHELL v. HELMS, 120 S.Ct. 2530 (2000), the Court fragmented into several camps in upholding against establishment challenge a program that provided publicly funded computers and other teaching aids to public and private elementary and secondary schools, including parochial schools. Justice THOMAS, announcing the judgment of the Court and writing for himself, Chief Justice Rehnquist and Justices Scalia and Kennedy, held that the only issue in the case was whether the program had an impermissibly religious effect, and outlined a broad approach to how neutrality should be assessed in challenges to parochial aid: "As we indicated in Agostini, and have indicated elsewhere, the question whether governmental aid to religious schools results in governmental indoctrination is ultimately a question whether any religious indoctrination that occurs in those schools could reasonably be attributed to governmental action. [In] distinguishing between indoctrination that is attributable to the State and indoctrination that is not, we have consistently turned to the principle of neutrality, upholding aid that is offered to a broad range of groups or persons without regard to their religion. If the religious, irreligious, and areligious are all alike eligible for governmental aid, no one would conclude that any indoctrination that any particular recipient conducts has been done at the behest of the government. [As] a way of assuring neutrality, we have repeatedly considered whether any governmental aid that goes to a religious institution does so 'only as a result of the genuinely independent and private choices of individuals.' Agostini. [For] if numerous private choices, rather than the single choice of a government, determine the distribution of aid pursuant to neutral eligibility criteria, then a government cannot, or at least cannot easily, grant special favors that might lead to a religious establishment." He rejected any test that would insist that aid to religious schools never be direct, or never "be divertible to religious use." Applying these criteria, he found the instructional aid program did not have the effect of advancing religion.

Justice O'CONNOR filed a separate concurrence in the judgment, joined by Justice Breyer: "I write separately because, in my view, the plurality announces a rule of unprecedented breadth for the evaluation of Establishment Clause challenges to government school-aid programs. Reduced to its essentials, the plurality's rule states that government aid to religious schools does not have the effect of advancing religion so long as the aid is offered on a neutral basis and the aid is secular in content. The plurality also rejects the distinction between direct and indirect aid, and holds that the actual diversion of secular aid by a religious school to the advancement of its religious mission is permissible. Although the expansive scope of the plurality's rule is troubling, two specific aspects of the opinion compel me to write separately. First, the plurality's treatment of neutrality comes close to assigning that factor singular importance in the future adjudication of Establishment Clause challenges to government school-aid programs. Second, the plurality's approval of actual diversion of government aid to religious indoctrination is in tension with our precedents and, in any event, unnecessary to decide the instant case." Insisting instead on applying the criteria set forth in Agostini for evaluation of religious effect, she found the aid program constitutional. Justice O'Connor concluded by agreeing with Justice Thomas that the Court's prior decisions in Meek and Wolmen (see 13th ed., p. 1534)' distinguishing the constitutionality of state loans of textbooks from state loans of instructional material, to religious schools, must be overruled.

Justice SOUTER, joined by Justices Stevens and Ginsburg, dissented.: "The plurality would break with the law. The majority misapplies it. That misapplication is, however, the only consolation in the case, which reaches an erroneous result but does not stage a doctrinal coup. But there is no mistaking the abandonment of doctrine that would occur if the plurality were to become a majority. It is beyond question that the plurality's notion of evenhandedness neutrality as a practical guarantee of the validity of aid to sectarian schools would be the end of the principle of no aid to the schools' religious mission. [The] plurality is candid in pointing out the extent of actual diversion of Chapter 2 aid to religious use in the case before us, and equally candid in saying it does not matter. To the plurality there is nothing wrong with aiding a school's religious mission; the only question is whether religious teaching obtains its tax support under a formally evenhanded criterion of distribution. [In] rejecting the principle of no aid to a school's religious mission the plurality is attacking the most fundamental assumption underlying the Establishment Clause, that government can in fact operate with neutrality in its relation to religion. I believe that it can, and so respectfully dissent."

†